What Is Family?

What Is Family?

Jaber F. Gubrium, *University of Florida*
James A. Holstein, *Marquette University*

Mayfield Publishing Company
Mountain View, California
London • Toronto

Library of Congress Cataloging-in-Publication Data

Gubrium, Jaber F.
What is family? / Jaber F. Gubrium, James A. Holstein.
    p. cm.
Includes bibliographical references.
ISBN 0-87484-878-4
1. Family—United States. 2. Discourse analysis—United States.
I. Holstein, James A. II. Title.
H0535.G83 1990
306.85'0973—dc20   89-39538
                                                               CIP

Manufactured in the United States of America
10 9 8 7 6 5 4 3 2 1

Mayfield Publishing Company
1240 Villa Street
Mountain View, California 94041

Sponsoring editor, Franklin C. Graham; managing editor, Linda Toy; production
editor, Carol Zafiropoulos; manuscript editor, Joan Pendleton; text and cover
designer, Jean Mailander. The text was set in 10/12 Garamond and printed on 50#
Glatfelter Spring Forge by Thomson-Shore.

We thank Tavistock Publications, for permission to quote from Elizabeth Bott,
Family and Social Network, London, 1957 and Sage Publications for permission to
include material from Holstein's article "Studying Family Usage: Family Image and
Discourse in Mental Hospitalization Decisions," *Journal of Contemporary Ethnography,* volume 17, number 3, 1988, pp. 261–84. Chapter 3 was adapted from our
article "The Private Image: Experimental Location and Method in Family Studies,"
Journal of Marriage and the Family, volume 49, number 4, 1987, pp. 773–786,
published by the National Council on Family Relations. A version of Chapter 4
appeared as Gubrium's article "The Family as Project" in *Sociological Review,*
volume 26, number 2, 1988, pp. 273–296, published by Routledge & Kegan Paul.
Chapter 7 was adapted from Gubrium's chapter "Organizational Embeddedness
and Family Life," which appeared in Timothy H. Brubaker (ed.), *Aging, Health, and
Family: Long-Term Care,* Newbury Park, California, Sage Publications.

Contents

Preface

Hardly a week goes by that newspapers or the broadcast media don't pose questions about what family is, was, or is becoming. Some of the concern, of course, pertains to the changing composition of the legal family. There is interest in, even alarm over, the high divorce rate, which may be accompanied by statistics about the high proportion of divorced who remarry. Those who value lifelong legal marriage decry the divorce rate. Those cherishing "marriage" of any kind, legal or informal, rejoice in the evidence that companionate domestic relations are still desired.

Whatever the status of marriage or the family and however it is valued, one thing is clear: the language of family life—family discourse— is very much in the air. Its messages cast family in different lights. It is a language we all use, day in and day out, to describe our relationships. We announce, for example, that a neighbor is like a sister or that a sister is nothing but a stranger, and thereby explain our various attitudes, sentiments, and actions. It is a language that persuades as well as informs. Family discourse tells us that, in practice, what being a sister is may be meaningfully described in ways entirely at odds with legal or biological definitions.

This book is about family discourse. It was written because we believe that to separate discourse from reality is to leave the object of concern—family—meaningless. In the following pages we focus on what people from various walks of life say about family in relation to themselves, others, and their interpersonal relations. The theme is that while family has its legal and biological definitions, the everyday reality cf the familial is produced through discourse. Thus family is as much a way of thinking and talking about relationships as it is a concrete set of social ties and sentiments.

In this regard, the title is telling. It was a deliberate decision to call the book "What Is Family?" not "What Is *the* Family?" We omitted the article "the" because it implies something given, concrete, set. Since our aim was to show how family derives its meaningful reality through inter-action, we chose a title that more nearly conveyed family as a socially constructed phenomenon rather than just a thing. In this context, asking "What is family?" focuses attention on the *process* by which we construe this thing—family.

Because we wanted to write for a broad audience—students, family scholars, and professional workers—we have chosen examples from a wide spectrum of family-related experiences. Students will recognize scenes drawn from home, school, and community life. Indeed, the information students encounter in standard family textbooks will take on additional meaning in the context of thinking about those texts as family discourse. Family scholars will recognize the familiar academic issues of how to define family and assess family life as very practical questions that family members and other concerned parties themselves are constantly addressing and sorting out. Human service professionals will be well acquainted with the field data presented, which were collected in a variety of service settings, from nursing homes to community mental health centers. Regardless of setting, all the examples and the data presented are significantly about home and community life. In that sense, the book speaks to all who are seriously concerned with the question "What is family?"

By focusing on process and family discourse, we intend to show each audience how the familiar is commonly taken for granted. From domestic scenes to court hearings and support group proceedings, we learn that, in practice, what is taken to be family is never something settled once and for all, but derives its meaning in relation to the conditions and understandings of everyday life. We might say that by talking family, we talk ourselves into its varied meanings. Our aim is to make visible the intimate connection in the realm of the familial between talk, meaning, and concrete reality.

Acknowledgments

We have introduced "process thinking" about meaning, language, and interpersonal relations in a variety of courses we have taught over the years, in particular those dealing with family living and everyday life. Students were quite forthcoming, presenting experiences out of their own lives and commenting on our interpretations. Their opinions, comments, and criticisms provided an important context for evaluating the presentation.

A number of colleagues, scholars of everyday life, have been helpful in clarifying our thinking: Robert Dingwall, Robert Emerson, Mel Pollner, David Silverman, and Carol Warren. They recognized the significance of the theme and point of view and in their separate ways showed concern for the importance of family discourse. In particular, our ongoing discussions with friends and colleagues Gale Miller and David R. Buckholdt have contributed immeasurably to this book. Last, but not least, we recognize the wisdom and artful practice which the many professional workers in our various field sites brought to bear on related work. In a manner of speaking, each group "talked" the book into a better product.

We also acknowledge the institutional support that made the book possible. The Department of Sociology at the University of Florida (Gubrium) and the Department of Social and Cultural Sciences at Marquette University (Holstein) provided supportive environments for the project. The Institute for Family Studies at Marquette University encouraged this work while Gubrium was director and assisted with a research grant to Holstein. The Division of Sponsored Research at the University of Florida, through its Research Development Award program, helped in many ways. Gubrium's fieldwork was partially supported by grants from the Midwest Council for Social Research on Aging, the Gerontological Society of America, and the Marquette University Graduate School. Holstein's fieldwork was supported in part by grants from the National Institute of Mental Health, the National Institute for Handicapped Research, and Marquette University's Graduate School.

We are grateful to the following reviewers for their many excellent suggestions: Robert M. Emerson, University of California at Los Angeles; Lucy Rose Fischer, St. Olaf's College; Anne Foner, Rutgers University; William R. Garrett, St. Michael's College; Donald E. Gelfand, University of Maryland; Mark Hutter, Glassboro State College; Jeanne Kohl, Pacific Lutheran University; Mary Ann Lamanna, University of Nebraska at Omaha; Lynn Lofland, University of California at Davis; Ralph LaRossa, Georgia State University; F. Philip Rice, University of Maine at Orono; Barbara Settles, University of Delaware; Kendrick S. Thompson, Northern Michigan University; Brenda Vander Mey, Clemson University; Patricia Voydanoff, University of Dayton; Carol A. B. Warren, University of Kansas.

For our families

What Is Family?

Chapter 1

What Is Family?

"When *I* use a word," Humpty Dumpty said in rather a scornful tone,
"it means just what I choose it to mean—neither more nor less."
"The question is," said Alice, "whether you *can* make words mean
so many different things."
"The question is," said Humpty Dumpty, "which is to be master—
that's all."

Lewis Carroll, *Alice Through the Looking Glass*

Professor Caswell, a renowned scholar of the family, quoted from
Lewis Carroll whenever he had the opportunity to make a point about
human nature. As he once concluded, "Alas, friends, big brass, and
pedestrians, words are what we make of them." Nevertheless, Caswell
expected more from the language of serious scholarship. Family studies
was a science, and he believed that science harbored clear thinking and
precise meanings.

Lately, though, Caswell had been bothered by a small figment of
his imagination, a curmudgeon of himself who talked back incessantly,
especially when Caswell railed over the place of words and meanings in
life and science. That little bit of himself seemed to emerge full-blown one
day when Caswell turned to a favored classroom technique for prodding
students out of their taken-for-granted view of things. "I shall assume the
perspective of an extraterrestrial visitor," he told his students, "and you will
see how your familiar world must look to a stranger." Caswell instructed
them to imagine him as an androgynous cyborg—a cybernetically operated
organism named "Borg."

Caswell had explained earlier that the family had taken many
different forms throughout history and across cultures, producing diverse

households. It ranged from what some call the extended family to its ever-popular nuclear counterpart of mother, father, and children. Caswell had been careful to point out that the varied configurations, in their particular historical and cultural contexts, were normal forms, not to be judged more superior or less desirable just because they differed from each other or from what is commonplace today. He added that, in some social contexts, the family had such strong connections with other social forms, like the workplace, that it was much less distinguished as a special unit of life than it is now. Caswell suggested that the family might take on any number of shapes and functions and launched into a lengthy discussion of "alternate family forms" such as the commune. As most textbooks on the family purported, an exact definition of family was out of reach.

Attempting to show his class how to sort through the variety of ties that have been called family, Caswell asked the students to put themselves in Borg's place. "Pretend that you don't know what words mean at all, that you don't know to what or how words should be applied. Now let's try to figure out what the family really is." Caswell wanted to show the students how the word "family," while highly variable in its historical and cultural meanings, nonetheless could be used to designate a concrete form of life, one he had studied for the greater part of his scholarly career.

Caswell started by talking about tables rather than households or homes. Using the classroom table next to him, he noted that, like the table, the family had parts and at the same time was a whole. Running his hand over the top of the table and down one of the legs, he explained how the whole held together the parts and implied each part's functions. Each leg held the top above the floor. The top, in turn, not only made the legs' collective functions evident but also provided a surface upon which objects could be placed.

Again referring to a table's analogy with the family, Caswell indicated how tables come in as many sizes and shapes as the family. "Some are big, some small, some do certain things—just as some tables hold dishes and others hold saws, different families do altogether different things." He cautioned that, nonetheless, they are all families. Caswell described structure and function as something common to all, even while he carefully denoted family's human variations. "And so that alien who looks across history and from one culture to another notices many, many differences. As Borg might ask, 'How can you have so many words for so many different things?'" Caswell's point was that, despite the variety across history and culture, *the* family was a continuous part of human experience.

Now Borg—that curmudgeon in Caswell's mind—emerged to speak in her own voice. Like Humpty Dumpty, she asked in a scornful tone, "But, Professor Caswell, I see the table, the students see the table, but I don't recall having seen *the* family, any family. If you ask me to find other tables using this one as a guide, I can probably find them; but I don't think I could do the same if you showed me a family or even gave me pictures of families." Borg added that, in her casual wanderings on Earth, she hadn't actually seen a family, only people.

Caswell picked up the assigned family textbook. Like most such textbooks, it included colorful pictures of diverse families and households, showing a variety of cultural and historical origins. Caswell opened the book to the appropriate pages and told Borg that the pictures would be her guide to a mission: to locate family in its many forms.

Before Borg left, she repeated that all she could see in the pictures were people and houses, just as she could see people in the classroom and people out in the street. Borg wondered how she would be able to distinguish just any collection of people from the collection that constituted a family; in particular, she wondered whether housing could help distinguish what these humans called "family." She asked Caswell how she could differentiate a collection that looked just like the people in one of the textbook pictures from what, on an earlier trip around Earth, she had heard called a "gang." Caswell responded that she had found the key; namely, that Borg had to combine looking with listening. He explained that she needed to discover how collections of people referred to themselves before she could locate families.

As Borg set out, she understood that this mission was going to be more difficult than finding more tables after seeing a table. What if people disagreed? What if they claimed to be family in one place and disclaimed it in another? Tables didn't talk to, or about, themselves. It crossed Borg's mind that speech might be the source of much trouble in her quest. She mused, "If only people didn't talk about themselves to anyone, even themselves; if only they stayed silent and remained what they were."

Several weeks later Professor Caswell announced to the class that Borg had returned from her search. He asked her what she had found. To begin with, Borg had found many collections of people whom other people referred to as families, but whose alleged members did not. She found that when she revisited the members of the gang she had mentioned earlier and paid close attention to what they said about themselves, she heard the members not only refer to themselves as family, but also call each other brothers and claim filial responsibility for their actions. Yet this "family" wasn't a household. She added, "And what about Laura, a teenage girl who shrieked that she didn't have a sister when her twin spilled grape juice on Laura's brand new cashmere sweater?"

Considering her difficulties, Borg explained that originally she had drawn a hint from Professor Caswell's own research and taken the legal status of the collections of people she observed as a convenient shortcut to their family status. But many of those who had legal family ties stated flatly that they were not a family. Some even remarked that they weren't family in any sense of the term and never had been; others complained that they were family in name only. On the other hand, she discovered a wide variety of people who spoke with equal force and sentiment about how they were family and held each other accountable for the claim, yet were not legally bound. The legal status of these humans, Borg found, was a very poor guide to what they said, claimed, felt, or did about themselves.

Borg didn't want to insult Caswell, but she thought maybe she would get a more definitive picture of the family if she consulted some other family experts. Dictionaries were no help because they offered dozens of variations. She found that scholarly texts were not much better. A few of them said families were persons living together and related by blood, marriage, or adoption. Others stated that this excluded too many of today's "contemporary" families, where couples lived together without being married. Still others complained that this included too many groups; a few relatives living together—say, two unmarried brothers running a trucking business and sharing an apartment because one was always on the road—really shouldn't be thought of as a family. Some texts stated that it was best to keep it simple and think traditionally: a family was a married couple living together with their children. But others claimed that this wouldn't do; wouldn't this definition exclude single parents raising their children or married couples living apart or childless couples for that matter? Finally, other texts concluded that there was no single definition of the family, just families, stressing the diversity of the phenomenon plaguing Borg.

Borg wondered how these experts could possibly study the family if there was so little consensus about what it was. How did they create a scientific literature on the family if they didn't define it in a common way? Could these experts have been looking at the same thing? Who did know what the family was and what it was like? Law books and family textbooks were not going to be much help in answering these questions.

Borg took delight in the confusion that seemed to rule the experts' search for the family. She teased Caswell that they were no better at it than she was. She enjoyed recounting the ways humans connected words and things; in general, it seemed to have no universal rhyme or reason. Yet everyone seemed to understand one another. She'd been keeping track of what people said when she asked about families, and it was clear that she had actually heard much more about the thing she was searching for—family—than legal status or biological kinship implied. What seemed most evident, she noted, was that people seemed to *use* family in ways that legal or biological definitions could not capture. She wondered aloud, "Could it be that what family is to people is how family is *used* by them?" Borg was beginning to sound like Humpty Dumpty.

Caswell was both surprised and annoyed by the question. Was Borg implying that family was nothing more than a human construct and that people applied family imagery and familial categories like brother, sister, and cousin to all sorts of human relations, in and out of homes? To make matters worse, Borg was starting to sound like those family therapists—called "constructivists"—who were beginning to show how important language, meaning, and process were to definitions of family, if not social reality as a whole. Was Borg saying that family was not so much a thing, but a way of interpreting interpersonal ties?

Caswell calmed himself and asked hastily, "Well, then, my skeptical alien sidekick, if that's all the family is—just words—then it's not much of anything! What are we to do? Study words?" Borg knew immediately that she had hit a nerve. She didn't want to be unfaithful to what she had heard in her empirical wanderings, and she didn't want to back away from Caswell simply because Caswell was unnerved. She was as committed to her studies as Caswell was to his.

Borg explained that no one she had talked with, or whom she had heard talk with others, acted as if family were just a word. She added, in a curious turn of phrase, that all the words she heard about family were words about "it" or some form of "it," something concretely part of experience. The people she heard were making statements about something either real, not real enough, or too real to them, and were not just uttering words. "It" seemed to link words to concrete aspects of life.

When Caswell accused Borg of making an intellectual exercise out of her search for the family, she replied, "Okay, wise guy, you claim to be a serious student of human affairs. You give me an accurate guideline for finding what we're looking for." But Caswell's every guideline or rule for discerning family broke down as Borg mentioned the diverse and sundry ways that humans seemed to assign the term to their interpersonal relations. Some called friends family; some called pets family; some called multinational corporations family; and some refused to call wives, children, and parents family. Who was right? Some stated that they knew better than others whether they were real family because they lived in the home; others claimed that they knew more objectively because they weren't members of the household. Having access to the inner privacies of the household seemed to provide no better picture of what a family was like than did the many voices Borg heard in public. And what of the experts, the family scholars? Should we take their word over the word of those who actually live out the domestic affairs studied by the experts? Were these ordinary folk wrong?

Borg pointed out that because people talked and communicated with each other about what they were, both in and out of their homes, they weren't like tables, and one couldn't establish a table-like guideline for discerning what they were to each other. (At the back of her mind, Borg suspected that the problem she was having locating families also existed with tables—not because tables talked back, but because people used the object in different ways. She saved that question for another day.) In order to "see" what people were referring to, one had to listen to the way they used words and described their social relations, paying particular attention to the factors that affected their descriptions. Looking straight at Caswell, Borg blurted out, "You have to listen in order to see, Caswell!"

This time, Caswell knew that Borg was annoyed, just as he had been taken aback earlier. He hadn't intended the listening business to become so central to locating the familial; he had meant it only as a handy guide. Yet, now intrigued by Borg's reasoning, Caswell was bent on learning more about Borg's thoughts on seeing and hearing. He turned toward her and asked warmly, "Well, then, my friend, what is family?"

Language Use and the Construction of Family

This book presents an answer to Caswell's question, which is telling in its own right. Caswell asked Borg not "What is *the* family?" but rather "What is family?" Was he on to Borg? What difference does the absence of the simple modifier "the" make?

In everyday life, we refer to many objects, both tangible and intangible. We speak of community, feelings, political allegiances, family, attitudes, households, and the nation, among other things. They are objects for us because, as Durkheim (1938) said, we experience them as *things*. As parts of our experience, we take things to be somewhere outside the standpoint from which we refer to them, existing apart from our attention to them. We experience our community as a feature of some population that surrounds us. The nation is presumably an even more heterogeneous object in the more distant environment. Our references to them indicate that we experience even feelings and attitudes as things separate and distinct from us. For example, we sense that feelings exist inside the body, perhaps lying somewhere near the heart or in the gut.

To speak of things as lying outside the standpoint of reference to them is a statement about experience, not physical reality. The world of experience is not the same as the physical world or the world of nature. The experiential world is made up of meanings and language, not just physical objects and space. Location is a matter of reference, not only of place. In the world of experience, what lies inside and outside of us has more to do with the *relationship* of the thing under consideration to a point of reference than it does to the thing's location in space. In experience, things are things because we think of them, act toward them, and speak of them as such; we confirm our references by responding to them as if they were objects. Thus whether feelings ultimately lie inside or outside the body, we nonetheless experience them as object-like.

Standpoint and the referencing process are integral parts of language use. Every utterance is about some thing, some object of experience. As we speak and indicate to ourselves and others, we inexorably create and construct objects. To do anything less would require silence; to be strict about doing less would require turning off that "internal" voice we call mind.

The connection between language, speech, and objects of experience was at the center of Caswell's and Borg's perplexities. Because Borg was an alien and didn't know what family was, Caswell attempted to give her a picture-like guide to finding it. But whenever she seemed to find an instance of what Caswell called family, she heard a cacophony of voices. Some affirmed its existence; others denied it altogether. Some voices referred to family while others referred to "empty shells" or "houses without homes" to convey the absence of family among a collection of individuals. People seemed to connect family to place (if place was mentioned at all) with terms like "household," "home," and "home base." Some voices not only affirmed the absence of family but also redefined linkages that Borg had heard others call "family." For example, some called their homes "prisons," the occupants "inmates," and acted as if that were actually the case, not considering that there were legal or biologically related families housed there. And strangely enough, she even heard prison inmates call the penitentiary home and their fellow inmates husband, wife, brother, sister—family.

Like "it," the simple modifier "the" flagged the problem facing Borg. When we speak of the character of *the* family, the structures and functions of *the* family, we imply a thing, a solid and evident, tangible or intangible object of experience, something with substance and boundaries. The implication applies whether our references are to the family as an entity or to particular families. For example, to speak of a specific family— say, *the* Martin family—is to describe a thing that is organized in a certain way, has an inside and an outside. Yet when we take the voices of those who speak for the Martin family into account, this thing loses its boundaries. As we listen to the father describe the Martin family, will he describe the same thing as the mother? Does the oldest child describe the Martin family similarly or differently? What of the youngest child? What of the maternal as opposed to paternal grandparents? What of the family physician, the social worker, or the oldest child's teacher, among a host of voices? Could it be that when we listen carefully and let those concerned define the Martin family, that "it" becomes many things, as potentially diverse as those who speak for it? And what of those ostensibly nonfamilial things that the Martins call "family" from time to time, like sorority "sisters" and lodge "brothers"? Even the family dog is considered to be and is treated like a true member of the family. Is this nothing but talk?

When Borg permitted herself to pay attention to what people said about family, she asked herself whether those she heard were speaking about *the* same thing. What disturbed Caswell was Borg's implication that neither she nor Caswell were in any position to state more truthfully than those concerned what was and wasn't family to them. As Caswell suggested at one point, could it be that what was said about family and the vehicle for saying it—words—were as much a part of the family as *the* family? Borg thought that was the case, but only partially so. She was concerned that Caswell might be implying that the family was a mere language game. Rather, she found people acting in good faith, using family language, and applying it to concrete social relations. People were not merely doing conversational contortions with the language. In their discourse, they were seriously sorting through observable signs of their relationships in order to figure what they were all about.

The article "the" seemed to prematurely objectify family—to impose boundaries on it before its potential breadth can be examined Borg had been prepared to observe family in the same way one might observe physical objects like tables. She eventually discovered that before she could find *the* family, she needed to pay attention to how modifiers like "the" were indirectly affecting her observations. Borg learned that she needed to pay very careful attention to how people used words to convey a concrete sense of family life in order to discern family. Thus she concluded that the simple modifier "the" was a sign of something much more important and that family discourse in general was quite telling of the status of the family in experience. Professor Caswell's reformulation of "What is the family?" into "What is family?" was indeed more profound than even Caswell realized.

Listening in Order to See

Borg claimed that one must listen in order to see. Let's expand on this statement. It's a statement about method, concerning how one goes about searching for the thing so many call "family." On her mission, Borg encountered people referring to many *things*. These things ranged from attitudes and feelings to families and communities. Borg could literally put her hands on some things, like tables and chairs, as Caswell had demonstrated in his lecture. Borg soon realized that this category also contained physical objects that were out of human reach, like distant stars or weather fronts that could be physically grasped by humans in principle. Other things, though, like families and communities seemed to defy both her own and humans' physical grasp.

Borg recalled reading that these objects that defied physical grasping were called social objects. Borg had just started to read Durkheim and guessed that what Durkheim (1938) meant by the term "collective representations" were the social objects she was pondering. Social objects were the ways a collection of people represented themselves and features of the social world—a family or a community, for example.

The more Borg remembered what people had said to each other about family and related matters, the more she began to feel that this thing family, like community and other things said to be social objects, was a class of objectless objects. This was very strange from a physical standpoint and posed many problems for Borg's attempt to locate and assess the thing she was looking for. The more she continued to treat what she was searching for as table-like, the less she was able to locate what people could so vociferously claim to be or not be family.

Borg recognized that humans had something in their lives that came between the things one could see (like tables and people) on one side, and their voices on the other. For lack of a better word, Borg called it what many of these humans did themselves—meaning. This reminded Borg of the statements she had heard like "They don't mean family to me at all, even though they're my brothers and sisters" and "She's a real sister to me; my own sister is really just a stranger." As Caswell had initially suggested without fully realizing its implication, the voices instructed Borg to combine looking with listening in order to decipher the meaning of "family." While Borg did not systematically search for other social objects at the time, she had noticed that "community" and "institution" had the same sort of relation to the "object" they represented. Furthermore, didn't Caswell refer to those deer antlers mounted on his office wall as a "hat rack"? And weren't diamonds referred to as "a girl's best friend"? These things were concrete, but they, too, could change in meaning as they were used. No wonder family was so hard to pin down.

It dawned on Borg that the key to understanding humans lay in deciphering how they, in their words and actions, *attached meaning* to the objects of their concern. Her reading of Weber (1947, 88) gave her the idea She decided that she could not straightforwardly refer to the object of her consideration as *the* family, nor simply look to households to locate it. She would speak simply of "family." This kind of "the-less" language assured Borg that she would not just search for *the* ostensible family, but always attend to the voices that spoke of the family in order to discern what any set of relationships *meant* to those concerned. Borg even thought at one point that she might use a special form of writing. She wouldn't write about the family, but rather, about family-according-to-brother, family-according-to-father, family-according-to-social worker, family-according-to-plant supervisor, and so on.

Borg was bent on turning her developing ideas about family into action. She could now organize her search for family according to the theory that family was a collective representation (a "social object") that was meaningfully revealed through discourse. Her theory would be her method. (She knew that Caswell was in the habit of treating theory and method separately.) Borg realized that in the world of social objects, the way to "see" the things of concern to people was to carefully attend to how people use words, to listen to what they indicate or define in speech and conversation. In short, she would analyze and document family discourse.

So, how did the project turn out? Unfortunately, the story ends here. But this is our own beginning. In the following chapters, we set out a new perspective on family, one combining theory and method. As we outline the conceptual framework and a terminology for analyzing the practical and descriptive process out of which family is constructed, we simultaneously demonstrate our method and present our findings. We do not lay out theory in one chapter, method in another, and findings in still another. Since the focus is on construction and construction is a process, being faithful to studying it requires us to proceed along with it.

We will end up with the theory and method of what we call a "social constructionist" perspective on family. It will be a description of description—our description of people's descriptions. Our analysis focuses on family discourse. We trace the process by which people actually assign familial terms like "home," "brother," "sister," and "parents" to the circumstances and relationships in their lives and highlight the conditions that affect the assignments. We document the way people literally *practice* family description and construct family meaning. Again, as Borg cautioned, it is important to emphasize that descriptive practice is not just about words. It is about what people *do* with words as they figure—indeed, create—the concrete meaning of their interpersonal relations.

Chapter 2, our point of departure, begins with the common view that the family, household, and home are a private domain of experience. We argue that this set of meanings is assigned by way of an essentially public discourse.

Chapter 2

A New Perspective:
Social Constructionism

Family. House. Household. Home. Privacy. It's a loaded set of concepts these days, when family concerns are anything but simple matters between kith and kin. These terms are as much political slogans as they are features of domestic relations. On the right, they signal the traditional values of family living, the preferred configuration of life's most precious bonds. On the left, they can convey a dubious arrangement of time past, associated with patriarchy, domination, and exclusion. Persons of all political preferences regularly use the terms but assign them different meanings according to their interests and objectives.

Public life comprises more than political concerns, however. Everyday living is conducted not only in the limelight of the mass media or in political forums, but also in the variety of locales where both celebrated and common men and women go about their ordinary activities—at work and school, in neighborhoods, houses, clinics, courts, offices, and social gatherings. So it is with the meaning of family, home, household, and privacy. Understandings of domestic life emerge from our commonplace interactions and communications with one another. The terms we've listed are part of the *discourse* each of us carries into the diverse enclaves of social life day in and day out. We speak and form opinions of house, home, and family while we are at work or play, when we talk business or gossip, when we are in the courtroom or with friends at the local tavern—wherever domestic affairs are taken into account in making sense of oneself and one's ties with others.

While we may think and speak of family matters in relation to the privacy of the household, familial concerns capture our attention across varied contexts of daily life. The discourse of the familial extends well beyond political affairs and the private confines of the household (see Donzelot, 1979). Our knowledge of domestic matters doesn't necessarily come from careful and detailed scrutiny of home life. Instead, it takes its shape and substance from the available concepts and categories we use to interpret home life. For example, a wife learns the possible meaning of the lifelong personal relationship with her spouse when a new category for interpreting the relationship is mentioned in a support group or emerging circle of friends. The public forums shed old and new light on privacy. We develop understandings of private household matters from quite public circumstances (see Mills, 1940; Gerth and Mills, 1953; Mills, 1959). Public life, if not public affairs, is deeply implicated in the way we formulate the meaning of domestic matters and privacy.

This experience contrasts with the common desire to categorically separate the public and private sides of life. Whether politically or ethically motivated, there are many who argue, for example, that what goes on in the household is a private matter and should be sheltered from public scrutiny and regulation. Family life, they say, is best left to families, not encumbered by institutions like the state, courts, and service agencies. Lasch (1979), for one, decries the extent that public affairs have infringed on what he calls the remaining "haven in a heartless world." He faults the invasion of the outside world for the ostensible demise of the family. From the separation of work and the household in the industrial revolution to domestic experts' ostensible assault on the home, Lasch sees the family as less and less able to socialize its children, provide much-needed intimacy, and perform other private functions.

The idea of a private family life parallels the notion of the private self. How often have we heard about the individual set against society? For better or worse, mainly worse, society is said to impose itself on the individual, compromising the individual's integrity. We take for granted that the private individual has a life of his or her own separate from public life, even while we acknowledge a primary socialization process. The implication is that, in principle, we go through life by ourselves, not together with, through, or by way of others. In contrast, in this book, we aim to take the familiar adage "no man is an island" to heart, substituting the word "family" for "man," and adapt it to a perspective on domestic privacy. We offer a view of family as a *socially constructed* object, a product of decidedly public actions and interactions.

Family Discourse

We are accustomed to thinking of *the* family as a specific set of social ties, a rather important set at that. Some would even say the family is the bedrock of society. But recalling Borg's earlier musings, we can just as easily think of family as a way of describing our social relations, some of which are formally kindred and others not. For example, we can all picture the teenage boy who insists that "everybody's against me; I got no family" to underscore his alienation from the parents who seem to thwart his every effort to grow up and his intention of leaving home or getting revenge. While he may be legally incorrect about his domestic ties, his claim nonetheless conveys his adolescent anguish over what he perceives as profound parental mistreatment. Parents remain parents; but at the moment of this utterance, the compassion that we take for granted as constituting the familial is called into question.

Conversely, we all recognize the myriad uses of kinship terms to celebrate the caring, loving feelings of close friendship. Carol Stack's classic ethnography of community life in a midwestern black neighborhood, *All Our Kin* (1974), highlights this usage. Consider the meanings that one of Stack's informants, Billy, bestows upon her diverse associates in applying and withholding kinship designations:

> Billy, a young black woman in The Flats, was raised by her mother and her mother's "old man." She has three children of her own by different fathers. Billy says, "Most people kin to me are in this neighborhood, right here in The Flats, but I got people in the South, in Chicago, and in Ohio too. I couldn't tell most of their names and most of them aren't really kinfolk to me. Starting down the street from here, take my father, he ain't my daddy, he's no father to me. I ain't got but one daddy and that's Jason. The one who raised me. My kids' daddies, that's something else, all their daddies' people really take to them—they always doing things and making a fuss about them. We help each other out and that's what kinfolks are all about. (p. 4)

The term "family" is part of a particular discourse for describing human relations in or out of the household. Among other terms like brother, sister, and son, this family discourse includes the terms listed at the start of this chapter. Yet family discourse is more than a set of terms: it also contains ideas about domestic life. For example, to speak of "being family" is not only to use the term "family" to describe a set of social relationships, but also to convey the idea that the relationships under consideration are, say, trusting and giving, not calculated (Gubrium and Buckholdt, 1982b). Such usage is clear in the following extract from a letter nominating an unmarried woman as an "outstanding family" in a contest sponsored by a community service organization:

> Although she is single and doesn't fit the definition of the
> traditional American family, [Elaine] is always reaching out to
> those around her and has become an extension of everyone's
> family. . . . She is sensitive to the needs of others and helps them
> whenever she can . . . she has given them room and board, but
> most importantly, she's given them the family support they needed
> at the time.

By the same token, relationships that cease to be trusting and giving raise
the question of whether they should any longer be referred to in familial
terms. Applied to the household, one might suggest that one house is
anything but homelike and another full of family life. Such ideas assign a
certain meaning to the social ties of the household, drawing a connection
between house and home. In their applicaton to people and their ties, the
terms and ideas give domestic shape and substance to what otherwise are
meaningless sets of interpersonal linkages.

Family discourse also includes various models and theories of
domesticity. For example, many think of the family as a nuclear comple-
ment of father, mother, and children. Others idealize the family in beliefs
about the quality of social ties, regardless of formal kinship. Some base
family life in the feelings people express for each other; for others, it's not
so much the feelings that count as the contributions individuals make to
a common good. In application, one folk model stands to discern family
in sentiments where another does not.

Family discourse is not just a mode of communication but also
assigns meaning to the actions we take on behalf of social ties designated
familial. In other words, it instructs us as to how we should think of and
react to related aspects of our everyday lives. When we speak of our
friends as "family," we not only publicly announce what they mean to us
and each other, but also simultaneously designate their interpersonal rights
and obligations. Stack (1974), for example, describes how kinship terms
both convey and substantiate personal relationships:

> When friends more than adequately share the exchange of goods
> and services, they are called kinsmen. . . . For example, if two
> women of the same age are helping one another, they call their
> friend "just a sister," or say that "they are going for sisters." (p. 58)

Elliot Liebow's (1967) description of street life in an East Coast metropolis
shows us how concrete the implications of kinship assignment can be:

> The social reality of the pseudo-kinship tie between those who are
> "going for brothers" is clearly evident in the case of Richard and
> Leroy. Richard and Leroy had been going for brothers for three
> months or so when Leroy got in a fight with a group of teenagers
> and young adults. Leroy suffered internal injuries and was hospi-
> talized for more than a month. One week after the fight, Richard
> and one of the teenagers who had beaten up Leroy, and with

whom both he and Leroy had been on friendly terms, got into a fight over a private matter having nothing to do with Leroy, and Richard killed the teenager. Richard was immediately arrested and the police, acting on information from the dead boy's friends, relatives, and others in the community, charged him with first-degree murder for the premeditate revenge killing of one who had beaten up "his brother." But when it was established that Leroy and Richard were not related in any way the charge was dropped to murder in the second degree. The dead boy's friends and relatives were outraged and bewildered. To them, and even to some of Richard and Leroy's friends, it was clearly a premediated, deliberate killing. Hadn't Richard and Leroy been going for brothers? And hadn't Leroy been badly beaten by this same boy just eight days earlier? (pp. 169-170)

Family discourse specifies the multiple dimensons of the familial. To state that household X or Y is a close-knit family despite what appears on the surface not only tells us what the domestic order of a household is like, but also urges us to look beyond what its occupants appear to do in order to discern what they feel. The various discourses concerning family life may direct us to actions, feelings, values, or commitments as signs of the familial. The sort of family that we may discover thus depends as much on the discourse that guides our search and shapes our reports as it does on the actual object of our scrutiny. For example, those who speak the language of domestic feelings instruct us to ignore mere activity in order to discuss sentiment, just as those who insist on the basic reality of behavior guide us away from what family members think of each other. Ironically, it seems that we can sometimes gain access to a particular home's domestic reality by ignoring much of what we observe. What we, as family members, concerned outsiders, or independent observers will choose to actually look for in investigating the private realities of the household is tied to how we sort and apply the offerings and options encountered in family discourse.

Family discourse, then, is both substantive and active. In terms of substance, we can think of its terminology, ideas, models, and theories as resources for both naming and making sense of interpersonal relations. When people speak of two friends as "brothers," they bestow familial meaning on the social ties, even though the men are not legally or biologically kindred. When they use another form of discourse to designate the ties, the interpersonal relations take on a different significance. For example, as applied to interpersonal ties, medical discourse designates the health or illness of social relations, not domestic rights, obligations, or sentiments. A doctor who remarks that he suspects child abuse, not normal discipline, in a household implies an unhealthy parent-child relationship, not just a mother or father punishing a son or daughter. Yet, discourses can be combined, too. As we will show later from data gathered among persons dealing with Alzheimer's disease patients, familial and medical discourses can be joined to interpret the limits of family responsibility in home care.

Family discourse is also active. Used in reference to concrete social relations, it communicates how one intends to look at, how one should understand, or what one intends to do about what is observed. Soap operas, for example, play on this all the time. A scene in which two people embrace one another may give the impression that one character is comforting or consoling the other. An abrupt change of scene that features the sudden entrance of a jealous wife or husband, however, easily reveals marital infidelity. The TV production has signaled to its viewers that, from this point on, a particular language for, and understanding of, these interpersonal relations will not be ignored, which of course has concrete consequences such as the married couple's estrangement, divorce, or reconciliation after a lengthy misunderstanding is worked out. Real life moves in parallel. Whether in fiction or in real life, as such scenes develop, we literally hear the existing or impending status of the familial in the actors' related communications. The point is that the definitions applied to our relations with others are not only ways of naming and making sense of them, but also provide courses of action.

There is, however, an opposite side to the coin. If discourse assigns meaning to everyday life and thereby instructs our actions, life's potential meanings are limited to the discourses available. Thus, for example, if in some circumstance we accord family significance to particular social relations, then those ties will not be seen in terms of whether they are, say, healthy or sick. Substantively, interpersonal ties are as potentially varied in their meanings as discourses permit. Furthermore, as circumstances and their available discourses change, so do the potential meanings of our relations with others.

Family Discourse in History

Family discourse and the imagery it carries is shaped socially, culturally, and historically. Indeed, it has become increasingly clear that "family" and related "domestic" concepts as we know them are relatively recent developments. While this does not mean that kinfolk did not live together in meaningful social relationships before now, it implies that different meanings have been applied to living arrangements. Many of the distinguishing features of contemporary family discourse—in particular the notions of privacy and sentiment—were either absent from or unimportant to the discourse of primary social relations prior to the last few centuries.

Social historians have noted the sense in which family and domesticity are recently "invented" interpretive structures. While we have always had biological mothers, fathers, and children, the public sense of their interpersonal configuration has changed dramatically over time. As Nicholson (1988) states:

> What existed prior to the sixteenth century was so different from what emerged later so as not to even properly warrant the label of family. Indeed, prior to the early modern period, there was not even the concept like ours of family. (p.4)

We can document this by tracing the development of the meaning and use of the word "family" itself. For example, as late as the end of the Middle Ages, the German language had no word for the private groups of parents and children that we currently understand as family (Mitterauer and Sieder, 1982). This is not to suggest that concrete arrangements like ours did not exist. They did, but it was a larger circle of persons that was regarded as a distinct social group. The present German word familie came into general use only in the eighteenth century, having been adapted from the French famille to convey the emerging sense of gratuitous sentimentality and privacy attached to the concept. The latter term derives from the Latin familia, which, in turn, comes from a common Indo-Germanic root, the Oscan term famel (Mitterauer and Sieder, 1982). The basic meaning attached to this root form is "house"; that is, the total number of cohabiting persons, including kin, servants, and slaves. The transformation of the word shows the development of family as a culturally meaningful category. It reflects the evolving centrality and connection of the concepts "home," "lineage," and "family" as categories through which domestic meaning is organized. While the linguistic and conceptual linkage of house and family is older than modern times, the private image is contemporary.

There seems to be some consensus among historians that the concept of family has existed only since the fifteenth or sixteenth century (Aries, 1962; Anderson, 1980). Yet its development cannot be described as a straightforward ascendance from nothing. Aries (1962) contends that most historians believe that precursors to the modern family were present in the ways that kinship was once understood. Ties of blood were thought to compose not one but two groups, "distinct, though concentric": the family or *mesnie*, which can be compared to our modern conjugal family, and the *line* which extended its solidarity to all the descendents of a single ancestor. The family and the line stood in opposition to one another, the progress of one weakening the other, in fluctuating cycles of ascendance up through the Middle Ages.

Aries, however, argues that relations between line and family may have been somewhat more complicated. He cites Georges Duby, contending that family ties in tenth-century France were, in Aries' (1962) words, "very loose":

> This is because they were useless: The peaceful organs of the old
> Frank state were still strong enough to allow a freeman to live an
> independent life and to prefer, if he so wished, the company of
> his friends and neighbors to that of his relatives. (p. 353)

However, the gradual dissolution of the state led to the strengthening of
lineal solidarity, with a lineage taking over the protective functions once
held by "other forms of human relationship and subjection: the vassal
homage, the seignoiry, the village community" (p. 354).

From 1000 A.D. through the Middle Ages, the importance of the
line relative to that of the family fluctuated in response to modifications
in the larger political order. Note that, as Aries (1962) argues in the
following extract, the line and family not only were relational, but also
constituted feelings and ideas:

> It is not so much a question of a progressive substitution of the
> family for the line . . . as of the loosening or tightening of the ties
> of blood, now extended, now restricted to the couple. One has the
> impression that only the line was capable of exciting the forces of
> feeling and imagination. That is why so many romances of
> chivalry treat of it. The restricted family community, on the other
> hand, had an obscure life which has escaped the attention of
> historians. But this obscurity is understandable. In the domain of
> feeling, the family did not count as much as the line. One might
> say that the concept of the line was the only concept of a family
> character known in the Middle Ages. It was very different from the
> concept of the family such as we have seen it in the iconography
> of the 16th and 17th centuries. It extended to the ties of blood
> without regard to the emotions engendered by cohabitation and
> intimacy. (pp. 355–356)

Thus, medieval society glorified the line, with its honor and solidarity. The
family was hardly recognizable.

It is only from the fifteenth century on that we can find "the rise
of a new concept: the concept of the family" (Aries, 1962, 363). The arrangement was continuously present, Aries contends, but

> the family existed in silence: it did not awaken feelings strong
> enough to inspire poet or artist. We must recognize the impor-
> tance of this silence: not much value was placed on family. It was
> only in the 15th and 16th centuries that we saw family's "long
> period of obscurity" come to an end with the "birth and develop-
> ment of the concept of the family." (p. 364)

Throughout Europe, "family" was obscure. Anderson (1980, 41) notes that
"Scandinavian peasants' everyday behavior was probably much more
oriented to the productive or residential group and to working and neigh-

borhood relationships than to the conjugal family," while Shorter (1975, 5) writes that "members of the family felt that they had more in common emotionally with their varous peer groups than with one another." The affective characterizations and sentimental attachments that dominate our contemporary understanding of family were virtually nil. Anderson reports that little evidence can be found of a duty to love one's spouse or children; instead there was a marked emphasis on respect, deference, and obligation, while affection and sentimental attachments were treated suspiciously and seen as potential disruptions to the larger social order. Marriage among the upper class was "remote," according to Anderson (p. 43), with spouses having separate sets of rooms, staff, and daily lives. They only rarely could be found together in private. Marital relations among peasants were also characterized by distance and formality, marriage being seen as an economic, productive, and reproductive, rather than as an emotional relationship (Stone, 1977). Kinship was thus vitally important in a range of instrumental ways, but "being together about the dinner table was not" (Shorter, 1975, 5).

Perhaps the sharpest contrasts between traditional and contemporary "families" shows up in relation to the concept of family privacy, a cornerstone of the contemporary family image that was all but absent in traditional society. Traditional households harbored a variety of residents and participants; close kin, relatives, employees, boarders, and near strangers shared the same quarters. People from the outside moved freely through the household, observing and monitoring. Seclusion, either from the outside or from other household members, was unheard of. All members of the family, for example, would sleep in the same room. It was likely that at least one person not a member of the immediate family would share this sleeping space and that this room would also house all other activities of the household as well (Shorter, 1975).

The contrast with today' s sense of family privacy is highlighted in the following description that Shorter (1975) offers of a typical German peasant dwelling:

> Inside such a dwelling there invariably lives a family of numerous offspring. Sometimes several generations are on hand, sometimes as well several unrelated families. Especially common in these rooms are lateral relatives, who also have children. The household's few beds, always very dirty and sometimes thick and sweltering, are found both in the main room and the dark, fetid side chamber, so that normally, 2-3 people, even of different sexes, sleep in the same bed. (p. 40)

And French peasants knew little more of privacy:

> the peasant family would eat, recreate, procreate, and slumber all in the same room . . . a single bed more commonly received the weight of the entire family. (pp. 41-42)

While the well-to-do were housed in more spacious accommodations, the lack of household privacy was not merely a function of impoverishment. Indeed, Shorter argues that neither rich nor poor ever thought to take advantage of the opportunities for seclusion—from either insiders or outsiders—that their homes may have allowed. The image of family privacy that underpins today's conception of family life and that pervades contemporary family discourse was simply absent from traditional ways of thinking and talking about everyday relationships and living arrangements.

It was not until the fiteenth century, writes Aries (1962) that the "reality and the idea of the family were to change: a slow and profound revolution, scarcely distinguished by either contemporary observers or later historians, and difficult to recognize" (p. 369). As the transition from medieval to modern family progressed, the family concept took on more of its contemporary sentimental meaning. Initially, "the family was a moral and social, rather than sentimental, reality. . . . The family scarcely had a sentimental existence at all among the poor . . ." (Aries, 1962, 369). The new and increasingly powerful concept

> was formed around the conjugal family, that of the parents and children. . . . It has less and less to do with problems such as the honour of a line, the integrity of an inheritance, or the age and permanence of a name: it springs simply from the unique relationship between the parents and their children. . . . What counted most of all was the emotion aroused by the child, the living image of his parents. (Aries, 1962, 364)

By the seventeenth century, "the sentimenal climate was now entirely different and closer to ours" (Aries, 1962, 370).

Shorter (1975) has characterized this change as a "revolution" in family sentiment. Modern notions of family, he argues, are tied to the rise of market capitalism and related "surges" in romantic love, maternal love, and domesticity. Property and lineage gave way, he suggests, to personal happiness and self-realization as criteria for choosing marriage partners; romantic love supplanted material considerations as reasons for marriage. At the same time, the mother-child relationship secured an unprecedented emotional primacy. While mothers in traditional society routinely placed many considerations—mostly basic survival concerns—above their infants' welfare, modernization allowed their counterparts to place an infant's well-being above all else. The seemingly spontaneous and natural attachment of mothers to their babies that we call "mother love" began to flourish as the changing economy liberated mothers from the desperate need to invest their time in other subsistence activities. And finally, Shorter argues, boundaries between family and community began to emerge as the household's role as an economically productive unit began to wane. Affection, empathy, and love—sentiment—took the place of productive considerations in relations between family members as the household formed into a "shelter" of domesticity.

According to Shorter, the modern image of family as a center of sentiment and domesticity emerged over the last three centuries, bringing with it a mosaic of family meanings associated with privacy and intimacy. Spontaneous, romantic love required a certain seclusion for its ideals to be realized. Maternal love elevated close and nurturant mother-child relations above other commitments to the larger community. It fostered the imagery of a sentimental nest that would shelter the family. The decline of economic activity in the home halted the traffic of outsiders within it. As links to the larger community weakened, the "inside" of the family was more clearly distinguished from the "outside." Members' ties to one another were reinforced, while nonmembers became "outsiders" against whom household barriers of privacy were erected. Thus, family's modern domestic image and discourse, which Shorter (1975, 227) describes as a "precious emotional unit that must be protected with privacy and isolation from outside intrusion" are only recently available as interpretive resources for social relationships.

The evolution of family's sentimental meaning continued as European culture spread to the Americas, bringing with it a concept of family that was to become one of the most potent and affectively charged images of the nineteenth and twentieth centuries. By the time of the Puritans' arrival in the New World, for example, the family was widely heralded as the guardian of the public as well as private good (Demos, 1970). And by the emergence of the Progressive Era (from about 1890-1917), American social reformers were practically obsessed with family issues as well as anxieties over the family's future. So strong and emotional was the image of the so-called "traditional" nuclear family by that time that, as Kennedy (1970) notes, "Practically everyone agree[d] on the paramount importance of the family in human life" (p.49).

The variety of familial meanings currently available and employed thus reflects particular times and places, not some intrinsic qualities of the familial that inhere in, or attach to, a distinct social arrangement. Still, our affinity for the contemporary family image—its centrality to our social organization and cultural tradition—often persuades us to regard the family as somehow natural and transcendent, to see and understand it totally in our own terms (Barrett and McIntosh, 1987). As Aries (1962, 364) asks, "Are we not ourselves unconsciously impressed by the part the family has played in our society for several centuries, and are we not tempted to exaggerate its scope and even to attribute to it an almost absolute sort of historical authority?"

We might be better able to comprehend shifts in family's meanings over time if we liken them to transformations in other, less emotionally laden concepts. For example, the term "civility" (or civilized) today connotes general politeness and courtesy; its most formal common usage might be "good manners." But from the Middle Ages through the eighteenth century, civility came to mean much more. According to Aries (1962), it was the "practical knowledge which it was necessary to have in order to live in society" (p. 381). The more generalized, nonspecific character attached to today's usage was preceded by specific and graphically explicit directives regarding the smallest details of daily living. Norbert Elias (1978) provides an extensive catalogue of rules and rubrics through which civility was expressed. It is a litany of axioms concerned with, among other things, speaking, dressing, undressing, sleeping, eating, defecating, urinating, flatulence, spitting, and relations between the sexes. The point is not that these activities have changed over the years, but rather that the way we conceive of civility or—borrowing from Elias—of civilization and culture has been transformed and generalized over the centuries. Its meanings, usage, and applications have changed.

Much the same can be said of family. Extending the historical record to contemporary usage, we can argue that what is available to us now as a configuration of domestic meanings to apply to everyday life was not always so. Time has transformed family's imagery and discourse, changing the way we think and talk about communal life and social relations. Family's meaning and usage, then, are tied to their historical context. Indeed, we will argue in addition that they are situationally sensitive—that is, influenced by their social and cultural circumstances as well.

The Social Distribution of Family Discourse

Family discourse is not randomly scattered on the plane of experience. People do not arbitrarily "break out" into just any kind of domestic terminology or wantonly apply familial models and theories. Rather, there are distinct domains and occasions recommending the use of select references and particular ideas about family life; usage varies in place and time. In some places, those concerned talk of family life in ways distinct from how they convey their thoughts about it in other arenas. For example, when middle-class husbands and wives talk of family, we regularly hear vocabularies of intimacy or child-rearing, or discussions in terms of the myriad daily activities that compose suburban home life. In contrast, one might expect that in certain treatment settings like psychiatric hospitals or rehabilitation centers, talk about, and references to, the family life of patients would take on a decidedly clinical tone. One might expect, too, that the particular clinical orientation of a treatment program would determine that the discourse of family life is articulated in a distinctive fashion. One approach might emphasize, say, the felt strength of interpersonal ties, while another one might focus the discourse of family life on the exchange of domestic goods and services. For participants in the respective settings, the fundamental realities of family life would be differently grounded, one setting presenting sentiment as the basis of domestic affairs and the other grounding domestic order in the exchange of resources. We refer to these differences in the use of terms and ideas about family life as *the social distribution of family discourse.*

There is an important point to be made about the connection between people's sense of the domestic order of the household, on the one hand, and the social distribution of family discourse, on the other. If family discourse is the mechanism by which we assign meaning to domestic affairs, then domestic affairs stand to be as diversely interpreted as the various settings in which our discourse takes place. For example, a middle-class environment conveys certain understandings of family life that might be altered, if not reversed, in working-class circumstances. Or, for instance, those who psychiatrically evaluate Sam—a delusional client at a community mental health center—stand a good chance of understanding his family life as it is linked to the causes and symptoms of Sam's mental illness; while the presiding court officials of an involuntary commitment hearing involving Sam are likely to interpret his family according to pressing placement and custodial concerns. The distribution of family discourse across the settings communicatively reveals contrasting domestic affairs in the household under consideration.

The connection between the sense of domestic life and the social distribution of meanings is not unique to domestic affairs. Answers to the question of who we are as persons, or what our peer relationships resemble, are derived as much from the various categories available to interpret lives and friendships as from the facts in their own right. We seem to know, for example, that one's measure of success depends as much on the way achievement is interpreted as on the achievements themselves. Those who see success in terms of the accumulation of honors, credentials, and material rewards, see entirely different things in conduct than do those who observe success in sociability.

When we ask whether perspectives and their related discourses can be separated from things like success and domestic affairs, we begin to see the importance of the connection between the two. Is it possible to "objectively" describe a thing like success or the domestic order of the household without some sense of what success or domestic order is? It seems not. The very realities both conceived and perceived through the discourse of one setting can differ substantially from the realities conceived and perceived in the discourse of another. This is not a matter of so-called objective differences; the same family, for example, encounters alternate interpretive agendas in various settings. Recall the many occasions when Borg heard different people make countervailing claims about the family status of specific relationships. What was spoken of as family from one point of view could be talked about quite differently from another.

The Household as a
Locus of Discovery

At the outset, we listed several terms—family, house, household, home, privacy—without distinguishing their relationship. Let us begin to do so by considering the term "household." There are, of course, various ways to think about the household: as an economic unit, a legal entity, or a shelter, among others. Perhaps the most common way to represent the household is as a physical structure of some sort that more or less provides a home for a collection of individuals. The adage that a house is not necessarily a home tritely reminds us that, while families often live in houses or their facsimile, houses to not necessarily contain what they allegedly should.

Even though house is not necessarily the same as home, there is considerable public sentiment about their connection—namely, that a house ideally should be homelike. Human service institutions, like nursing homes, trade on the connection. A quick glance at the ads for nursing homes in the yellow pages, for example, shows an abundance of references to homelike atmospheres and family substitutes: "you'll find a new home and a new caring family"; "discover a warm homelike environment"; "family-style retirement living"; "pleasant, homelike atmosphere." The implication is clear. Home and family are variable qualities for institutional dwellings, qualities that must be assiduously cultivated and consciously conveyed.

Household commonly is conceived as a kind of link between house (or another physical structure for housing people) and home. Unlike house, household is about both place and people. Accordingly, we can ask at least two kinds of question about households: where are they located, and what is life like within them? Having located a house, we can appropriately ask whether it provides a home for anyone. By the same token, addressing the second question informs the first. Having discerned the meaning of home, we can reasonably ask whether a particular place, such as a skilled-care facility, can sustain a quality home life.

These considerations reflect genuine practical concerns and interests. For instance, the issue of institutionalizing a demented elderly family member presents relatives and significant others with a double-barreled question regarding two potential homes—the family household and the nursing home. Can a particular nursing facility provide a home for a loved one and, if it is concluded that neither this facility nor any other one can, will the household continue to be a home to anyone, given the strains caused by caring for the patient in the home? In addressing the question, those concerned center their attention on the experiential linkages between house, household, and home, especially as they bear on the possibility of continuing to be family. In the Alzheimer's disease experience, for one, family caregivers worry about whether there will come a time when the stresses of continued home care will start to erode the household's family life in general to a point where the house is no longer a recognizable "home" to anyone, neither the patient nor its other occupants.

The linkage of house and home—of physical structure and social sentiment—is so prevalent that its terminology and ideas have been incorporated into the contemporary public culture of the household. Following Geertz's (1973, 1983) conception of culture as a way of assigning meaning to experience and Gerth and Mills' (1953) decidedly public interpretation of privacy, we conceive of a public culture as a commonly recognized sphere of understanding about human affairs, notably personal and interpersonal affairs. Public cultures may emerge around diverse issues like a disease, the family, or even such mundame activities as outdoor recreation or video games. In turn, at the interpersonal level select experiences are named, repeatedly communicated, and recognized as a distinct domain of everyday life (Berger and Luckmann, 1966). Any parent knows just how impenetrable the "realities" of childhood can be if one does not share in the local childhood cultures of "My Little Pony" or "G.I. Joe." The same is true of diverse family realities and their associated public cultures.

If we think of the terms house, household, and home as featured in a public culture and articulated through family discourse, we begin to discern a perspective on the household that contrasts with the view that the household is the concrete embodiment of domestic life. From our perspective, household is less a concrete place for family living than it is the idea that some place might be more or less homelike. Putting it in terms of family discourse, we use the term "household" as a way of speaking about place, one taken for granted as the likely location of a home. As such, the household can be thought of as a locus of discovery for home life, more specifically for family life. It is a place where people believe family life might reside.

The distinction between the household as a concrete place and the household as a locus of discovery is important methodologically; the way we choose to study domestic life is affected by which view we take. As a concrete location for finding family, the household is presumed to actually contain the facts of home life. Should our task be, let's say, to assess a household for the quality of its family life, we would rightly aim to get as close to its internal workings as possible and not be fooled by outward appearances. With due respect for ethical considerations, we would muster whatever means we could to directly or indirectly obtain the private facts of the home (see LaRossa, Bennett, and Gelles, 1981). This might even mean living in a household in order to learn its daily, yet inner secrets. Needless to say, this would present numerous tactical problems, as our daily presence in the household would no doubt alter it significantly.

If we think of the household as a locus of discovery, our orientation is less to the interior, interpersonal contents of a physical structure than it is to the *process* by which the household's domestic realities are discovered and described, regardless of whether that process occurs in or out of the household proper. One need not be physically present in the household in order to discover how social order is assigned to its domestic affairs. As we shall show in greater detail later, even family members who have lived in a particular house and shared their lives together for years learn and relearn what kind of family they are, were, and will be, in locations far removed from the household proper. For example, a mother who in postparental life joins a support group for widows may learn that "what went on" in her home for "all those years" is entirely different from what she had thought all along. Her participation in the group presents an interpretation of domestic affairs at odds with her existing one. Close attention to family discourse in her support group shows that what had been, to her, the concrete "facts" of a private household can be quite publicly reconfigured to reveal an entirely different sense of domestic order. The new version challenges the prior understanding of her family life, which—until her participation in the support group—she hadn't given much thought to.

Family discourse shows that those involved in the inner workings of the household are not the ultimate arbiters of what is or is not its family life. Rather, the household is an "envisioned" place, where those concerned typically focus their attention when aiming to understand family life. Household as an envisioned place does not mean that observers have no factual knowledge of domestic life, only that what is believed about the actual domestic order of a household is not necessarily warranted by having physical access to it.

As private as they are said to be, if the facts of the household take on their meaning in diverse places, both in and out of the physical household, then the household is less a concrete place for locating domestic order than it is a kind of cognitive anchor—something that fixes our attention as we seek the meaning of domestic life. In practice, household, then, is something *used* to specify the location of what we believe to be authentic dometic activities, whether or not we have ever been on its premises.

Studying Descriptive Practice

To study family discourse as it applies to concrete domestic affairs is to focus on what we might call "descriptive practice." Descriptive practice is the situationally sensitive, communicative process by which reality is represented. In studying descriptive practice, we come upon veritable, cognitive, and interactional practitioners of family order—people who are inspecting, witnessing, evidencing, deriving, and theorizing about the internal domestic organization of the household. In virtually "doing things with words," these practitioners assign meaning to what they more or less know goes on in the household (Gubrium and Lynott, 1985; Bernardes, 1987).

Descriptive practice is our field of data—family discourse in use. Its practitioners fashion answers to diverse questions of familial order: What type of family is this? Who are its "real" members? What are its boundaries? How did it come to be what it is? As we encounter the field of data, we witness practitioners of familial order building bridges between the possible domestic affairs of particular households (that is, the public culture of family) and what a particular household's hidden facts seem to tell.

This bridging process is situationally sensitive; what people do with words does not take place in a vacuum. In representing the domestic affairs of the household, they take account of understandings and interests in their immediate circumstances. For example, in attempting to discover the domestic order of household X in the context of a psychiatric conference, speakers are likely to discuss family in terms of affective relations. The conference, as a set of local understandings for how to think—and talk—about family life, provides its participants with a way of communicating and assigning meaning to the household. The discourse is a feature of the setting where domestic life comes under consideration, not of the household itself. Each situation, as a descriptive context, serves to construct its own domestic affairs.

If domestic order is socially constructed, then our task as analysts of family's descriptive practice is to "de-construct" the many versions of domestic reality into its diverse languages and the processes through which household truths are produced (see Derrida, 1977). Deconstruction is a kind of working backward, from the taken-for-granted social realities of everyday life to the descriptive practice that produces them, documenting the process by which reality is constructed. Our aim in analyzing family discourse and descriptive practice is to *make visible* the ways in which the affairs of the household come to be publicly recognized and understood as they are.

Because the interpersonal privacies of the household are tied to public understandings of family life, there is no reason to assume that family members have privileged access to the meaning of their own domestic affairs. As do others, family members engage in descriptive practice. They inspect, witness, offer each other evidence, and theorize about their lives together. Like others, their descriptive practice is context-bound, producing situationally sensitive versions of family order. How they conceive of the social order of their own households in one circumstance may be at considerable odds with how they think of the social order in another one. Their versions are not closer approximations to the truths of family life than others' versions are. We don't stand a better chance of discovering the domestic realities of the household by asking kindred or occupants than by being witnesses to others' testimony. In principle, all descriptive practitioners equally represent the domestic affairs of concern to them; only their particular representational claims differ. Thus, our conception of family-as-descriptive-practice directs our family studies to any situation where family is made topical. It grants no special status to descriptions obtained within households, nor does it privilege the reports of insiders. We look at (and listen to) family discourse, wherever it may occur, to discover the domestic meanings that persons employ to organize and make sense of their social relations.

Since family formulations may arise anywhere, we will find the data of family discourse both inside and outside families. Ironically, such discourse may occur rather infrequently inside families as compared, say, to what transpires in a family therapy agency. This is because families' considerations of the meaning of family and domestic order are likely to be prompted by troubled relationships. For example, it might take an exasperated father's complaint to his teenage daughter ("We never see you around here. This place is just a place for you to crash.") to cause a discussion of what parents and children mean to each other as family: "You know you owe it to us as family to spend some time with us." The presence of such troubles, of course, does not necessarily mean a family is deviant or in need of therapy; they are simply family troubles.

The Evidence and Research Settings

The evidence and examples we present to illustrate the relationship between the discourse of the family and the social order of the household are taken from three sources. First, we draw upon the myriad instances of family discourse that we've encountered in our own lives or that others around have shared with us. Some have been generated as part of our university teaching activities, mostly from the students who variously brought family constructions to light for us. Some were found in letters, advertisements, newspaper accounts, formal reports, and other documents. Anyone who attends carefully to the swirl of communication that engulfs everyday life will discover family discourse to be ubiquitous.

A second source is a variety of existing studies of social interaction where domestic issues have become topical. While many of these have not intended family to be the main topic of research, family discourse has nonetheless insinuated itself into both the interactions being analyzed and the analyses themselves. Stack's and Liebow's work, which we have already cited, are examples.

Finally, we have collected data through our own field research in a variety of human service and community settings. These include nursing homes (Gubrium, 1975, 1980a, 1980b), a residential treatment center for emotionally disturbed children (Buckholdt and Gubrium, 1985), a physical rehabilitation hospital (Gubrium and Buckholdt, 1982a), support groups and a self-help organization for the caregivers of Alzheimer's disease (senile dementia) victims (Gubrium, 1986), and community mental health settings and involuntary commitment hearings (Holstein, 1984, 1987a, 1987b, 1988a, 1988b; Grusky et al, 1986, 1987; Miller and Holstein, 1989, forthcoming; Holstein and Miller, forthcoming). We did extensive fieldwork in each setting, combining participant observation, informal or focused interviews, and the analysis of personal, professional, and institutional documents. While each setting presented lives in terms of local or official categories, the discourse of the familial was always present and important.

Murray Manor was a nursing home studied in the early 1970s (Gubrium, 1975). (Throughout this book, the names of all persons and field sites have been fictionalized.) The Manor was known locally to be one of the finest facilities in the area. It was church-related and, at the time, housed 130 patients and residents; it had a few uncompleted floors that eventually were occupied by patients. Residents housed on the facility's first floor were ambulatory and officially only in need of personal care. Patients constituted the remaining care population and occupied the third and fourth floors. Two-thirds of the patients and residents paid for their care privately; others were supported by Title 19 (Medicaid). Like many nursing home facilities, the Manor provided an activities de- part- ment, occupational and physical therapy, pastoral care, medical and nursing services, and a beautician, among other daily, weekly, and seasonal programs.

The nursing home research eventually extended to other facilities, with a focus on professional decision making (Gubrium, 1980a, 1980b). Of particular concern was how the diverse professional languages of staff members, from physicians and nurses to social workers and activity therapists, were integrated into coherent descriptions of care and clinical intervention. Also of interest was the effect of external accountability on the process by which care plans were formulated.

In 1976, groundwork was laid for a field study of the descriptive organizaton of emotional disturbance in a residential treatment center for children (Buckholdt and Gubrium, 1985). Named Cedarview, the facility was nonprofit, nonsectarian, and officially committed to a treatment-by-objective approach, stressing behavior modification. Other treatment perspectives, however, entered into the facility' s programming. While one or two of the social workers were partial to behavioral methods, others considered themselves to be more Rogerian or person-centered. Some thought themselves eclectic. The three regular psychological consultants were a psychoanalytically oriented psychiatrist, a behavioral psychologist, and a psychologist who took the eclectic approach. Even the special education teachers held varied views of treatment, although they were, on the whole, not known to be as individually partial as the consultants and social workers were to particular approaches. Cedarview, more than Murray Manor and the other nursing homes studied, combined rather diverse, formal theoretical orientations in its staff, even while it officially dedicated itself to behavioral programming.

The children ranged in age from six to fourteen years and were regularly placed in the facility for two years of treatment. During an eighteen-month period, Cedarview' s census fluctuated between thirty-five and sixty children. Both boys and girls were treated, although the residential program was limited to boys. Girls participated in the day program, which included schooling, counseling, behavior modification, and selected cares and activities. The boys were housed in four cottages (dormitories) and supervised by live-in child-care workers.

A growing interest in the descriptive organization of care led to research on the impact of audience on the communication of treatment and recovery at Wilshire, a physical rehabilitation hospital where fieldwork was conducted in 1979–80 (Gubrium and Buckholdt, 1982a). The hospital treated the physical dysfunctions associated with stroke, brain traumas, spinal cord injury, amputation, and hip fracture. Its treatment staff included physical and occupational therapists, social workers, speech therapists, nurses, physiatrists, and leisure therapists. The average length of stay was four to six weeks.

During the fieldwork at Wilshire, it became evident that what was said about treatment and how it was communicated depended significantly on whether the audience was the patient, the family, or outside agents like insurance companies. For some audiences, staff members communicated in medical terms; for others, they formulated descriptions and explanations of progress in decidedly educational terms. The family figured significantly in varied aspects of clinical practice.

In 1983, the fieldwork moved outside of formal treatment facilities and into Alzheimer's disease caregivers' homes, support groups, and local chapters of the Alzheimer's Disease and Related Disorders Association (ADRDA) in two different cities (Gubrium, 1986). Description and discourse continued to be the research focus, this time centering on how the borderlines of the normal and pathological were communicatively sustained. In one of the cities, participant observation also was conducted in a structured day care program for Alzheimer' s disease patients, which was organized and staffed by a geriatric institute affiliated with an acute care hospital.

Holstein's (1984, 1987a, 1987b, 1988a, 1988b; Grusky et al, 1986, 1987) fieldwork in community mental health settings, like the Alzheimer's research, bridged the household and community with the formal treatment facility. This continuing study of community responses to mental illness began in 1981 and has examined treatment and support settings, as well as involuntary commitment hearings, in several communities across the United States. These include urban metropolitan areas in the western, upper midwestern, eastern, and southeastern United States, as well as more rural sites in the Northwest, the upper Midwest, and New England. A multicommunity, descriptive evaluation study of community support programs for the chronically mentally ill (Grusky et al., 1986, 1987) provided the opportunity to observe and interview in community mental health centers, within inpatient and outpatient psychiatric facilities, diverse rehabilitation and socialization programs, patient and family support groups, and legal and law enforcement settings. As in Gubrium's field settings, concerns for home and family were commonplace as psychiatrists, psychologists, mental health administrators, social workers, therapists, clients, and others confronted the contingencies of community and institutional care for a chronically troubled population. Especially problematic was the role that family could be expected to play in delivering community-based care and providing community-based custody for persons who frequently were socially disruptive, had long histories of psychiatric problems and institutional treatments, and whose reinstitutionalization was often imminent.

A separate but related observational study of involuntary mental hospitalizaton procedures was concurrently conducted, primarily in California, but also in several of the sites mentioned above. The California research focused mainly on those *habeas corpus* hearings in Metropolitan Court through which persons who had been hospitalized on initial fourteen-day commitments sought their release. More limited observations in four other jurisdictions focused on the occasional involuntary commitment hearings that were handled through municipal, county, and state court systems.

Civil commitment decisions under reformed mental health legislation are guided by fairly standard criteria. Laws varied somewhat in their wording across study sites, but were quite similar in their application. California' s Lanterman-Petris-Short Act is prototypical in that it allows for commitment based on a diagnosis of severe mental illness *and* danger to self and others, or grave disability (the inability to provide for one' s basic personal needs of food, clothing, and shelter). Two of the other jurisdictions had essentially the same commitment requirements but did not employ the grave disability terminology. The others had no corresponding formal criterion; but, in practice, persons seen as unable to provide for their basic needs were commonly judged dangerous to themselves. Hence, a *de facto* grave disability standard was in effect in all of the sites studied.

Regardless of the formal statutes, involuntary commitment proceedings typically orient to the candidate patient' s ability to establish some workable living arrangement outside the hospital that can contain the havoc—both internal and external—associated with mental illness (Holstein, 1984). While a diagnosis of psychiatric disorder is required, civil commitment depends more on decision-makers' practical asessments of the "tenability" of candidate patients' proposed living situation than on formal assessments of their mental conditions. Issues regarding food, clothing, shelter, medical and psychiatric care, as well as questions about who will look after and manage the released candidate patient, are central to most decisions. Images of family and home care were integral to such discussions, both in terms of family's availability as a custodial and treatment resource, and as a standard of concerned care against which alternatives could be assessed. Family discourse was consequently ubiquitous as parties to the commitment process argued the various possibilities and prospects.

The strategy of reinterpreting data originally gathered for other purposes is well established in the social sciences. Each of our settings was the focus of research objectives that only partially bore on questions of family, home, and household. The nursing home research, for instance, initially centered on the manifold worlds of care embedded in a single facility and suggested that quality of care could not be understood separately from how the nursing home experience figured in the institutional lives of patients, families, and floor and administrative staff. The research on community mental health care originally examined the process by which issues of competence and care were interpreted and organized among persons with varied interests in the cases under consideration, some of whom were family members. In their original formulation, the studies took domestic matters into account in describing patterns of social organization, primarily because those persons being studied spoke about family. Family matters were generally assumed to be important ingredients of care, custody, and commitment. There was always much conversation about family life, home, and household, which combined ideas, theories, and models of domestic relations. While it would not be correct to state that the relation between the discourse of family life and the domestic affairs of the household was a primary interest from the start, we do note that descriptive practice and its social organization were always topics of the research. Thus, as we reflect back on the familial data gathered in the various settings in the following chapters, we now treat the data as family discourse and present its descriptive practice.

Much of the family discourse we analyze is drawn from human service settings dealing with what some would call "deviant behavior." In a sense, settings of this sort insure the discovery of family discourse because contemporary Americans seem thoroughly convinced that most troubles in some way relate to family life, either as causes or potential remedies. Moreover, as a last resort, they commonly bring the troubles to the attention of professionals. Family is therefore likely to be quite topical in settings where troubles are treated. Accordingly, the data of family discourse are more efficiently collected where one can anticipate routine discussions of domestic issues. Of course, this still raises the question of whether the patterns and generalizations derived from the data apply only to troubled families. We offer two reasons why they do not.

The first reason is empirical. Time and again in the field sites, family members, disease victims, troubled children and adults, service providers, and significant others cast their references in speaking of domestic affairs across the broad spectrum of living arrangements. Their judgments and comparisons took on their meaning from both "deviant" and "nondeviant" frames of reference. It was never as if their lives were continually conceived as troubled. In practice, deviance was not so much a given framework for interpreting domestic affairs as it was one category, among others, more or less known to be a relevant frame of reference for understanding family, home, and household. A major theme of the Alzheimer' s disease experience, for example, was resolving the question of whether the disease is part of the normal aging process, the answer to which was far from obvious in practice (Gubrium, 1986).

In all field sites, there were times when and places where people acted out their lives and spoke about them in categories altogether separate form those officially connecting them with the agencies under consideration. Those whose lives we studied directly and indirectly subjected themselves and each other to questions such as "What is family?" "Where is family?" "When is family?" and "Who is family?" Their answers reflected their varying circumstances. Because their responses arose out of descriptive practice, the bounds of the normal and the pathological, the nondeviant and the deviant, among other oppositional categories, were never completely set, but took on their reality in relation to what was done with words. Their interest in family questions went beyond the issue of the deviant or pathological status of certain aspects of their lives or troubles. Rather than their lives falling into one category or another, they actively used *each* pole of these binary opposites to assign meaning to what ailed or interested them. In other words, the categories were taken into account in interpreting domestic affairs but they did not determine descriptive practice (see Gubrium, 1988a, chapter 2). In this sense, then, the field data cut across the margins of the normal and the deviant.

What is more, as we show throughout the book, the organization of family usage in the service settings reflects usage in diverse "nondeviant" settings. Discussions of issues ranging from the relation between family values and running for public office to accounts of a sports team's morale show how descriptive practice displays the familial in varied domains of daily living. Many of our illustrations from human service settings will resonate with the family discourse that readers encounter in their own lives. For example, we will discuss at length several instances in mental health and support group settings where family membership is discussed, contested, and negotiated as persons try to make sense of the circumstances and social relations confronting them and come to some practical decisions about courses of action to pursue. The ways that family comes up in these conversations can also be found in cordial chats or marital spats between husbands and wives, when neighbors gossip across the back fence, or when two friends meet in the checkout line at the supermarket. We invite readers to consider how similar the instances of family usage described in this book are to the occasions when they hear people "talking family" in their own daily lives.

A second reason our data speak to the full gamut of the familial is more theoretical. It seems that we social scientists too readily accept official or formal categories as our own, without taking a close look at the way the categories are organized in the diverse experiences of all concerned, not just officials. We assign lives to categories such as deviant, sick, and normal, treating those we label as if they were the categories' virtual puppets. Garfinkel (1967) once stated that social scientists tend to address people as if they were "cultural dopes." What he meant was that people are not given credit for being concerned at all with the fundamental meaning of the categories in their own right, those in which we social scientists handily place them. We tend to act as if people were passively subject to so-called social forces. For example, we orient to the category "broken home" as if the condition had an objective, wholesale impact on delinquency. But the social sciences rarely examine how those concerned—divorced parents, children, police, service providers—themselves use such categories to account for delinquency .

In contrast, our analysis of family discourse treats persons' interpretations of their circumstances and their understandings and uses of official categories as its topic. "Deviance," "senility," "sickness," and "mental illness" are not taken to be objective features of the settings we've studied. Rather, we treat them and their opposites as emergent constructions. They are end products rather than starting points of the people in question, who come to understand and categorize who and what they are and what is happening to them notably in relation to the interpretation of domestic order and family life.

We have now laid the conceptual groundwork of a new perspective for addressing the question "What is family?" Before we turn to family's descriptive organization, let us examine in detail the three fundamental assumptions of conventional studies of domestic life. The assumptions combine into what we call the "private image" of the family.

Chapter 3

The Private Image

Facts are not the only arbiter of truth in human affairs. The way we frame the facts or choose to interpret them also determines what is known about people and their relationships. In this chapter, we turn to a common way of framing the facts of household, home, and family—the private image. In Chapter 2 we discussed how the private image developed throughout history in Western culture, how barriers of privacy erected as links to the community were weakened over the last three centuries. In this chapter we consider the general conception toward which this has evolved. We examine how the image is articulated in relevant areas of family studies, setting the background for later chapters where our data give rise to important questions about the image's assumptions concerning the reality of family life.

The Concept of Image

An image is a working conception, an impression, or a model of reality. We regularly hear people ask if something might not have appeared differently if it had been approached in some other fashion, from some other perspective. Would we have formed another impression had we begun from a different viewpoint? The questions apply to diverse matters, from the perception of which Super Bowl team "got all the breaks" to the portrayal of family life and public affairs. We might guess, for example, that one whose image of the family rested on the values of prestige, appearance, and influence would see and convey the political, status-building patterns of home life when describing family matters. On the other hand, we might expect one whose image emphasized common values and interdependence to focus on close domestic relations or the lack thereof. It is not too difficult to discover a child's version of household issues that contradicts a parent's version. A refusal to buy a third family car for a teenager's use could, from the parental perspective, be framed as an expression of sound family values; a family must live within its means and members should acquire only what they have earned. But from the teenager's point of view, this might be just one more instance of the tyranny of two parents who run a "prison, not a home." Whether we call them theoretical differences or, more casually, alternate perspectives, the manner by which we approach things and issues seems to be part and parcel of what we actually find. In the course of our everyday lives, we take into account both fact and perspective. Indeed, it would not be surprising to hear facts themselves spelled out as the facts from one point of view or another. The proper grammar to use, if it were not so awkward, would be to specify, say, the facts-according-to-X, the facts-according-to-Y, or the facts-according-to-Z, and so on.

Yet the scientific penchant to be objective about matters of fact distracts us from the effects of perspective; we are often so buried in facts that we forget that facts are always presented according to someone's point of view (see Raffel, 1979). Scientific protocol tends to dissociate facts from perspectives, although in everyday life we regularly apprehend them as mutually dependent. The quest for objectivity seems to demand the separation.

We don't mean to suggest that social scientists are unaware of differences in perspective. As far as family studies is concerned, any number of theoretical compendia show that diverse points of view exist and inform programs of research. For example, the two most recent comprehensive reviews of research and action in family studies published by the *Journal of Marriage and the Family* outline alternate theoretical frameworks (Broderick, 1971; Berardo, 1980), as does the important two-volume collection entitled *Contemporary Theories about the Family* (Burr et al., 1979). Nonetheless, once theoretical diversity is acknowledged, it seems to be set aside when matters of fact are considered. Perspective or image is treated far less seriously than it is in our ordinary lives, where we can go so far as to conduct interpersonal warfare over the claimed realities of objective fact (see Gubrium, 1988a).

Image affects not only the interpretation of facts, but also the way we actually communicate them. For example, to preface questions about family life with the article "the," as one might do in asking about the status of *the* family, implies that family is a separate and unique entity. The implication is that it is a thing, to be found somewhere, and is a possible object of study. (Borg, we recall, was rather troubled by that implication as she attempted to locate families.) As some feminist scholars and others have recently asked, what do we mean to convey about family life when we preface family with "the" (Thorne and Yalom, 1982; Bernardes, 1985a)? Do we perhaps inadvertently signal a reality that, had our words been chosen otherwise, might suggest that family is a configuration of entirely different facts? Regarding the connection between household, home, and family, such questions imply that family is not just a thing located more or less in the household, but is something we commonly think of as connected with matters of house, home, and privacy in a particular way. These matters are as much ideas as entities. Just as anthropologists Clifford and Marcus's (1986) collection of papers on the poetics and politics of ethnography thematizes how anthropologists have "written culture," we might say that students of family studies have not only theorized family in terms of the private image, but have *written* family accordingly.

If we consider family to be as much an idea about the connection between people as it is a concrete set of social relations, we are less inclined to inquire about "the" family as we are to ask about how family, as an idea (without the "the"), is *used* to specify people's relations with others. While the latter approach might not be shared by most students of family life, we know from our everyday experiences and from reports about what are sometimes called "fictive families" that family usage is indeed commonplace in everyday life.

A Distinct Domestic Order

Let us consider the first of three assumptions underlying the private image of family life—the assumption that there is a separate and distinct domestic order. While this assumption admits that the family is influenced by so-called social forces as well as the characteristics and activities of members, it nonetheless construes the family's distinct domestic order as an entity in a category of its own. Families are taken to be real, the "things" that family studies and lay descriptions merely report about, not create in the process of communication. The family is not actually the figment of anyone's imagination; it just may seem to be at times. Some have called this the problem of "reification," meaning the unwarranted assignment of a separate and distinct reality to something.

The Family as a Superpersonality

From the outset, the scientific study of the family had a tendency to take family to be a distinct entity, casting it into a particular shape. Consider an extract from an early description of the family entity, by Ernest Burgess, a pioneer in family studies. Reporting how he developed the broad outline for a field of study, Burgess (1926) wrote:

> This study of the patterns of personal relationships in family life led directly to the conception of the family as a unity of interacting persons. By a unity of interacting personalities is meant a living, changing, growing thing. I was about to call it a superpersonality. At any rate the actual unity of family life has its existence not in any legal conception, nor in any formal contract, but in the interacting of its members. (p. 5)

Burgess informs us not only that members are involved in the formation of the thing he calls family life, but also that the "unity" is living and changing. Although it is not clear in the passage what the precise relationship is between the interacting personalities, on the one hand, and the unity, on the other, Burgess nonetheless is tempted to cast the unity in the form of a personality writ large. Following this, he empirically locates a possible "superpersonality" in the social relations of its components, seemingly suggesting that, whatever the precise relationship between members and the unity, it is members taking account of each other that is the family's existential source.

Although Burgess does not elaborate on the superpersonality, the idea has a number of implications. Following the analogy to personality, we might assume that the family had some form of consciousness, separate and distinct from the consciousness of individual members. Putting it differently, we might presume the family to have a particular way of thinking about the world, which is not necessarily coincident with that of its membership. We might even distinguish families according to their particular world views and develop a typology of family worlds.

What Burgess found tempting, others have actually attempted or at least descriptively indulged in (for example, Hess and Handel, 1959; Berger and Kellner, 1970; Reiss, 1981). As in the quotation from Burgess, it is not often clear what these authors consider the precise relationship to be between individual members' senses of family life and family consciousness or world view in its own right. Nonetheless, they describe the family (or marriage) as a kind of personage with a virtual life or mind of its own.

Hess and Handel (1959), for example, entitle their case analysis of five families *Family Worlds*. They begin by stating, "However its life spreads into the wider community, there is a sense in which a family is a bounded universe" (p. 1). This informs us that family is both a thing and a totality. As a thing, it has boundaries and is separated from other social forms or entities in "the wider community." Thus it can be described and studied as subject matter in its own right. As a totality, it constitutes a world of its own, harboring its own reality.

The authors' very next sentence informs us that, as Burgess implied, the family world or bounded universe has its source in members' actions. The mechanism by which this comes into existence and changes is what Hess and Handel refer to as "an endless process of movement in and around nonsensual understanding, from attachment to conflict and withdrawal—and over again" (p. 1). While the superpersonality that Burgess mentioned does not quite have a life of its own, we see the entity more fully developed as we move along in Hess and Handel's text.

We also learn that families have "themes." The authors explain that a "family theme is a pattern of feelings, motives, fantasies, and conventionalized understandings grouped about some locus of concern which has a particular form in the personalities of the individual members" (p. 11). Later in the same paragraph, however, the family that has a theme is seemingly granted greater sovereignty over members, even while themes are admittedly drawn from members. Hess and Handel write, "In the family themes are to be found the family's implicit direction, its notion of 'who we are' and 'what we do about it'" (p. 11). From this, we find that the family has a kind of identity that organizes courses of action much as personality organizes the conduct of the person.

We might ask if this way of referring to family is just a shorthand, not the specification of an actual entity—the family—separate from members. For purposes of communicative convenience, we all regularly accept the convention of writing and speaking of "things" in the large, to which we do not mean to assign concrete reality. We speak of world opinion, for example, but don't mean to imply that there is a world that thinks and forms judgments separate from world leaders and others. Indeed, the tendency to actually give life, as it were, to the larger communal things we are as people, is sometimes denigrated as anthropomorphism. Still, shorthand or not, in the course of being used, shorthands, like other habits, easily take on lives of their own.

It is not clear in Hess and Handel's text whether family world, family theme, and other family characteristics are shorthands as such. But, reading on, we learn that each family has a "stance," which is the "position it has taken vis-à-vis the outer, non-family world" (p. 14). More to the point, we are told that "families differ in their inclination to permit members to make unique personal evaluations of and responses to stimuli" (p. 15). Whether or not this is explicitly a shorthand, it now seems that families must be some entity separate from members in order for families to be variously inclined "to permit members" to make personal evaluations. Shorthand notwithstanding, the distinct domestic order assumption of the private image, in Hess and Handel's text, seems to virtually cast family as a superpersonality, writing it as much as discovering it, as it were.

Berger and Kellner's (1970) "family" takes on a life of its own in their discussion of marriage and the construction of reality. Where Hess and Handel describe the family theme or world, Berger and Kellner refer to the marriage's "nomos," which is the symbolic by-product of "a social arrangement that creates for the individual the sort of order in which he can experience his life as making sense" (p. 50). As we follow their discussion, we find that the emphasis is less on social arrangement than it is on order. The order is cognitive, a configuration of *consistent* ideas or symbols about the nature of the reality that constitutes social entities. Still, as Berger and Kellner state, marriage is "only one social relationship in which this process of nomos-building takes place" (p. 50). One might then substitute the term "marriage" where the authors write of society and derive the following description of what they refer to as a socially constructed "world":

> Every [marriage] has its specific way of defining and perceiving reality—its world, its universe, its overarching organization of symbols. Erected . . . is a system of ready-made typifications, through which the innumerable experiences of reality come to be ordered. These typifications and their order are held in common by the members of [a marriage], thus acquiring not only the character of objectivity, but being taken for granted as *the* world *tout court*, the only world that normal men can conceive of. (p. 51)

While Berger and Kellner's nomos or world is conceived as a product of a social construction process, its by-product seems to take on its own life. Even though, as Berger and Kellner state, "the social constructed world must be continually mediated to and actualized by the individual" (p. 51), the authors refer to it as an object, a thing, against which its members wholly identify themselves as partners in marriage. In turn, this thing—the marriage as a nomos or "little world" (p. 57)— provides a sense of relationship, an overall meaning to those concerned.

It is important not to underestimate the uniformity and orderliness of the nomos described by Berger and Kellner. The stability of the marriage relationship rests on orderliness. The nomos keeps things together, even while its source continues to be the principals' continuing cognitive contributions. Referring to the exchanges that realize (make real) the little world that consolidates marriage, the authors explain:

> The reconstruction of the world in marriage occurs principally in the course of conversation, as we have suggested. The implicit problem of this conversation is how to match two individual definitions of reality. By the very logic of the relationship, a common overall definition must be arrived at—otherwise the conversation will become impossible and, *ipso facto*, the relationship will be endangered. (p. 61)

More recently, David Reiss (1981) has derived the idea of the family's distinct reality from laboratory experience. According to Reiss, while he initially set up the social interaction laboratory to measure the problem-solving skills of the family group, it soon became evident that each family shared assumptions about the world in which it lived, assumptions that organized the way the family dealt with the world.

From the very start, we find that Reiss writes of "the" family, even though, at the same time, it is evident that what the family becomes as a thing is linked with its continuing relationship to the environment:

> This book presents a new model of the family. The model explores how relationships between the family and its social environment are related to the ways the family regulates and orders its own inner life. The central idea around which our model is built is that the family, through the course of its own development, fashions fundamental and enduring assumptions about the world in which it lives. The assumptions are shared by all family members, despite the disagreements, conflicts, and differences that exist in the family. Indeed, the core of an individual's membership in his own family is his acceptance of, belief in, and creative elaboration of these abiding assumptions. (p. 1)

As in Hess and Handel's "world" and Berger and Kellner's "nomos," family members not only have assumptions about the world they live in but also, insofar as they maintain membership, share the same assumptions.

The totality of Reiss's usage is apparent when he compares the family's common assumptions with Kuhn's (1962) concept of paradigm. Each family, he argues, has its own paradigm or approach to life. As Kuhn's sense of paradigm connotes both theory and practice, so Reiss's usage suggests that each family has a distinct and uniform way of dealing with the world. Translating this usage into a grammar of action, we virtually hear Reiss describing an entity—the family—that encounters the world and figures its daily challenges. The description resembles the superperson that Burgess nearly indulged in. Admitting to its metaphorical tone, Reiss nonetheless takes the "family paradigm" to be the thing in the large that rationally acts for its membership:

> We now speak of the *family paradigm* as a central organizer of its shared constructs, sets, expectations, and fantasies about its social world. Further, each family's transactions with its social world is guided by its own paradigm, and families can be distinguished—one from another—by the differences in their paradigms.

Note that families share not only constructs and expectations, but fantasies as well. Not only does the family entity conceive of things in a distinct way, but it also can deceive itself. We shall return to the deception theme when we address the scientific attempt to penetrate the household in order to decipher the actual shape and form of the family entity.

Whether it resembles a superpersonality or is an actual world, a nomos, or a paradigm, the *distinct* domestic order of the family (or marriage) is evident. The distinctiveness assumption leads these and other family scholars to write of *the* family, *the* family world, *the* nomos, and so on. The homogeneity of each distinction is evident, too. Whether, as Hess and Handel suggest, every family has *a* theme or is *a* world, or, as Berger and Kellner argue, each stable marriage is *a* consensual conversation informed by *its* nomos, the idea is that the family is something meaningfully and uniformly active in its members' lives. In a manner of speaking, the "the-ness" of the family entity is both distinct and clear. Entity and writing seem to be mutual realizations; the thing cannot exist without descriptions of it.

The contrasting idea that the family is a practical achievement of a variety of circumstances and interests, which would diversify its nomos or worlds, is not evident. The possibility that each family is, in practice, a family-for-this-member, a family-for-that-member, a family-according-to-that-organization, a family-in-the-judgment-of-this-expert, and so on, is meaningless. This would not accommodate the superpersonality theme, for it would at the very least require thinking of family in its own right, separate from its members, as having multiple personalities. For Berger and Kellner, such a state would signal a family's (or marriage's) instability.

Boundedness and Ritual

The assumption of distinct domestic order comes with a language of boundaries. The self-contained familial entity is signaled by an internal-external demarcation of what it is and isn't. Evidently, the family entity in the large has an inside and an outside, which makes it altogether reasonable to distinguish its interior from its environment.

Hess and Handel's (1959) specification of family worlds and themes not only refers to boundaries, but also presents boundaries as the product of a kind of familial labor that others have called "boundary maintenance" (for example, Aldous, 1978, 33-36). As one of Hess and Handel's subtitles maintains, a primary task is "establishing boundaries of the family's world of experience" (p. 13). Note the language in which the argument is conveyed, which includes such terms as "close," "admissible," "domain," "external," "space," "outer," and "limits":

> The significant themes consequently not only subsume the psychic content of the family's life but also indicate something of the breadth of its world. A family constitutes its own world, which is not to say it closes itself off from everything else but that it

determines what parts of the external world are admissible and how freely. The family maps its domain of acceptable and desirable experience, its life space. The outer limits of life space for any family are well marked. There are signposts for goals and signals for danger. (p. 14)

Hess and Handel seem to recognize a tendency to reify when using words like superpersonality. Following their earlier remarks, they state, "But these metaphors fail because the boundaries lie within persons, and however firm they may be, there are always areas of inexperience not adequately charted" (p. 14). Nonetheless, the caution is glossed over as the narrative again picks up the now tacit metaphor of something (some thing) seemingly writ large, beyond members, which, as the preceding extract suggests, "constitutes its own world," does not "close itself off," but "determines" admissibility and thus "maps" a domain of experience. The authors can't seem to shake the grammatical enticement toward metaphor, which perhaps suggests that metaphor itself constitutes the objects of experience as much as objects themselves present us with their evident boundaries and respective internal orders (see Manning, 1979; Lakoff and Johnson, 1980).

The admitted, yet lost, metaphor of a bounded entity is found time and again in family studies. Bott (1957, 1), for example, writes of families as interacting with external persons and institutions. Adams (1986, 11) describes structures, functions, and the "other internal aspects of family life." Handel (1985) even entitled his popular anthology *The Psychosocial Interior of the Family.* For some, families are even bounded in time. Rodgers and others (Rodgers, 1964) refer to the family as an entity whose inner dynamics and outer conditions regulate its course of development over time. According to some developmentalists, families have "careers" (see Aldous, 1978) that present distinct stages of growth with their respective developmental tasks. The family's stages and developmental tasks are distinguished from the individual life cycle. As Aldous (1978) writes:

> In this chapter we have been talking thus far about the individual and the developmental task concept; let us now turn to the family and the developmental task concept. . . . The family developmental concept gives content to the various stages of the family's lifespan, whereas the individual developmental task relates to the life course of the individual. Within the time covered by a given family stage, family members may take on a variety of individual developmental tasks. (p. 108)

Once the family life cycle has been separated from its individual counterpart, it is then reasonable to raise questions about the relation between the two, something regularly done and empirically addressed.

For others, borders are ceremonially secured. Describing the way family sustains its reality, Reiss (1981) puts it this way:

> This concept pictures family behavior as a sphere. At the center are a set of family ceremonials which organize and shape a set of routine pattern regulators at the periphery. Family ceremonials are episodic, highly routinized sequences of family life which ordinarily have little affective charge or symbolic meaning. We propose that ceremonials conserve the family's conception of the outer world. Pattern regulators reinforce, often subliminally, the role of ceremonials.

Variations in Tone

The overall tone of the domestic life contained within the boundaries of the family has varied. Most commonly, the family entity's interior is idealized and sanctified. Some, however, view the borders as the virtual portals of an inner sanctum, whose interiors are prowled by dark and sordid forces (see Laing, 1969; Laing and Esterson, 1964). If not physically secure, the family's borders are often so psychologically closed as to tie their members in "knots," to paraphrase Laing. In contrast, when the inner reaches of the family are not idealized nor their traditional order nostalgically pined, they may be cast dramaturgically. In her important textbook, Skolnick (1983), following Goffman (1959), titillates us with the kind of theatrical game that shapes the family's natural, "backstage" demeanor.

The actual extent to which the family entity's separateness forms a private domain of experience has been the source of some controversy. Lasch (1979), while certainly not one to dismiss the social influences on domestic affairs, nonetheless decries the increasing contemporary deprivatization of the home. Laslett (1973), however, argues that, historically, changes in the composition and physical segregation of households have increasingly sequestered family affairs. The separation of the workplace from family living thus enhanced the privacy of the household. Challenging this view, as well as what he refers to as Berger and Kellner's (1970) "maximum privacy" model of marital conversants, Wiley (1985, 29) writes that "the long, historical rise in family privacy has crested and is sliding in reverse," to some extent reflecting Lasch's sentiments. Wiley maintains that the empirical support for Berger and Kellner's insular, consensual view of the marital conversation has changed to the point where contemporary conversations about domestic affairs are more "loosely coupled," so to speak. Descriptions of the realities of marriage and family life are not confined to the household but spread in several directions outside the private domain of the home and are articulated in the context of a variety of concerns and interests.

Household Location

In the private image, a geographic twist is given to the relation between house, home, and family life. This brings us to the private image's second assumption. While family members carry on their lives in many places, the private image assumes that the most authentic experiences are displayed at home. There is a clear methodological imperative here—namely, that genuine knowledge of domestic affairs comes by way of the household.

From laypersons to social scientists, from clinicians to counselors, knowledge of family life is evaluated against this standard. It is assumed, for example, that facts of domestic life gleaned from what is known of a woman's work performance are not as authentic as knowledge derived from a close scrutiny of her home life. Indeed, a telltale sign of the assumption is the enduring question of whether what is inferred from a distance about the family squares with what actually goes on in the household.

The methodological imperative to study the family in its household is a directive that is easier said than done. It assumes that the most authentic picture of family life is derived from the home, but that life is presumed to be private. It is not just the household that locates actual domestic affairs, but the *private* household. The family is most authentic in its private moments, some have said "behind closed doors." As such, a physical barrier to authentic knowledge presents itself. To make matters worse, the physical barrier is coupled with a normative one. While some say that privacy has gradually eroded (Lasch, 1979; Wiley, 1985), there is considerable sentiment for conceiving of, and sustaining, the household as a private domain. Whether the actual state of home life is now more or less private than it once was, the normative side of the household location assumption makes public access to the home as much of a methodological problem as physical barriers do. Beyond this, of course, is the problem of the effect of an outsider's presence in the household.

The link between geography and authenticity is not unique to family studies. One might expect, for example, that the connection between gang life and territory would lead those concerned to seek knowledge of the gang's social organization in the proverbial "streets," that is, where gang life is supposed to naturally occur (see Hammersley and Atkinson, 1983: Schwartz and Jacobs, 1979). This admittedly motivated Whyte's (1943) fieldwork in an Italian slum, which was launched in part to challenge the prevailing "armchair" (inauthentic) belief that gang life was lawless and normless. As in the private image of family life, the idea of native territory inspired a geographic interpretation of close scrutiny.

A Natural Habitat

Consider the natural habitat theme in the family studies literature. Bott's (1957) pioneering network research was inspired in part by the household location assumption. Writing about the central place of the family in social life, Bott noted that despite the family's importance, very little is known about it, especially how its relation with the environment figures in the family's internal workings:

> There is an enormous literature on the family in Western society—a reflection of its importance for the continuation of society and the happiness, and misery, of individuals. The family, we are constantly told, is the backbone of society. But actually not much is known of the relationship between families and society. There are very few studies of the way families interact with external persons and institutions, and there are not even very many studies of families in their natural habitat, the home. (p. 1)

Bott not only informs us that the home has not been very well scrutinized for its domestic affairs, but also implies that what families do naturally, they do in the household. With the proper substitutions, Bott might just as easily have stated that household studies provide the most authentic measure of actual domestic life.

In the second chapter of her book, which Bott entitled "Methodology and Field Techniques," she immediately turns her attention to the procedural implications of the natural habitat theme. She says it is imperative that families not be studied at a distance, nor by way of family members' reports given in other social settings. At the same time, she admits that the methodological challenge of studying the household has played no small part in its avoidance. As Bott explains:

> The reasons for the lack of intensive field studies of ordinary families are not hard to find. Family life goes on inside homes, not in the street or in universities, schools, clinics, churches, factories, or any of the other institutions to which research workers might have easy access. (p. 6)

She then notes how privacy also acts as a hurdle to the study of the household:

> Unless one is invited inside a home one cannot learn much about a family as a working group. But ordinary families are not likely to ask a research worker into their homes since they have no particular motivation to come to a research team. . . . It is difficult to interest people in a study that probes into their private affairs, especially if interviews continue for a long period of time. Contacting families by knocking on doors is inappropriate when one is asking for extensive cooperation in the exploration of matters that are felt to be private. (p. 6)

As Bott specifies the methodological difficulties of getting into households, she indirectly raises the question of how to gain a full, not partial, view of the family. Outsiders' views of the household are clearly partial ones, mere versions of *the* distinct domestic order of the household. In this regard, Bott writes, for example, of what outside agents might learn about family life:

> such agencies usually have contact with some members of the family, often with a single individual, and only for certain aspects of the family's affairs. Thus the doctor is sometimes concerned with the whole family, but often he treats only some of its members, and in most cases he deals only with health, not with all aspects of family life. Similarly the church, the school, maternity and child welfare clinics, birth-control clinics, lawyers, etc., deal only with certain aspects of a family's life. (p. 7)

The procedural implication is evident. What is needed is a full interior, not a partial or exterior, view of the family, not a representation provided by one member or another. This requires direct access to the household. Bott's research was limited to intensive household interviews with family members (couples), and she laments not being able to conduct extensive participant observation in the home, implying the ideal means of capturing the natural habitat of the family:

> It would have been a great help in the research if we could have relied more on observation and less on interviews. In comparison with most anthropological field work, there was very little observation. This came about partly because of our research aims, but also because of the structure of urban society. Of course we observed the couple while we were interviewing them, and the interview when we met the children was particularly instructive. On that occasion family life went on more or less as usual and we observed and took part in it without asking questions or taking notes. (pp. 23–24)

While Bott obtains glimpses of the family in its natural habitat—the way "family life went on more or less as usual"—she soon stresses that even participant observation, or being in the household, would have its limits. Although family life admittedly goes on in the home, not in outside institutions like universities, Bott reminds us that family life extends from the home into the community. She remarks that even though she witnessed aspects of the natural affairs of the household,

> we could not observe the total social life of the family. We could not follow the husband to work, and we could not interview friends, neighbours, and relatives, partly because these people were scattered all over London . . . for the most part observations of the family's relationships with other people were very sporadic and incomplete. (p. 24)

Still, to extend one's observation is not to displace the family's essential domain—namely, the home.

In her final methodological section, Bott elaborates the ideal means of studying not only the family's natural habitat (the household), but its virtual natives (family members) as well. She uses the terms "natural" and "native" liberally, but now distinguishes the household as natively experienced from the household as witnessed by outsiders. While participant observation would be preferable to interviews, the former does mean, as noted earlier, that there is a visitor in the household. The implication is that, in the final analysis, observation would not be of families "at home" but families merely in the home in the company of a nonmember:

> In home interviews we observed the family while we were there, but we saw them chiefly as they would behave when entertaining a visitor—although a visitor of a special kind. One could observe a more varied range of behaviour if one lived with a family, but few families would permit such constant observation. (pp. 48-49)

Falling short of the ideal, Bott considers the validity of the glimpses of home life she did obtain. As she explains, "Because there was relatively little direct observation of behaviour, we often had to take the couples' descriptions of their behaviour as actual fact" (p. 49). She goes on to specify the conditions that had to be met to take what was observed at face value:

> We considered it reasonably safe to take their behaviour at face value if four conditions were met: first, if the events described were simple and concrete rather than complex and abstract; second, if the events described took place in the present or the recent past rather than the distant past; third, if both husband and wife agreed on the description and neither seemed emotionally upset about it; and fourth, if the description seemed consistent with the behaviour we had observed.

The standard of validity is close to a snapshot criterion and, in some ways, resembles the consensual view described earlier. And note how it invalidates a "perspectival" understanding of family by attempting to "triangulate" on the family as an entity with a singular appearance.

Bott's elaboration of the natural habitat theme is neither idiosyncratic nor dated. There are numerous recent examples of the same theme. While some, like Henry (1971; 1985), Howell (1973), and Speedling (1982), have felt the need to actually reside in homes for a period of time, others have lived in close proximity to the households being studied, if not in the actual physical structure (Lewis, 1959, 1961; Stack, 1974). Still others have tried to discern the family's domestic order through intensive interviews with family members, preferably as near as possible to native habitats (Bott, 1957; LaRossa, Bennett, and Gelles, 1981; LaRossa and Wolf, 1985). Several have noted that the validity of domestic data is enhanced by joint, especially couple, interviewing in depth (Bott, 1957; Bennett and McAvity,

1985; Hess and Handel, 1959; LaRossa, Bennett, and Gelles, 1981; Thomas and Calonico, 1972). Finally, there are those who have simulated the household in the laboratory by placing members in ostensibly real-life situations (Reiss, 1967; Strodtbeck, 1951; Strauss, 1964; Miller, Rollins, and Thomas, 1982).

Henry's (1985) study, in which he actually did take up residence in the homes of families with psychotic children, is instructive regarding the perceived value of proximity. Cognizant of the methodological uncertainties of his effort, Henry reasons much as Bott did. Once again, the terms "natural" and "native" abound. For example, in describing how he happened to study psychotic children, Henry explains:

> For many years it had been my conviction that the etiology of emotional illness required more profound study than had heretofore been possible, and that the best way to new discoveries in the field was through study of the disease-bearing vector, the family, in its natural habitat, pursuing its usual life routines—eating, loving, fighting, talking, taking amusements, treating sickness, and so on; in other words, following the usual course of its life. (p. 51)

After describing an event in the domestic life of the Jones family that took it outside the home, Henry points out:

> Although I was part of the event, I did not experience it as a member of the family did, yet since I was literally in it, I was acutely aware of all its objective features. Thus, in close proximity to the members of the family living in their native habitat, I was able to observe their actual life and arrive at some reasonably probable inferences. . . . I believe it reasonably certain that the circumstances and spirit of this expedition [the Jones family's trip into the country] could never be recovered from an interview. Thus naturalistic observation, by placing the observer in the midst of real family life, provides insights impossible to attain in any other way. (p. 60)

Finally, and most recently, LaRossa and his associates (LaRossa, Bennett, and Gelles, 1981; LaRossa and Wolf, 1985) have offered understandable pleas for the qualitative study of families as a way of gaining access to what they, too, take to be the richest grounds for discovering actual domestic affairs—the home. The natural habitat theme rings clear as they write of tracking families in their native environment:

> Qualitative family research is almost always conducted in the home because it is assumed that natural geographic and social milieus provide the richest possible context for the study of family life (Kantor and Lehr, 1975; Henry, 1965). . . . (LaRossa, Bennett, and Gelles, 1981, 307)

The household location assumption of the private image has presented a compelling methodological hurdle for generations of family scholars. Ironically, family studies has reified the assumption of a private geographic domain to such an extent that the assumption itself keeps family researchers outside the family's natural habitat while at the same time preserving their belief that this is the ideal family study site.

Backstage

Even when physical access to the household is obtained, an outsider's presence serves to constrain the ways that families might behave. Indeed, natives might unwittingly work to retain the secrets of their private affairs. The very idea of the natural state of a setting precludes formal investigation. As Bott (1957) notes just before she presents four conditions for assessing the validity of her data, "There is no reason to suppose that they [family members] were not telling the truth as they saw it, but it is well known that people sometimes distort things without knowing it" (p.49). And as Henry (1985) implies in his conclusion, "Naturalistic observation of the families of psychotic children is feasible because a scientist can be admitted to their homes and because for a variety of reasons distortions of the usual mode of life of the family are not serious enough to make observation fruitless" (p. 66).

This brings us to a second theme of the household location assumption: that domestic life has a hidden side or "backstage." In presenting his dramaturgical approach to the self, Goffman (1959) wrote of a dilemma that parallels the problem of naturalistic observation. Goffman argued that, on the one hand, self is a thing each of us believes more or less organizes our courses of action, but, on the other hand, it eludes direct observation and reveals itself only by way of interaction. In practice, then, the self is both object and representation. What we and others know of it derives from a combination of tacit appreciation and communication. In his inimitable way, Goffman described the dramatic labor associated with the communication that "gives off" the self (p. 2). It isn't that what is given off is necessarily less authentic than the actual self, only that we derive the self by way of communication. In this early writing, Goffman was inclined to present the dramatic labor of the self, and of everyday life in general, against a geographic background. There was a space where actors formulated what would eventually become the appearance of things; it was called, appropriately, "backstage" or the "back region." There was also a space where, as Goffman put it, "accentuated facts make their appearance" (p. 111); it was called a "front region" or "frontstage."

The parallel with the private image of family life turns on the dramatic metaphor. Substituting domestic affairs or family life for the self, on the one side, and the household for backstage, on the other, one might say that the natural state of the family is found in the household (the natural habitat theme), but what we know of it is communicated to us and received frontstage, not directly from its most private domain (the back-stage theme). Just as Goffman portrayed duplicity, guile, and other mechanisms of deception, as well as mechanisms of sincerity, as veneers over what is essentially a communicated reality, the backstage theme of the household location assumption draws our attention to the contrast be-tween what is thought to actually go on behind closed doors and what seems to be happening "up front."

Skolnick's (1983) discussion of the nature of family life is exem-plary in relying on the dramatic metaphor. Asking "What really is happening to the family?" (p. 14), she describes "two new areas in the study of the family [that have] given us particularly important new insights" (p. 15). Referring to the first (1967) edition of Handel's (1985) book *The Psychosocial Interior of the Family,* one area is the history of the family and the other is studies of the psychosocial interior of family life. Regarding the drama of family living, Skolnick explains that the psychosocial interior refers to "the emotional worlds of particular families and the ways they speak to and act with one another when they are together" (p. 15). Skolnick conveys a domain that seems to resist public inspection. Those few observers who have successfully penetrated the household had to negotiate its dramatic barrier. As Skolnick puts it, they had to "observe live family interaction from behind the looking glass—the one-way screen that is a mirror on one side but transparent on the other" (p. 15).

The dramatic metaphor is expanded as Skolnick introduces what she calls the "dark underside" of ordinary family life (p. 16). While Skolnick does not present the psychosocial interior in a totally negative way, she does portray the geography of the household as a clandestine location for domestic affairs. Although the term "dark" resounds with things sinister, it also signals the unseen. And, of course, the term "underside" conveys something hidden—private, not public.

While there are traces of the private image in early family research, Skolnick informs us that recent empirical studies have begun to seriously examine this aspect of family life. The methodological problems associated with this examination are highlighted in a chapter entitled "In Search of the Family" (p. 53). Once again she introduces the language of the hidden, framed in terms of a distinction between the public and private sides of domestic life:

> One of the discoveries of recent family research is that families
> have myths, secrets, and information-processing rules that deter-
> mine the kind of communication that goes on—what can be said
> and, more important, what can't be said. Families filter informa-
> tion not only about the wider culture, but also about their own
> functioning. Or, as Laing puts it, families practice mystification: they
> have complicated stratagems for keeping people in the dark about
> what is going on, and in the dark that they are in the dark. (p. 55)

A particularly telling section follows, entitled "Sanctity and Secrecy," and is worth quoting at length for the way it combines the ideas of public concern and private experience to form a methodological issue. The issue centers on the moral and observational barriers of the family's backstage:

> Besides familiarity and mystification, other obstacles handicap the study of the family: it is morally sacred, and it is secret. The family in America includes two moral dimensions, a religious one based on Judeo-Christian family ideals and a legal one relating to the laws of marriage, economic obligations between husband and wife, parents and children, and so on (Ball, 1972). Thus the happenings of family life are the concern of others besides the family members themselves; they have a public dimension.
>
> Paradoxically, however, because privacy is also a cherished value, the family is perhaps the most secret institution in American society. To a greater extent than in other societies and in our own historical past, American family life goes on behind closed doors (Laslett, 1973). The home is a "backstage area" (Goffman, 1959) where people can be relaxed, informal, and off guard precisely because they cannot be observed by outsiders. (pp. 55–56)

Combined with the natural habitat theme, the backstage theme informs us that the household location of family life is not only something intrinsic to domestic affairs but also something to be camouflaged and preserved as well. As far as human affairs go, especially family life, nature takes a moral character. LaRossa and his associates (LaRossa, Bennett and Gelles, 1981; LaRossa and Wolf, 1985) have put this directly in the context of both methodology and ethics, especially as the two bear on naturalistic studies:

> There are two important reasons to devote special attention to the ethics of qualitative family research. First, the private and intimate nature of the family imposes unique constraints and raises distinctive ethical issues for investigators using qualitative methods; and second, although qualitative techniques have been infrequently used in family research (Hodgson and Lewis, 1979; Nye and Bayer, 1963; Ruano et al., 1969), the increased interest in system level analysis (e.g., Kantor and Lehr, 1975) has made it likely that more family studies will be employing qualitative designs (see Waxler, 1977). (LaRossa, Bennett, and Gelles, 1981, 303–304)

Privileged Access

If the natural state of the family lies in the inner reaches of the household, its members would seem to have privileged access to it. This is the third assumption of the private image. Even while family members' knowledge of domestic affairs may be obscured at times by family myths, the image assumes that insiders at least unwittingly carry knowledge of the actual goings-on of the household. Outsiders like service providers, neighbors, and family researchers can only approximate what native members, in principle, know best.

Secret Knowledge

Describing the family household as a back region, Skolnick (1983) highlights the insider's privileged access. She informs us that the household retains secrets known only to family members. This, of course, suggests that those who study domestic affairs can rarely be satisfied with having full, intimate knowledge of the home:

> Because family behavior is a backstage kind of interaction, it is, of course, extremely hard to observe. As Goffman noted, people in backstage regions know about their own unsavory secrets, but they are not in a position to know about those of other people. Thus families may think of themselves in terms of their backroom knowledge, but judge other families by their onstage performances. This may be why the discoveries of the new family interaction studies are at one and the same time so shocking and so familiar. By observing backstage family behavior, these studies have opened up for public discussion aspects of family life that could never be reached by means of questionnaires and formal interviews. (p. 134)

Family truths, Skolnick suggests, derive from actual observation of backstage family behavior, not from indirect methods that would likely tap only the household's front regions, that is, what family members wish outsiders to know.

There can be a distinctly unsavory flavor in what is taken to be the hidden character of the household. As insiders, members are more likely than outsiders to possess negative knowledge of "real" family life. Here the language is quite telling. Its terms reveal a sinister underworld: hidden, secrets, dark, unsavory, shocking, closed doors, impolite. Better than others, members of households know about this, the household's inner sanctum, a region best kept secret.

Whether the dark, inner sanctums of households are ever found, we nonetheless seem to expect that members, but for their reticence, know of these matters. Even while we might never actually encounter dark secrets, we sense the dangers associated with the hidden disorders of the household. Something about this seems impure, perhaps because it is the conceptual opposite of what it is believed families should be—orderly, loyal, intimate, giving (see Douglas, 1966, 1978).

As the preceding extract from Skolnick's popular textbook suggests, the domestic secrets held by family members are recent "discoveries" of the new family interaction studies. The studies have set the familial record straight, so to speak. The implication is that what family members have always known is just now becoming generally acknowledged.

Not only is the discovery of familial secrets a result of looking closely at the household, but—according to some—the secrets are also as varied as the secrets' keepers. Some students of domestic affairs have come to recognize that the domestic order of the household can have as many versions as there are family members. While not dismissing the household location assumption of domesticity, Safilios-Rothschild (1969), for one, has taken issue with the belief that the relative amount of time spent in the household serves as a standard for who best knows its affairs. Criticizing what she calls "wives' family sociology," Safilios-Rothschild questions the presumption that homebound wives necessarily provide the fullest information about the family's domestic life. This has led a number of researchers to formulate methods for obtaining and comparing several members'—especially couples'—interpretations of family living (Bagozzi and Van Loo, 1981; Bennett and McAvity, 1985; Neal and Groat, 1976; Thomson and Williams, 1982).

Hidden Knowledge

Some students of family life distinguish between domestic knowledge held and domestic knowledge known. This seems to be the point of Henry's (1985, 60) argument for the "better accounting" an outside observer can offer of household realities. His point is not that the careful outside observer knows more than family members themselves do, but that the observer can be more objective and clearly convey what may be more or less acknowledged, but nonetheless concealed, by insiders. Family members are likely to be concerned with practical familial, not methodological, matters. It's not that family members don't have privileged access, but that what they know better than anyone else is seldom systematically documented. The domestic experience of family members holds the knowledge that an objective outsider can come to discern better than members themselves.

Scholars who are therapeutically inclined are more skeptical regarding the hidden nature of members' familial knowledge. For them, it is not member's lack of interest in the documentation of domestic life that hides the social order of the household, but tacit "conspiracies of silence" (Laing, 1969; Laing and Esterson, 1964). Jackson (1957) refers to the "fog of family fictions" (p. 80). In contrast to Henry's view, this less benign view sees family members as engaged in practices that, unbeknownst even to members, serve to keep family secrets secret.

In documenting the "politics" of family interaction, Laing and Esterson (1964) show how such everyday minutiae as the subtle and regular winks of some members behind the backs of others can be telltale signs of tacit collusions. In the Abbott family, for example, it was evident that Maya's parents were unaware of the enduring part they played in their daughter's mental illness. In her own way, Maya knew that something was "going on" between her parents, but what that was escaped her. Laing and Esterson put it this way:

> An idea of reference that she [Maya] had was that something she could not fathom was going on between her parents, seemingly about her.
>
> Indeed there was. When they were all interviewed together, her mother and father kept exchanging with each other a constant series of nods, winks, gestures, knowing smiles, so obvious to the observer that he commented on them after twenty minutes of the first such interview. They continued, however, unabated and denied.
>
> The consequence, so it seems to us, of this failure by her parents to acknowledge the validity of similar comments by Maya, was that Maya could not know when she was perceiving or when she was imagining things to be going on between her parents. These open yet unavowed non-verbal exchanges between father and mother were in fact quite public and perfectly obvious. (p. 40)

The signs of the hidden are less concrete in others' work. For Jackson (1957, 1965) and others (Anderson and Bagarozzi, 1983; Bagarozzi and Anderson, 1982; Ferreira, 1963; Haley, 1967; Perlmutter and Sauer, 1986), family members keep things hidden by distorting domestic truths through "family fictions" and "family myths." While family members are thought to have privileged access to domestic life, what they know lies buried beneath obfuscating beliefs. The methodological (clinical) aim in this circumstance is to penetrate fictions or myths by taking family members' public testimony about domestic affairs with a grain of salt. Therapeutically, the object would be to persuade family members to confront what they know, which untruths otherwise keep from them and fuel related family troubles. As a pioneer in taking the family as a unit of analysis and treatment in psychotherapy, Jackson (1957) describes hidden truths as a kind of collective self-deception:

> "family" refers to the group with which the psychiatrist becomes acquainted through his distillation and translation of the patient's recollections. The individuals include real people of today. . . . The view of "how it must have been" is obscured by the fog of family fictions—the family, as members tell themselves they were, usually contrasts with how they actually were. The family first presented by the patient is usually the version offered for public consumption; and, only after several interviews does the real family emerge for the psychiatrist's scrutiny. (pp. 80-81)

Having now "deconstructed" the private image as conventional family studies have "constructed" it, we turn to family discourse and descriptive practice in everyday circumstances. Our aim is to demonstrate the analytic utility of our social constructionist perspective on family. This approach offers a way of rethinking what family is and how it comes into being in our experience. (For related work from this perspective, see Bernardes, 1985a, 1985b, 1987, 1988; G. Miller, 1987; L. Miller, 1987, forthcoming; Smith, 1985.)

Together, the following chapters show how the private image is not just a vision held by researchers of domestic affairs, but informs the search for family order by persons dealing with practical daily matters as well, from social scientists and social workers to friends and family members themselves. The private image, indeed, is culturally compelling, a prevalent means of conceptualizing the substance and place of the familial in our lives. People use, as well as challenge the use of, varied facets of the image as they try to discover the meaning of family and domestic privacies. And they do so under the auspices of manifold roles, offices, and organizations. We present the private image as a kind of collective myth in search of its own experiential bearings, diversely realized in place and time.

The next three chapters focus on the three assumptions of the private image. Chapter 4, "The Family Writ Large," challenges the assumption that the family is a separate and distinct entity, reconceptualizing it as a "reality project" of those who describe it. Chapter 5, "The Descriptive Usage of the Household," concerns the experiential borders of family life and is an empirical commentary on the geographic inclination of the private image. Chapter 6, "Privileged Knowledge in Practice," addresses the assumption that members of the household have the most authentic understanding of domestic affairs.

Chapter 4

The Family Writ Large

Challenges to our understanding of things like community, personality, and family have a way of bringing them into focus and giving them life. For example, because we commonly take for granted that each of us has a personality, its shape and substance are largely unattended. Personality remains somewhere in the nebulous background of experience. A demand to consider one's character, however, compels one to discern what had been tacit and undistinguished, prompting a consideration of what one is or might be as a person. Challenges serve to give structure to things.

As a distinct object of experience, the family can be similarly understood. It's not that family emerges completely anew with each challenge. After all, it has long been in our vocabularies. Rather, challenges invite us to assign meaning to the familial. We can discover something about ourselves and our social bonds when it is suggested, for example, that a history of tenuous family ties explains personal insecurity. Whether or not we agree, the suggestion nonetheless compels us to entertain the possibility that personal history has been significantly affected by an unstable family. This draws the family from the background of everyday life and presents it to us as a separate and distinct object of reckoning (Berger and Luckmann, 1966; Berger and Kellner, 1970).

    This chapter is about the family writ large, this ostensible thing that might or might not have an impact on its members' lives. Contrary to the distinct entity assumption of the private image, we argue that the shape and substance of the family, as known to those concerned, are constructed from its concrete challenges and responses to the challenges. As a thing in its own right, separate from its component members, the family writ large is a *practical* accomplishment. It is a virtual project of experience (Gubrium, 1988b).

The Challenge to Family of Commonplace Questions

While familial matters are myriad and no list could claim to be exhaustive, we offer brief illustrations of three common familial challenges. Framed as family matters, the following questions about the *affectional, custodial,* and *durational* character of interpersonal relations challenge family's presence, form, and function: Who cares? Who takes care? For how long? In practice, family seems to take shape in response to the questions.

Who Cares?

To start, let us consider the way challenges concerning affection prompt persons to specify the meaning of family. During a particularly heated discussion in a family/patient support group studied in the community mental health fieldwork, a schizophrenic, 22-year-old's father questioned his son's filial sentiments, casting doubt on the son's loyalty to his parents. The father complained bitterly that, despite all he and his wife had done for their son, the son was indifferent and ungrateful, displaying no emotion toward them except when he needed help:

> You're always willing to drop in any time they toss you out of the [transitional living] home, but you never show us any appreciation at all. You don't keep in touch. You won't even talk on the phone. Or when you do, you're just plain disagreeable. We never know how you're doing or what you're up to. You don't care about your mother's feelings; you don't feel for her at all. Do you realize what she goes through, worrying about you? You know you don't give us a damn thing. You could be a stranger. No consideration. No warmth. Nothing. You only act like a son when you need us. Where's your family loyalty, anyway?

    The son was at first defensive, blaming the parents for driving him away. But he soon became more conciliatory, almost apologetic, and tried to establish the ways in which he was, in fact, a son:

Come on. You know that I care. It's just hard for me. I come by, but I don't want to start you worrying, so I don't say too much. I don't want to complain because I don't want you to think I'm not doing okay. I thought I was doing something good for you by trying to stay out of your hair. We had all that talk about independence. . . . I get pretty screwed up sometimes, so I try to stay away when I might have a bad day. I know what it does to Mom and I don't want to do that to her. I don't want to hurt her. It may not look like it, but I keep away because I thought that was best for you guys. I got my problems and I know that they get to you, but you're all the family I have.

The father's complaint regarding his son's filial sentiments conveyed an eroding sense of family. In response, the son assembled evidence to counter his father's depiction of sundered family relations by explaining that his suspect family feelings and commitments were actually intact. Both challenge and response made family topical, producing an object to be openly contested, something constructed and reassembled, not merely contemplated.

As further illustration, note the complex connections that produced family in a challenge to a board-and-care facility resident's network of intimate relations. Conrad Moore, a 27-year-old who had been diagnosed as chronically schizophrenic, had been involuntarily hospitalized when his bizarre behavior and delusional speech disrupted business at a fast-food restaurant, frightening a number of patrons and employees. At the legal hearing to determine whether Moore's hospitalization should continue, the presiding judge made an uncharacteristically impassioned attempt to convince Moore that a "short vacation at the hospital" would be in Moore's best interest. The judge suggested, among other things, that life would be easier for him as an inpatient. Moore would have less to worry about, and everything would be taken care of for him while he "got himself back together." Beyond that, the judge argued that the hospital was the most caring, compassionate environment that Moore could hope for:

They care about you at the hospital, Conrad. Those people really do. They can give you the kind of love and attention that you seem to be missing when you're living on your own. You don't have any family to love you, so it might be best to take what you can get.

There were multiple challenges implicit in this plea, particularly the assertions that Moore's life lacked "love and attention" and that he had no loving family around him. Moore's response addressed the issues:

You can't tell me they care about me like my people. I got people at Briarwood [the board-and-care facility], man, they care. They're my family, man, my people. We're all in the same boat out there.

We got each other, man, just like a family. Why can't you just let
me stay?

The judge's comments had challenged the existence of affectional bonds in Moore's life in the board-and-care home, which Moore
countered by invoking family imagery to characterize the nature of his ties
with fellow residents. His living arrangements took on a familial cast in
direct response to the affectional concerns; fellow boarders were assigned
family status as a means of conveying their care and attention. Moore produced a sense of caring and compassion for his circle of co-residents by
depicting them as family, simultaneously instructing the judge about how
to understand their meaning for him in his life outside the hospital.

Who Takes Care?

Family ties also are commonly constituted in terms of the willingness and/
or ability of members to take care of one another. A direct challenge may
question one's right to claim family status in matters of custody, inviting,
in turn, efforts to substantiate a family tie. For example, in one community
support program studied, a mental health social worker questioned a
mother's filial responsibility and, thereby issued a family challenge as she
attempted to elicit the mother's cooperation in getting the son to adhere
to his treatment regimen. The social worker derided the mother's custodial
concern for the son, framing its absence in familial terms:

> I just don't understand how you cannot care about Jimmy [the
> son]. Don't you want him to get better? Don't you want him to
> make it on his own? He's got no one else. Somebody has to show
> some concern. Somebody's got to look after the boy. He needs
> your help and, right now, you're not there for him. Tell me this,
> Mrs. North, where is the boy's family when he needs you?

The social worker appealed to family's custodial quality, using its implied
absence as a way of influencing the mother to attend to the son's welfare.
Conversely, custodial challenges may bring family imagery to
bear in legitimating the concerns of caretakers. Consider the implications
of the following familial claim made during an involuntary commitment
hearing in Metropolitan Court. Asked where he would stay if he were not
hospitalized, James Robinson said he would live with Sophia Mills, a
woman identified by Robinson's public defender as Robinson's "common
law wife." Robinson elaborated his argument that there would be
adequate supervision in the household:

> I got a whole family there, and family takes care of its own. I got
> my old lady and her sister and some cousin or somethin'. Name's
> Esther. That kind of family ain't gonna let nothin' happen to me.
> Hell, they don't let me do nothin' period.

The ability and willingness of this household group to care for Robinson was underscored by descriptively consolidating them into a family unit, cast in the large ("that kind of family") as a source of unquestioning care and support.

For How Long?

The quality and duration of social relations also are commonly questioned, formulated, and underscored in familial terms. Family itself may be doubted if its manifestations are not apparently enduring. Brothers, for example, who are said to have been out of touch for years may be descriptively stripped of fraternal bonds, their formal kinship notwithstanding. Conversely, questions of how well or how long one person has known another may borrow from the language of the familial to convey a sense of continuity and permanence and to maintain existing linkages.

When a support worker in a community mental health program was asked how long she had known one of her clients, her reply "Long enough for me to be her mother" used the family metaphor to emphasize the quality and duration of the relationship. The kinship reference capitalized on familial meanings, using them as a resource to secure an appreciation of the relationship's history. Or, for example, near the end of Conrad Moore's commitment hearing, which we discussed earlier, the judge expressed doubt about how long Moore would be able to continue living at the board-and-care facility. The judge's concern was expressed in terms of "how long it will take for you to wear out your welcome with your buddies down at the board-and-care home." Moore was adamant as he asserted that his cordial, supportive relations would continue indefinitely, replacing the judge's characterization of his co-residents as mere "buddies" with a claim to "family":

> Why do you think they'll turn on me, man? We're tight. These are my brothers. You know what I mean? Brothers. They won't disappear on me. They can't. Family is *always* family, man.

Questioning the likely duration and endurance of this arrangement invited Moore to substantiate his claim to everlasting support through a family connection.

Local Resources

While the family writ large is referenced as a thing in a category of its own, separate from those who perceive it, its particular formulations are socially distributed. Formulations correspond to locally available understandings. The family writ large is imparted with its working character through ways of thinking, seeing, and speaking about domestic reality that are known-in-common to members of separate and diverse social realms. Using "local resources" gives a distinctive tinge to family depictions so that family meanings and characterizations of domestic life vary across social locations—from one social class, group, or organization to another, for example. In the following discussion, we draw at length from the experience of members of support groups for the family caregivers of Alzheimer's disease victims to show how the disease's public culture combines with group folklore into "local cultures." These continually expanding and changing local cultures, in turn, serve as interpretive resources for shaping members' understandings of the family writ large. As we document the related family discourse, we see how the abstract family entity is a circumstantially produced ensemble of meanings.

According to some support group facilitators, the groups were charged with the task of "raising consciousness" among caregivers regarding the appropriate place of the family in caregiving. They were especially concerned with the limits of familial obligation to the deteriorating patient. The family was the object of repeated challenge as support group participants turned to one another for help in comprehending alternatives in the emotionally charged situation. As participants reflected on their home care experiences, they admittedly became aware of the meaning of burden and familial responsibility in ways they had not previously considered. It was not just the support groups themselves that offered a stock of new and provocative questions and experiential resources for assigning meaning to caregiving, but the groups' reflection of a related public culture. From the broadcast media, frequently shown documentary films, chapter newsletters of the Alzheimer's Disease and Related Disorders Association (ADRDA), popular caregiving handbooks, and the commentaries of participants knowledgeable about Alzheimer's disease, caregivers were regularly offered ways to think about domestic and familial affairs, as well as being given examples of individual caregiving and patient experiences. In attempting to make sense of home care as a domestic experience, members of the support group drew from both local and national formulations.

In one group session, a particularly forceful facilitator, Gilda, referred to a variety of well-known sources of information about the Alzheimer's experience as she pointed out how families might affect the burden of care. As was common in support group proceedings, participants shared experiences and responded to each others' concerns and difficulties. Two caregiving wives, Sheila and Sandra, described at length their worry over how they would manage alone to see to their husbands' increasing confusion and physical needs at home. Both spoke of their love and devotion, of how, as one of them put it, "I'm going at it alone and, so far, I'm holding up." Yet they also expressed fear that it might be just a matter of time before each would collapse from the overwhelming burden of it all. Gilda responded sympathetically but firmly:

Look, I know what you're going through. I've been through it myself. I really feel for you, as we all do I'm sure. But you have to start thinking a different way about it. All I've been hearing just now is "I this," "I that," "*I'm* taking care of him," "*I'm* holding up until now." Well, my dears, are you ever going to stop and think that it's not all *you?* Sure, it's all very hunky-dory that Sheila's daughter is supportive and has been very complimentary, "a perfect daughter," you said? Well, my dears, there's a *family* here. Let's turn this around a bit, please. You've all seen *Someone I Once Knew* [a popular documentary film portraying five families' experiences with Alzheimers's]. Well, then, what's the family really doing? After all, it's not just your husband; it's their father. It seems to me there's a bigger problem here. What should the *family* be doing?

Both Sheila and Sandra were reluctant, as Sandra stated, "to bring them [family members] into it." They felt their duties as wives obligated them to see to caregiving alone. What was more, Sheila added, "My son and daughter have families of their own to think about." Nonetheless, Gilda insisted on drawing their attention as well as that of others who had offered similar sentiments to what Gilda repeatedly called the wider picture. Her comments soon made it evident that the wider picture was the abstract family entity in the large, separate from each and every one of its members. As Gilda spoke, select sources of a family challenge were again referenced, some of which admittedly had earlier affected her own "thinking about things." As she put it:

Ask yourself this, will you? You've both been around for a while. Right? You read the newsletters from National [ADRDA headquarters] and the *36-Hour Day* [a popular Alzheimer's caregiver handbook] and you saw those films we show at chapter [meetings]. Did you ever stop to think that you all might be one of those families? Forget that sister for a minute, or that daughter of yours, Sheila; what kind of *family* are you? Just ask yourself that.

I remember how I was. It wasn't that long ago either, I might add. I'd read the stuff and poured over it. Over and over. But I kept saying to myself, "No, that's not us." Well, my dears, it took Judy here [another facilitator] to nearly pound my head against the wall to wake me up to the fact that one of those pathetic devoted wives I had read about was really *me!* I remember Judy telling me, "That's *your* family all right." It struck me like lightning because I hadn't really thought of us [her kin] as any kind of family at all.

Another participant, John, whose experience partially echoed Gilda's, then recollected how he had learned his wife's diagnosis and thought at great length about what was happening to her, to himself, and to his three adult daughters as their spouse and mother slowly became "the shell of her former self." John presented his own thoughts in relation to the familial experiences of a temporarily absent support group participant who was well known to all. John's remarks showed how group folklore, like the many familial cases and kinds of families presented in the disease's wider public culture, served as a resource for cognitively transforming a collection of kindred into a type of family. As John remarked:

> It was like that for me, but sort of in reverse. I hadn't thought of how we were all, really, in this together. When Katie [his wife] was fine, we were happy, of course. But you know how families are; you each just did your own thing. Matt's [the absent member] not here today but I can remember that I was a lot like him. You know how his kids have pulled themselves together and how they all pitch in to see to Corinne [Matt's stricken wife]. I'm sure you all remember that time when Matt did his presentation at the [ADRDA] chapter meeting. Something he said really brought it together for me. I'll never forget it. He said, "You never know what a family is until something like this happens." That's when I started to think that, by God, we're the type of family he's talking about.

In the course of this session, as in other ones, the remarks and discussion became descriptive resources for the participants' own unfolding discoveries and attributions of family life. Their particular formulations of the familial emerged from, and were conditioned by, the diverse sources of family understandings available. Through descriptive practice and family discourse the participants constructed the concrete meanings of the family writ large.

Interpretive resources, of course, have no life of their own. The developing awareness of the particular types of families and family members the caregivers were, were functions of resources put to work. It took someone like Gilda for example, with a particular purpose in mind, to make use of the disease's public culture to construe and specify the family relations of the caregivers. Moreover, resources have no particular order of application. The conceptualization of the family writ large that caregivers' kindred represented did not unfold in distinct stages, even though it was frequently reconstructed as doing so in subsequent reports and testimony. What kinship and its related obligations meant in overall familial terms depended on the context of their consideration. Comparing contexts, it was evident that where at one moment participants produced *the* family entity, at another time they could raise doubts over whether it ever existed (Gubrium, 1987b; Lynott, 1983; Gubrium and Buckholdt, 1977).

As caregivers' testimony in the preceding paragraphs indicated, the challenge of caring for an increasingly demented victim meant that caregivers needed to figure conditions and events in terms of domestic responsibilities and their limits. In this regard, support group proceedings centered on the question of how to bridge the gap between an emerging awareness of the family entity and prevailing definitions of responsibility.

Consider, for example, how this question was addressed in one of the day hospital's support group sessions. Participants had just taken up the question of how much a family like Adele's, a caregiving daughter, "can take." Adele's mother had Alzheimer's and attended the hospital's day care program for patients. At one point, Adele recollected how her mother's worsening dementia had made it necessary some months earlier to bring the mother into Adele's own home to live:

> I could see how it just wasn't going to work leaving Mother in that apartment. She'd forget to turn up the heat in the winter and to turn it off in the summer. It was just awful in there, freezing or like a steam bath.
>
> To make a long story short, we moved her in and, as you might guess, it wasn't easy. We start having "those family problems." You know the scene—"grandma-griping," I call it. And my brother . . . the one who lives in Square Lake [some 30 miles away] . . . well, now, was he ever strange. It was like, just as soon as Mother moved in with us, I heard neither hide nor hair of Claude [the brother].
>
> I remember Dan [Adele's husband] saying something that really hurt, when things were going pretty awful. He said, "What kind of family do you have anyway, putting the whole thing on you?" It really bothered me because I had been thinking for some time that I was getting to feel just like Claude about Mother and wanted to just get away. It started to really sink in: what kind of family were we anyway?

Several participants presented similar thoughts, feelings, and questions. As they did, they engaged in a task that was repeatedly undertaken in support group sessions. The family entity conjured up, the issue became what kind of family was it, if it was "family" at all (see Gubrium and Buckholdt, 1982b; Gubrium, 1987a). Adele had turned the question she had originally asked herself at her husband's behest into one for general consideration by support group participants. It was at this point that the variety of resources came into play, as it did on numerous other occasions and would do on still others. A domestic challenge and response to it were substantively articulated through shared and public formulations.

Responses at first suggested that Adele's brother should not be too readily dismissed as unconcerned; for, as Myra, a caregiving spouse pointed out, "He just might not know what you're going through or he might be afraid to ask." Others confirmed that this also had been their own experience and that when they had bothered, as one put it, "to lay it all out, real clear," some consensus about the obligation to pull together as a family resulted. Indeed, by referring to "hidden family strengths," one of the facilitators, a social worker, bridged the particulars of the experiences and so categorized the families. The social worker explained:

> I hear what you're saying and I've seen it many times. Many
> families just don't get it together as a group, like working together
> as a team. There are many with hidden family strengths that just
> never get expressed for some reason. Something like Alzheimer's
> disease can really test a family and, if someone just takes the time
> to express the feeling, it can come out. [Turns to Adele] Like
> Adele, if you'd take the time to talk it over with your brother and
> share your feelings, it just could very well be there. It seems like
> we mostly just take things for granted and you just don't know
> what kind of family you are until a crisis like this happens. And
> that's what we're here for, really, to help you sort it out.

The social worker's final sentences tacitly revealed the task of a veritable
family project.

As the discussion unfolded, it was evident that other sources of
familial definition presented further options for discerning the particular
realities of Adele's family. What had been called possible "hidden family
strengths" between sister and brother took on other meanings. Velma, a
caregiving wife, spoke at length of a family she had read about in a copy
of an ADRDA chapter newsletter her daughter had sent her from new
Jersey. Repeating what Adele had said earlier, Velma stated that a story
in the newsletter "really sunk in." It was about a devoted wife who, like
Velma, continued to care for a very confused and forgetful husband at
home but was ignored and virtually forgotten by the husband's own
brothers. Velma reported how each time "the family" (she signaled
quotation marks with her fingers) got together, which was rarely, her
husband's brothers avoided him and, what made her angrier, chose to
ignore any references Velma would make to her caregiving burden and
occasional need for respite care—just like in the newsletter. Expressing
her deep feelings about the matter, Velma turned to Adele and asked:

> I wouldn't call that hidden family strength, would you? I'd call it
> total lack of responsibility! After all, it's a brother. It's family!
> Donald's [the confused husband] as much their family as he's my
> husband. Adele, I wouldn't be too sure about how your brother'll
> respond. You might just get the old slap in the face, you know
> the it's-*your*-problem routine. It just makes you really wonder if
> they ever really were a family, doesn't it?

The discussion following this made it evident that Adele and
several others had begun to think about the possibility that Adele's "family"
was, as Adele herself later repeated, "no family at all." Admittedly
saddened by the thought, Adele wondered aloud about how she could
"take it" much longer, whether in fact her ostensible familial ties with her
brother had ever "been there" in the first place. Velma's story and experience cast a distinctly disappointing shadow on what several had specu-

lated could actually be secure sibling bonds, which Velma, referring to her own case, had expected to be "above personal selfishness."

As participants offered both similar and contrasting experiences against a familiar background of related knowledge, Adele's brotherly "family" took on varied forms, some negative, others more positive, some altogether unfamilial. The abstract family entity she and her brother represented was a working accomplishment that was never conclusively defined. Rather, it acquired a variety of meanings depending on the various practical concerns with it.

Family Conduct in the Large

The consideration of family conduct in the large prompts a virtual leap in experiential reality. One moves from the concrete particulars of domestic relations to the *behavior* of the abstract family itself that the particulars represent. In the preceding section, as John and others had testified, "I hadn't thought of how we were all, really, in this together," the realization signals the possibility of a family project writ large. The entity under consideration transcends family's individual components. Those concerned attend to a social form that is both distinct from, and greater than, its parts. Changes in modes of address, such as shifts from personal kinship designations to collective family references, hint at a cognitive transition to a way of thinking about family as a collective "thing." When a transition serves to juxtapose members, on the one side, and the larger familial entity they constitute, on the other, the transformation is further secured.

In the field sites, family discourse showed that the family writ large was conceived as an active, willful agent, capable of thinking, feeling, and acting. Accounts of what families, as opposed to members and others, do indicated that family conduct was divided into at least three parts: cognitive, affective, behavioral. Interestingly, this is a folk facsimile of the tripartite behavioral structures commonly designated by human scientists.

Just as attitude theorists and researchers (see Katz and Stotland, 1959; Krech, Crutchfield and Ballachey, 1962) specify an attitude as having a cognitive component, discussion of what *the* family thought or said described the same component. A particularly well-informed geriatric nurse, who frequently facilitated the support group connected with the day hospital studied, often discerned family conduct along cognitive lines. On one occasion, in attempting to explain how her geriatric experience guided her work with caregiving families, she pointed out to support group participants:

> I've been at this for a long time, as most of you know, and from what I've seen, there are two types of families here. You can read

about it in the [Alzheimer's disease] handbooks. There's the family that thinks they can do everything, that needs no help at all. And there's the family that thinks the world owes it a living. And believe you me, most of us just don't stop and think which kind we belong to. I've worked with both types of families and sometimes it's a real job getting them to see what their families are really up to. Right? Really hits home, doesn't it?

The nurse went on to further differentiate the two types, again in terms of the cognitive component of family conduct, elaborating the types' respective thought styles. She was joined by select participants who, in like manner, offered examples of the designated types of family thinking. All made use of prevailing familial resources, from group folklore to the disease's wider public culture, to exemplify the cognitive categories. As the categories were applied to their personal familial experiences, the family writ large took on its concrete shapes. The participants, in turn, used what they both learned and constructed to understand the familial sources and consequences of their individual thoughts and conduct in matters of care and responsibility!

Family conduct also had an affective component. As separate and distinct entities writ large, families were said not only to think but to have feelings as well. It is important to note that family feelings, like the other components, were not the same as individual members' feelings, even though the related feelings of individuals were used to exemplify family feelings in the large.

For example, Muriel, who was a facilitator as well as an experienced caregiver in her own right, claimed that the "frustrated" family can impose its feelings on its members so that virtually all are equally affected:

> I know how a family like that gets to feeling. Deep down, you can see them wrestling with it, even though they just can't admit it to themselves. It's there and they're really feeling the frustration. That's what causes each and every one of them to feel guilty. Sometimes, maybe if you're lucky, one of them's a survivor and doesn't get overwhelmed by it, maybe like Evelyn [a local caregiver who is "going it alone" caring for her vegetative father at home]. But you just don't see much of that. It's pretty unusual, I'd say. I'd say a family like that can really do it to you. That kind of family would give anyone a case of the crazies.

Responses to Muriel's comments showed that the separate domains of familial and member feelings could be markedly disjoint. An outspoken caregiving daughter, Riva, who was never totally convinced of the contribution of families to patient care and support, challenged Muriel's depiction of pervasive affect:

> Come on, Muriel. If you could just see my own family. My father—God bless him—he was a tough nut. Well, he had a heart,

I have to give him that much credit. But it wasn't an easy life for us. It still comes. My sisters and my brother . . . they're each wonderful, very smart people. But when we're together, you just know. It's the same old feeling. Everybody's afraid to say anything about anyone, like no one wants to hurt no one. You just can't believe it. Me too! We just begin to be different people. I feel it. The old feelings come. As a family, it just doesn't work. So, I says to myself, I take care of Mama. So mostly we stay away from the family and get away from it [old feelings].

Other participants had different opinions about the impact of the family's feelings on individual members. Some classified families according to types based on the felt depth and strength of their bonds and used the types to explain differences in individual members' responses to the burden of care. The typology used by others centered on degrees of consensus in sentiment concerning the organization of the caregiving burden. For example, some said that the family in full consensus was easier to handle than one at odds with itself.

Like other components, family feelings were personified by way of the disease's related public culture. When a particular family's affective status was said to exemplify a type of family feeling, the message also was heard as an affective category in a more general system of classification— as the feeling of a kind of family. The Smith family's anger exemplified anger in the family—and the angry family as well. In turn, the general system was enlivened through the concrete familial experiences that exemplified the kinds of family under consideration. In this way, support group participants learned and relearned the family feelings they were subject to, allowing them to discover, explain, or contrast their individual emotional statuses in comparison.

The third component of family conduct was behavioral, concerning what a family did as opposed to what it thought and felt. Again, what a family did was distinguished from what individual *members* did and was consequently used to explain members' conduct. There were many telltale references: "what the family does," "how the family acts," "what the family has always done [or is expected to do]." The range of family behaviors was constrained only by what was conceivable. Families of chronic mental patients, for example, were variously described as "jumping through hoops," "standing on their heads," and "bending over backwards," metaphorically underscoring the lengths to which the families had gone to help a troubled member. Indeed, on occasion, the thoughts, feelings, and behaviors of the family in the large were combined to form a family personality, as when troubled and confused families were said to be "schizophrenic" or "delusional."

In the field sites, the discourse of the family project was at times charged with the parallel obligations of service accountability (Gubrium, 1987a). Social workers, psychologists, nurses, psychiatrists, and physicians, as well as support group participants themselves, referenced and delved into the thoughts, feelings, and behavior of the family writ large. For example, the day hospital service providers who attended the Alzheimer's support group sessions met separately in periodic patient care conferences dealing with the patients and family caregivers in their program. Their discussions regularly addressed the family as a category distinct from its individual members. Family thoughts, feelings, and behavior were used to explain why and how individual caregivers presented the family troubles they did, with the extent and limits of family responsibility providing a theme for the discussion. Again, in turn, participants offered the knowledge of cause and circumstance that they had constructed as a basis for helping those in trouble! Presented with, say, the type of family whose thoughts and behavior resembled what was said to be "classic" (such as the classic paranoid family), the service providers' intervention was accordingly guided. Participants even used published research descriptions of family conduct to articulate the ostensible facts of family living, as a psychiatrist did when he claimed that one family's behavior resembled Laing's and Esterson's (1964) portrayal of the Abbotts.

Denotation Devices

Just as society, community, institutions, and other social entities are not directly available to us, the family is an abstract thing more or less perceived through its signs. While attitude researchers, for example, study attitudes through opinions, opinion is merely representative of attitude's inferred reality. This brings us to the question of *how* those concerned concretely designate the conduct of the family entity. Our concern with descriptive practice and family discourse leads us to see this as an issue of descriptive technique. The question is what descriptive devices are used to actually denote the meanings of the family writ large? In other words, how is the abstract displayed in concrete experience?

Metaphorical Denotation

The process of denotation involves two rhetorical modes: metaphorical and metonymical. Metaphorical denotation is the process whereby family conduct is designated through comparisons with other related conduct that is not literally that of the family under consideration. For example, describing an Alzheimer's family's caregiving feelings in terms of the bereavement individuals experienced at the death of a loved one characterizes and communicates the inner loss that a family experiences as Alzheimer's disease debilitates a living victim.

Alzheimer's disease's growing public culture regularly offered the death metaphor as a way of conveying the disease experience. Bobbie Glaze, a renowned caregiver and nationally active member of the ADRDA in the United States, coined one of the now-popular slogans used to describe what it is like, day in and day out, to witness the mental degeneration of a loved one, even while the victim is alive and physically fit. According to Glaze, Alzheimer's disease is "like a funeral that never ends" (Glaze, 1982).

The death metaphor was frequently used in the Alzheimer's support groups by service providers, facilitators, and caregivers to concretely illustrate "what it's like"— that is, what a family feels at the mental demise of a loved one. Occasionally, a support group session was devoted to caregiver education. Typically, an expert, professional, or experienced family member would be scheduled to talk on some aspect of the disease experience. All made use of the death metaphor in explaining or describing the course of the illness and the family's emotional response to it. In one session, for example, a popular and articulate caregiver, Ruth, spoke of her family's experience in witnessing the slow and painful mental degeneration of a husband and father. Ruth conveyed in vivid detail how it felt for a "once crack salesman" and devoted father to lose his whereabouts and uncharacteristically viciously attack his sons and wife. Ruth began her talk this way:

> I don't have to explain it to you. You've all felt it. For us, it's like Bobbie Glaze said, "a funeral that never ends." And it still hasn't ended even though Barry's [the victim] been at the VA home in Claremont for over a year now. Even though it's four hours away, I visit him every couple of weeks. Sometimes you think you've gotten over it, but, my friends, the funeral goes on. Barry's alive, sure, but he doesn't recognize me. He gets around but he doesn't know where he is. I try to get his attention and call his name: "Barry, Barry, Barry. It's me, Ruth. Ruth, Barry." Maybe deep down he knows it's me. I hope so.

Ruth went on to describe how it felt as a family to have a loved one "mentally fall apart right before your eyes," as she put it. She returned to the death and funeral theme, applied it to the Alzheimer's experience, and elaborated it. She soon became pointedly didactic in conveying what all families go through and feel:

> Let me tell you exactly what you're going through. Some of you, especially the family members who don't see the patient every day, might not realize it right away, but the whole family, everyone really, goes through the relentless mourning. It's there . . . the feeling of loss. But you can't let go. You just can't. You can't just have that funeral and get it over with and try to lead a halfway normal life, I tell ya. The family's still in mourning. We might as well all be wearing black.

Ruth then turned to the course of the family's affective experience. She spoke of the way it is "at first" and what the family's feelings are like as time goes on. As she had often heard from service providers and concerned others, Ruth explained that family feelings came in distinct stages. Elaborating the death metaphor, Ruth referred to the Kübler-Ross (1969) stage theory of the dying experience as an apt model. Without applying the model stage by stage, she described and reaffirmed what many of those in attendance, caregivers and facilitators alike, had heard and themselves used before as a means of assigning temporal organization to family sentiment.

Ruth's presentation metaphorically linked the disease's public culture with caregiving biographies of particular families, a common enough undertaking (Mills, 1959). Familiar metaphors and slogans served as a stock of resources available to convey the substance of a real but unapparent entity—family feeling. Other popular slogans attested to the shared loss: the disease "stealing the mind," a disease that "dims bright minds," which "makes shells of former selves." This served to further elaborate the metaphor and, in its concrete application to family feeling, ramified the family's emotional status as a developing entity.

Family thought and behavior were likewise metaphorically substantiated. For example, not only was the Kübler-Ross model used to construct the organization of feelings in the family writ large, but the model's five stages also designated the course of the family's rationalization, too, as well as how the typical family would behave over time. What for the individual experience of dying was characterized as the initial denial of death, in the Alzheimer's disease experience became the family's initial insistence that nothing was happening to the victim other than the normal decline common to aging. What in dying was bargaining over a terminal status, in the Alzheimer's experience was the family's vacillation over institutionalizing the patient. Thus, in support group talk, the family entity progressively thought and behaved as the dying person did, even while individual members could vary considerably in their respective thoughts and deed.

Metonymical Denotation

Metonymy is a rhetorical device in which an attribute or commonly associated feature of some thing is used to name or designate the thing. It substitutes attributes or components for the name of the thing itself. Referring to a king as "the crown" is a simple example. Metonymic denotation designates the substance of family conduct by means of family's concrete components. Again, the latter are not taken literally to be the entity under consideration. For example, the known denial of a family member might be used to exemplify the "denying family," thus giving substance to what the family is like writ large.

Support group participants made use of a broad range of metonymic devices to reveal family conduct. While the Bobbie Glaze story, for one, metaphorically likened the Alzheimer's disease experience to a never-ending funeral, Bobbie Glaze's personal conduct metonymically represented what the family went through. It's important to note that, metonymically, her family's conduct was not a mere aggregate of its individual members' experiences, but that one member, at least, represented what the family, as such, was like. Disagreements over the status of the family entity, as opposed to the counter-status of select members, were telling in this regard.

Caregivers frequently used celebrities to represent types of family conduct. They cited stories of now-deceased Alzheimer's disease victim Rita Hayworth, the former Hollywood actress, and her daughter Yasmin's devoted care and custody to show what the accepting and responsible family was like. For example, asked to describe that type of family, an active support group participant responded:

> Just take a look at Rita Hayworth's daughter. She's a "princess." [Gestures with quotation marks] She's taken complete responsibility for her mother's care, I hear. It was hard at first but she's doing it, in a caring and loving way, and she doesn't resent having to do it either. That's what I'd call a really devoted family. They've all pulled together and are doing it. You can read about it.

The individual family members portrayed in a popular film *Do You Remember Love?* also served as metonymic resources for giving substance to the kind of family depicted. The film touchingly documents a husband's desperate yet tender response to the effects of the disease on his wife, who is a college professor and poet. While the family entity, of course, was not physically evident in the film, this did not keep a support group participant from pointing out that the husband in the film showed "that there's a devoted family." Interestingly, another participant immediately responded, "I wonder if they realize just what they have?"

Not all exemplars, of course, are national celebrities. The wide variety of individual stories contained in the disease's available local culture was used to reveal family conduct. Support group participants and concerned others, for example, used what they knew about each other to exemplify the families that undesirably affected or infringed on their domestic affairs. A geriatrician's description of one of his Alzheimer's patient's "really depressed caregivers" became a way of portraying the depressed family. A social worker's classification of select caregivers into devoted, unrealistic, and irresponsible types served to substantiate the respective forms of family conduct. What was taken to be a particular caregiver's characteristically erratic concern for his mother, in metonymic application, pinpointed arbitrary family behavior. Metonymy, like metaphor, brought the family project to life.

Negotiation and Denotation

Denotation through metaphor and metonymy did not conclusively define family conduct. While the form and substance of family conduct writ large unfolded rhetorically, they were articulated against a variety of perspectives, social ties, agendas, and sentiments. In the settings studied, participants commonly negotiated at length, let's say, over the particular type of family from which someone under consideration hailed. For instance, what some once construed to be a substantially guilt-ridden family, others considered to be "really" only presenting a remorseful front for public consumption.

Perspective came into play because persons brought different background experiences to the family project and thus imported different ways of seeing family conduct in terms of parts and wholes. In one support group, a husband and his adult daughter were known to disagree over the family's conduct regarding the demented wife/mother. Their disagreements were linked directly with kinship as one occasionally prefaced his remarks with the phrase "speaking as a husband" while the other presented herself with "from a daughter's point of view." The phrases indicated that understandings of family conduct were embedded in the social relations chosen as descriptive frameworks.

Family Usage

Perhaps more than any other aspect of the family project, it was family usage—that is, practical family descriptions used to produce family meanings and to motivate courses of action—that showed how "real" and distinct, not fictive, the family could be as a collective representation. Time and again, the facilitators and service providers studied used what they claimed to have discovered about family type and conduct to design effective support group formats and interventions. Speaking of what she labeled a "denier" (a person who denies reality), one facilitator explained how she would set a different tone at the next session, to "get her [the denier] to see what they're [the family] really like":

> Harriet's denying. That's it. What we have to do now is to get her to see what they're [the family] really like. She's a classic denier all around. The family's got her bugged. You [JFG] saw yourself what's happening, what that kind of family can do to you. I would be surprised if they're not all [family members] deniers, really. None of them can face up to the fact that Mother's [the patient] gone [demented] and their obligation is over. Kaput! Done! Over! I can see it. You can see it. The problem is, can they? We'll work on it. I'll set a different tone next time.

Family usage often entered into rather momentous decisions about matters of care and custody. The familial responsibility theme repeatedly emerged in determinations of when it was no longer feasible to care for the Alzheimer's patient at home. Support group members often entertained the question of what a family's ultimate obligation should be and when the obligation had been met against the background of members' varied senses of family conduct. Many thought members who were "denying" their family's fundamental reality required counseling to make them realize what the family was actually like. Thus family conduct in the large was used, in part, to explain and justify intervening in members' lives. As one geriatrician explained:

> You stand a good chance of getting them [family members] to start thinking of themselves for once and not the patient. If you can get some of them to just look hard at the family and what's happening to it, they'll see what's happening to each and every one of them—the guilt and all.

Other families' conduct was used to explain the ineffectiveness of intervention and influence. For example, some families were said to be "committed," meaning that no manner of persuasion would alter their allegedly unrealistic self-reliance in caring for the patient. The committed family might even work against its members. For instance, while individual members might privately entertain thoughts about limiting familial responsibility, for the so-called "sake of the family," all acted as if the family were fully committed and would never, say, place a mother or father in a nursing home.

The idea of family conduct, as the categorically distinct action of a family entity, is considered bad form in standard sociological discourse. Warnings against giving human shape and substance to any social form are ample; some family theorists and researchers warn against "anthropomorphization." Society does not think, we are told. The family per se does not act; only members do. Still, this sort of description does creep into family studies, as discussed in Chapter 3.

Moreover, it is evident in everyday conversation, in which the family and other social forms are spoken for and acted toward as if the forms did indeed think and behave. People tell us as much in phrases like "society thinks . . . ," "society says . . . ," and "society does . . . " Descriptive practice seems to acknowledge, appreciate, even defer to, these social things. Similarly, members of households, support group participants, and others who are concerned with family matters populate their worlds with behaving and thinking families, abstract entities larger than, and in a category separate from, individual family members.

Because the family writ large enters into everyday experience as a discursive formation, its conduct cannot be revealed by methods exclusively focused on individual experience. Accordingly, we have examined family discourse to reveal the collective ways that family is constructed and brought to life as a thinking, feeling, acting entity with human shape and substance. These practices combine in what we call the family project. As two senses of the term "project" suggest, family is both a practical undertaking and an extending outward, a way of objectifying an aspect of our experience.

While the family is a thing in a descriptively practical sense, things are expected to be located in some *place*. Yet how can an objectless object like family be found? In the next chapter, we again turn to descriptive practice for an answer.

Chapter 5

The Descriptive Usage
of the Household

"Now this one is an absolute gem," gushed the real estate agent as she ushered her clients—a young couple, the wife obviously pregnant—up the walk to the front door of a four-bedroom, two-bath, red brick colonial. "Can't you just tell by looking at it that a happy family has lived here? I think it may be just the place you're looking for to get that family of yours started."

The real estate agent in this scenario was doing something many of us do from time to time. As she talked about the house and people dwelling within, she was reading (and telling) signs of family life from the physical features of the structure that she believed housed real family life. Of course, she was trying to make the house seem attractive; but at the same time, she was conveying to her listeners the sense that the structure and condition of the brick colonial revealed important information about the quality of the domestic life within. Moreover, she clearly implied that a congenial house—indeed, this house—was the place where family life would flourish. Although unwittingly, the real estate agent was articulating the second assumption of the "private image" that we discussed in Chapter 3: family's natural location is the home.

What makes the real estate agent's descriptions understandable, if not compelling, is the assumption that the most authentic experience of the family is found at home. The essence of domestic life emerges within the household, and the physical features of that household reflect the family within. In the course of daily activity, persons are constantly using images of house and home to impart diverse and distinctive domestic meanings to the lives of occupants. To state, for example, that a family "barely has a roof over its heads" can describe more than just marginally adequate shelter. The statement can convey familial insecurity, inadequate parenting, or fiscal irresponsibility as well.

In this chapter, we turn to the descriptive usage of the household, focusing on how interpretations of the appearance of a physical structure, its environs, space, and location figure in discoveries about home and family. As the vessel that contains family life, the household can set the stage, as it were, for discerning family themes, plots, and actors. We will examine how household signs are taken and used to impart meaning to domestic life within.

Descriptive Imperatives of the Household

In discussing the household location assumption of the private image in Chapter 3, we noted that some family scholars were oriented to the household in general as a natural habitat. Others divided the home into more and less authentic regions, dramaturgically distinguishing frontstage and backstage. Some focused on the core of the household, calling it the "psychosocial" interior. Still others presented the "dark side" of family life. Their language offered tacit understandings or images of things to come. The household as a gloomy container of human affairs compelled the discovery of domestic pathology, from the winks and implicit gestures of the Abbott family to the subtle interpersonal imaginings of the Lawsons (Laing and Esterson, 1964). In contrast, Lasch's portrayal of the household as a "haven," not of dark secrets or sordid goings-on, but of rejuvenating private life, prepared us for a history of the ways domesticity has been spoiled.

Our tacit understandings not only orient our attention, but also organize what we believe we see when we look at things. Laing's dark and sordid concept of the household, for one, not only introduces what we expect to hear about its domestic affairs, but also interpretively designs the facts of mystification and pathology that are presented. Understandings extend to conclusions, too. After the facts of the household have been both introduced and presented according to a particular set of themes, the conclusion is conveyed along the same lines. The imperative of rational description would make something less consistent seem irrational.

Understandings also shape our feelings. Lasch's household-as-haven, for example, is not only a way of presenting de-privatization, but is a lament for lost privacy as well. Laing's household-as-inner sanctum is not just a means of concretely situating sanity, madness, and the family, but also a forceful condemnation of the family's unconscious tyranny over members. Thus, while household, through its imagery as a vessel, both figuratively and literally contains domestic affairs, it also adds flavor to the brew.

The descriptive imperatives of the household are not just about communication, but about experiential reality as well. In asserting, for example, that certain households are overcrowded and tense, we not only inform our audience of an understanding, but also announce an expectation of facts such as domestic violence. Of course, we might be right or wrong about what is eventually discovered, but we nonetheless provide a set of expectations as well as a particular standard for making that judgment.

In terms of descriptive practice, we can think of household as an expression of the common cultural linkage of house and home. The assumption that houses are the natural sites of domestic life—that is, homes—provides a set of guidelines for interpreting and describing family life; a house's physical features are signs of the lives within. For example, in their study of child abuse in England, Dingwall, Eekelaar, and Murray (1983) found that service workers conceived of the possible violence of the home in terms of a variety of physical, geographic, and subcultural indicators. Environmental signs like a tidy garden behind a home suggested that a family's domestic life was intact. As the authors imply, the material environment is an important system of quite public signs for interpreting the private affairs inside the home. Indeed, the authors contend that some service workers took the material environment to be a more valid sign of domestic life than actual observations of the family's interactions with one another:

> This part of the social evidence may itself be further divided into a number of subsidiary categories. These include the physical condition of the home (the state of the property and its furnishings) and the physical condition of the occupants (the state of their clothing and self-care). . . . In some sense, these data may be considered to be "harder" than the observations of the interpersonal environment. They are more publicly available and their evaluation requires no specific training or esoteric knowledge. At the same time, the frameworks of interpretation incorporated within particular occupational licences may discount their significance. (p. 57)

As Dingwall, Eekelaar, and Murray caution, while the household signals what life is like within, it can signal different things to different people. In this regard, it is important to link the descriptive imperatives of the household with actual descriptive practice. For example, while some refer to the physical appearance of the household as the reason that its children, say, are withdrawn or always tense, others might dismiss it as being the cause of the children's behavior. While there are those who interpret dilapidation, say, as a sign of familial irresponsibility, others might recognize it as understandable given the age of the neighborhood. The point is that the household is offered as explanation or clarification within the overall descriptive work of figuring the domestic order of the household. The household's status as cause, effect, or judgment is more a matter of descriptively working it into ongoing arguments and sentiments about domestic life than it is a necessarily definitive sign in an objective sense.

The descriptive imperatives of the household have two important, interconnected sources. One is usage; the household is regularly used, more or less successfully, to provide clues to the inner workings of the home. The other source is cultural; considerations of family life are regularly linked with house, home, privacy, and domesticity in culturally anticipated ways. The terms are part of the everyday discourse of domestic life. Their meanings are so intertwined that anything we learn about one of them almost surely informs us about the others. Just as we take for granted that something about love might tell us something about tender feelings—because the terms are regularly linked in the language of sentiments—it seems to make sense to turn to the home to learn about family life, and vice versa.

Still, what may be intelligibly used need not ultimately persuade us of its merits. A common plausible connection readily provides good reasons for figuring the meaning of family affairs in a certain way; and so the momentum of established ways of doing so, like reading domestic violence from a house's state of repair, must be overcome in putting forth new connections. Conversely, we are not as readily persuaded by clues to domestic order that are culturally strange—such as reading marital satisfaction from the number of steps leading to the home's front porch—until the descriptive merit of such clues is convincingly established. Because signs have no definitive life of their own, both usage and cultural intelligibility are ultimately more or less persuasive components of descriptive practice.

Physical Appearance

To start, let us consider how the physical appearance of the household serves as a sign of domestic life. Keep in mind that, as far as descriptive practice is concerned, our attention is not on whether household signs correctly represent familial order, but instead focuses on how the household's physical appearance is *used* to assign meaning to the family and its activities, thus constructing domestic life.

Disarray

While the families, service providers, and significant others we have observed did not usually utter the term "disarray" in describing the households of concern to them, they did use phrases like "messy homes," "noisy environments," "everything out of place," "everything everywhere," and "the aftermath of a tornado." The references pertained to both the internal and the external environs of the home. Some claimed to notice a messy home from the very moment they approached it, an impression easily drawn into the home's interior. Others were taken aback by a relatively orderly outer appearance belying rooms that looked as if they had been "hit by a tornado." In the Alzheimer's support groups studied, the physical appearance of the victim's home was regularly taken by family members as a possible sign that "things were coming apart." The messy apartment of an elderly husband who cared for his demented wife at home could show that their relationship was disintegrating. For others, it could signal the husband's fortitude in caring more for his spouse than for his own belongings. In community mental health settings and in the residential treatment center for emotionally disturbed children, the "noise level" of the household was used by staff members, especially front-line workers, as a sign of familial control. Did noise represent weakened domestic bonds or did it show remarkable interpersonal tolerance? What might the judge of an involuntary mental commitment hearing make of a report that a two-room apartment strewn with catfood cans and litter served as home for a candidate patient, her 21-year-old son, and her eleven cats? Was it evidence of disorientation and an inability to adequately provide for a family's basic needs, or was it a courageous adaptation to the conditions of poverty and social isolation that plague the deinstitutionalized mentally ill?

Let us consider in some detail the use of household disarray as an interpretation of domestic disintegration in the Alzheimer's disease experience. In some of the support groups studied, certain family members would attend sessions together. For example, in one group, an adult daughter often attended with her father. The father cared for his demented wife at home. On one occasion, the father described the various methods he used to monitor his demented wife's needs. Because the wife was virtually mute, her husband had to "second guess" her, as he put it, which meant he had to rely on his own judgment in deciding whether she was thirsty, hungry, or needed to use the toilet, among other needs. He spoke at length of how much time this took and said he wished she could simply tell him what she wanted because that would make life much easier. At one point, the husband, Mike, remarked:

> and, as you can guess, the house has gone to pot. It takes all my time just to see to Bev's [the wife's] needs. But, you know how it is, you have your priorities.

Mike's adult daughter, Cynthia, who lived in an apartment in the vicinity of her parent's home, was not as cavalier about the "house [going] to pot." She cautioned Mike that he should not so glibly dismiss what had become of the house. According to Cynthia, a house going to pot was sometimes a sign of "other things happening that you don't care to think about." Cynthia explained:

> I don't want to make a big thing out of this, but it's known to happen that what's happening all around you, you just don't realize that it's affecting your life. I'm a bit worried about Dad. I go over there [to the parents' home] and find all this stuff all over the place, like a tornado's hit the place. Dirty, moldy dishes in the sink. Newspapers all over. You name it. [Cynthia turns to her father] Dad, I know you say that you're hanging on and doing it, but from what I see all around whenever I'm over, I think something's giving.

Mike smiled and warmly expressed appreciation for his daughter's concern. He also told her not to jump to conclusions about the physical appearance of his home:

> Cynthia, we've talked about this before. It's nothing, really. I'll get it when I have time. It's your mother that's my top priority and, of course, seeing to the groceries and the bank and all that. To hell with the house. You can't keep up with everything; it's first things first. I really don't think you should make so much of these kinds of things. Really. It's just a house.

It was evident in Cynthia's response that she wasn't convinced that a house was simply "just a house." Indeed, in her father's later remarks, he even began to "think twice" about what was going on at home when things got as "messed up" as his own house was. While both father and daughter understood the connection that could be made between physical appearance and familial disarray, the father had initially dismissed it as inapplicable in his own case while the daughter attempted to make good on it.

Other support group participants contributed their own perspectives. Some elaborated the connection and offered concrete suggestions for what might be happening to Mike's domestic affairs, more or less reflecting the father's or daughter's views. For example, another husband-caregiver commented how "that kind of thing," meaning the condition of the household, was the first sign of domestic strain. He noted further that he'd even seen that kind of thing actually lead the caregiver to hate his or her spouse for what the household was becoming—a home to no one. Other participants cautioned that too much was "being made" of the matter. One even explained that what was physically evident in the home had no relation at all to what family members felt for each other.

As father, daughter, and others exchanged views on the meaning of the household's disarray, several levels of concern developed. Not only did group members debate the actual extent of physical disarray in specific households, but they also discussed the particular domestic meaning of Mike's household in relation to them. They described the principle of making a connection between physical and domestic disarray. As the exchanges continued, it was evident that the practice of describing itself, together with the shared understanding of the linkage between physical and domestic disarray—process and principle, respectively—revealed what was actually seen in a household.

Dilapidation

Just as familial disintegration was regularly linked with the physical disarray of the household, the home's dilapidation also could be a more or less convincing sign of the lack of domestic tranquility. As the community mental health data showed, for a social worker making a home visit, the ramshackle exterior of a client's small frame house— peeling paint, rotting clapboards, cardboard covering broken windows— could be an obvious indication of the crumbling family life within. As one such social worker noted:

> Zandie [the client] has been raising her two sons by herself for years, but things seem to be getting away from her more and more lately. She's lost control of the boys; they're just hanging around waiting for trouble. Nobody's doing anything to keep the place up. Look at this dump. You can see it's no place to be bringing up kids. I mean it's only a matter of time before the roof falls in and we have to hospitalize her and put the kids in foster homes.

The social worker spoke both literally and figuratively as she linked the family's future to the disintegrating structure that housed it.

As with physical disarray, while some saw the connection between dilapidation and social integration causally, others took dilapidation to be only a clue to what remained hidden in the home. Whether causal, suggestive, or otherwise intelligible, the rhetoric of descriptive practice itself was a significant factor in convincing those concerned that dilapidation actually represented family disintegration.

Take the following example from a psychiatric staffing at Cedarview, the residential treatment center for emotionally disturbed children that was studied. Staffings are the professional conferences in which staff members (consulting psychiatrists and psychologists, special education teachers, social workers, child-care workers) review the sources of children's troubles and the children's progress in treatment, among other aspects of care and custody. Ricky, a 12-year-old boy in treatment for approximately one year, was being staffed. At one point in the proceedings, Ricky's social worker recalled household comments that Ricky's father had made in a parent effectiveness training session held at Cedarview a few evenings earlier. The goal of such training is to help parents become more effective in dealing with their children. At Cedarview, staff engaged parents in role-playing, encouraged them to share family experiences, and taught them behavior management skills.

Following a detailed description of Ricky's family's household and its environs, which Ricky's social worker claimed were abysmal, and an earlier plea by another social worker to not stereotype neighborhoods, Ricky's social worker cautioned:

> but don't get me wrong. I'm not trying to say that dilapidated housing like that makes these kids go crazy. I've seen the best of them burn their brains out in a place that none of us would ever live in and others make it in flying colors no matter what the condition of the house. I really don't think that it makes much difference overall. Sometimes, you know how you go up to one of those places and you think to yourself, "I can see why this or that kid's acting out all the time . . . like if I lived in a place like that, the whole family would suffer, really." But I've seen it too many times . . . like when I go in and really check things out, the family's not as bad as you figured.

The participants' exchanges following the social workers's initial comments showed that all recognized the connection being made between the home's state of repair, familial disintegration, and emotional disturbance. Indeed, the special education teacher remarked at one point, "You just wonder sometimes, don't you, how any one of those kids can even think in some of those places they live in." Yet, despite their recognition of the connection as well as what it told them in other cases, neither the teacher nor the other participants agreed that it applied in Ricky's case.

Even a consulting psychologist, himself a behaviorist, could not persuade the others to think differently. At one point, the consulting psychologist had explained:

> I hear what you're saying and understand your feelings about it. But I wouldn't dismiss the environment too quickly. You all know from working with these kids what a simple change of scene can do. Sometimes it's really true that a broken-down house can make a broken home. I wouldn't be too surprised if some of that wasn't happening to Ricky's family and having an effect on his ability to handle it. Think about it.

Nonetheless, while several of the participants responded that they understood how house and home could make a difference in emotional development, they were not convinced that what was generally understood and suggested by the consultant was a compelling source of Ricky's problems.

Still, as the proceedings turned to the general effect of physical environment on the emotional growth of children, it was evident that all participants confirmed what dilapidation could reveal about family life in general. None was ready to dismiss what all understood to be a possible sign of domestic order (or disorder). As a principle of representation, dilapidation, like household disarray, was a significant sign. It was only the particular case under consideration that suggested to all but the psychologist that the principle did not apply. In the course of the deliberations even the psychologist saw the merits of looking at this particular case from a different angle; Ricky's case was an exception to the rule. As it turned out, the new angle was the household's neighborhood location, not its state of repair.

Location

The neighborhood location of a household can have a contagious quality. Families risk "catching" their neighborhoods' putative characteristics. A so-called "bad neighborhood" can be the source of any number of undesirable familial characteristics, from "broken homes" to child abuse. The contagion is sometimes benign. A "good neighborhood" might explain why one household remained intact while another household, located in a bad neighborhood, had all manner of misfortune. Again, exceptions prove the rule. For example, a family believed to have kept itself together despite the malevolent influences of the community might be considered unique, as is the family that surprisingly falls apart in the best of circumstances.

Consider how the concept of "fresh air," as a characteristic of location, served as a sign of what the future could bring for a recently paralyzed 18-year-old boy named Gary and his domestic caretakers. In this case, the connection between location and domestic life was not considered exceptional. Gary had been in a motorcycle accident, suffered brain trauma, and had a spinal cord injury that resulted in paraplegia. The staff at Wilshire, which was the rehabilitation hospital where Gary was placed for physical and occupational therapy, expected him to spend the rest of his life in a wheelchair. In all such cases, the rehabilitation strategy was to bring the patient to maximal physical functioning despite the handicap.

Before the accident, Gary lived with his grandparents in a modest house located in an older, industrial section of the city. According to the hospital social worker, it wasn't the best environment for a kid, let alone the grandparents. The social worker had suggested that everyone in the neighborhood seemed to be "on edge." The air was often thick with industrial pollutants from local manufacturing plants. The major thoroughfares bordering the grandparents' home added to the dust and grime, with buses, cars, and trucks spewing their fumes into open windows. To make matters worse, odors from a nearby sewage treatment plant had a way of continually fouling the atmosphere despite its pollution abatement program.

In planning for Gary's discharge from Wilshire, which typically begins soon after admission, his treatment team considered the parents' quieter and cleaner neighborhood and home. It, too, was an older home, but was located away from the grime and bustle of the inner city. According to a nurse familiar with the parents' neighborhood, the air was fresher there and didn't give rise to the domestic tensions associated with a polluted environment. Gary hadn't lived with his parents for three years, partly because he had attended a vocational high school that was more convenient to his grandparents' home; he didn't own a car and could walk to school. Now that Gary was permanently disabled, the hospital treatment team felt that the parents' home offered a better overall environment. Gary needed all the domestic support he could get. Convenience took a backseat to the purported connection between fresh air, domestic tranquility, and individual outlook on life.

In the team's conferences with the parents and grandparents, participants discussed the so-called fresher air of the parents' neighborhood in relation to Gary's future. While financial considerations, household space, and custody were taken into account, what the particular discharge location of choice would bode for the years ahead was a constant theme. As the physical therapist once explained to the mother and grandfather:

> I really feel that you can't just look back in cases like this and think that what's coming up is going to be just like it was before. Like we talked about before, Gary's future is going to be different. I'm not saying it's gonna be bad, just that it's gonna be different. So we have to think about the neighborhood and all, and what's best for him in the long run.

The possibility of moving Gary back into his parents' home was discussed openly. An important factor broached by all was the matter of fresh air. Even the grandfather admitted that the fresher air might, as he put it, "do him [Gary] some good and give him a better outlook." All hoped that Gary would manage to keep his habitual optimism despite his recent misfortune. Fresh air, it seemed, was a sign of the future; it stood for whatever Gary could personally actualize in a new environment.

Neither the treatment team nor family members questioned the viability of the parents' domestic life. While some felt it was not an especially exciting household, it was congenial and responsible. What is more, according to the social worker and occupational therapist, the fresh air "made a difference" in everyone's overall mood and predisposition in the household. Exactly how was not clear. What was evident, though, was that conference participants agreed that fresh air could breathe new life into family living, which, in turn, could have a positive effect on Gary's outlook. Fresh air signaled something about domestic life that would affect Gary's future in its own right.

Now it is important to note that no one reasoned in detail about the place of fresh air in domestic life nor about how household location and residence figured in the connection. If there was a causal sense to the matter at all, it was that something about fresh or foul air as a characteristic of neighborhood location could have an impact on domestic life. Fresh air was nonetheless a sign; in Gary's case, it was taken to be a positive sign of the future for a family member. As a nurse put it, "You can just tell that it'll make a difference," referring to fresh air and its associated interpersonal conditioning.

The use of household location as a sign of domestic life was not unique to Wilshire's world. Correctly or not, location represented the privacies of the household in all the field sites. Not only staff members, but also friends, significant others, families, consultants, even bystanders understood the application of location as a means of representing the family. Like other factors appropriated to the description of domestic life, location was part of a culture of signs for the private affairs of the home.

Transiency

The permanence of the family's residence was yet another sign of a family's domestic order and stability. Constant changes of address suggested negative familial consequences. While residential permanence was taken as significant in all field sites, its use was especially noteworthy at Cedarview. In sorting through the sources of a child's emotional disturbance, transiency was an important consideration; a child's psychosocial stability was often read from his family's changes of address.

In this regard, let us consider the interpretation of 13-year-old Marcia Thompson's emotional disturbance. Like other girls at the facility, she was not in residential care; only boys remained in the institution around the clock. But she did participate in Cedarview's special education program. She had been at Cedarview for over a year and attended school there from approximately 8 A.M. to 3 P.M., when a schoolbus drove her home. The public school's multidisciplinary team had referred Marcia because of what were reported to be unmanageable outbursts and lack of motivation. According to her referral documents, Marcia manifested a "definite lack of self-control and presented a lackadaisical attitude toward her schoolwork." The team recommended that Marcia enroll in a facility with a structured environment and a controlled learning experience, the very things Cedarview's goal-oriented, behavior management program provided.

Participants in Marcia's latest semiannual psychiatric staffing focused on Marcia's home life as a possible source of her present problems. The home was a commonplace consideration in all staffings. What stood out in this particular staffing were Marcia's frequent changes of address. From the time she was placed in the institution, her family had moved four times. This presented Cedarview with some administrative difficulties. The office and treatment staff both complained that it always was difficult to reach the parents at home because they moved so often. At least twice, Marcia's social worker had attempted home visits only to find that the family no longer resided at the address. The family's telephone was so frequently disconnected or out of order that so-called chance visits to the home had to be made. The social worker remarked that the problem was "really frustrating."

In the staffing, the social worker went into considerable detail about the unsuccessful home visits. On her most recent visit, she found that the current occupants of the home she had listed as Marcia's address weren't the family she was looking for. The occupants informed her that the previous tenants had moved out the week before, adding that they believed it was to a nearby trailer park. The social worker decided to look into the matter and went to the trailer park to find the family. She soon located them and learned that Marcia continued to be transported from school by bus to her previous address, from which she then walked home. As the social worker recounted her difficulties, she repeated how "really bizarre" it all was. She explained that, for some reason, the family was either suspiciously secretive about where they lived or "too lazy to keep in contact."

Throughout the proceedings, members of Marcia's treatment team stated several times how exasperated they had grown with the situation. The worst part, they claimed, was what "all this moving" conveyed to them about the family's domestic life. While none of them admittedly knew much about the family except what they surmised from telephone conversations with the mother, all felt that the family's transiency told a great deal about what was probably going on in the home.

The trailer was a particularly telling sign of the unsettled domestic affairs believed to be at the root of Marcia's emotional disturbance. Centering their attention on the trailer, staffers combined their ideas into a rather complex chain of reasoning. The trailer was a concrete and paramount sign of transiency, which, in turn, represented domestic instability. These conditions easily explained Marcia's outbursts, which the psychiatric consultant convincingly argued were Marcia's way of getting attention. The consultant's rather humorous comments, at one point, conveyed the relevance of the household:

> My God, now a trailer! What next? Do you think we might find them [the family] living under a viaduct the next time? You know, if you put all of this together, it makes a whole lot of sense. No wonder she [Marcia] blows up. Anyone would blow up if they

never knew where they lived from one week to the next. I know I'm exaggerating a bit, but. . . [Explains the dynamics of the process described]. I'll bet that trailer is a real nightmare to the child . . . I mean what it tells her about her family and all. I think what it's telling us is that we've got to work on the bonding end of things. Marcia needs a secure home life. Maybe we should consider foster care?

Other participants responded by further elaborating on the trailer's significance. It was evident that the trailer not only represented transiency; but, in the connections made, it was also taken to be the source of Marcia's emotional disturbance. In turn, the emotional disturbance, especially the outbursts, were accepted as visible evidence of "what could easily happen" when a child lacked permanence in his or her home life.

Personnel in each of the field sites took change and permanence into account in evaluating residential prospects. At Wilshire, for example, discharge planners considered residential stability an important factor in assessing which destinations were most likely to provide a rehabilitation patient with a supportive home life. In the support groups for caregivers of Alzheimer's disease patients, an enduring issue was the domestic meaning of institutionalization. In decision making regarding nursing home placement, support group participants weighed the advantages and disadvantages of the continuity in family support derived from continued home care, the domestic impact of the burden of caregiving, and the discontinuity and possible dysfunctions in support that would come from institutional placement (Gubrium, 1989a). Indeed, a major theme of the scholarly literature concerning nursing home relocation is the question of whether residential changes affect mortality, an important consideration being the discontinuity in support that results from relocation (see Tobin and Lieberman, 1976; Schultz and Brenner, 1977).

Concerns about transiency also were central to involuntary commitment decisions. In particular, court personnel believed that residential stability was an important ingredient in effectively caring for released mental patients in the community. This factor was taken into account, for example, when Ozzie Glover, a mental patient, petitioned for release and community placement. He claimed that his symptoms had abated to the point where he could live in the community with his parents. The psychiatrist who testified at the hearing, Dr. Ratik, acknowledged a remission in Ozzie's symptoms, but attributed it to the chemotherapy Ozzie was receiving while hospitalized. Ratik confirmed that the parents had offered to take Ozzie into their home, but he expressed strong reservations about the sort of care and supervision that this particular home might provide. According to Ratik, the parents moved from community to community several times a year as Mr. Glover, Ozzie's father, sought work in the construction industry. In the psychiatrist's view, this fact posed problems for a community treatment regimen because it signaled the sort of unsettled, disorganized household and family life that accompanied frequent uprooting and resettlement. "There's a constant state of confusion in homes like that," Dr. Ratik had noted. Ratik explained that "that kind of family doesn't know who's coming or going. I'm afraid Ozzie's treatment will be just one more thing that gets lost in the shuffle." Again—whether or not this reasoning was correct in an objective sense—like others, Dr. Ratik descriptively used the household as a possible sign of domestic stability and offered his recommendation accordingly.

Personal Space

In the social science literature, the density of interpersonal relations has been a favored explanation for social organization. Durkheim (1947), for one, argued that as human density increased, so did a kind of organic interdependence with its specialization of function. Simmel (1950) and Wirth (1938) linked the sheer density of interpersonal contacts with the condition of mental life, noting that city living seemed to increase cognitive indifference.

Both too little and too much personal space have signaled social travail. At one end of the spectrum, crowding within households has served to explain domestic tension, among other familial stresses and strains. In the field sites studied, it was a common idiom to refer to the connection between the home's density and individual freedom as "[personal] space." Assertions such as "you just know that the family suffers when things are that crowded" and "the kids are alone in that big house" were descriptively revealing. A crowded household, for example, might be said to offer family members very little space. A small house, a household with too many children, or a combination of the two were signs of domestic trouble. At the other end of the spectrum, lack of supervision or too much personal freedom has been used to signal possible family disintegration. There could be too much personal space. Either extreme could represent an undesirable condition of domestic life. It was uncommon for household crowdedness or its opposite extreme to be associated with domestic bliss. When it was, however, it was treated as a surprising exception to the rule that nonetheless left the rule intact.

Crowdedness

While crowdedness could be a simple matter of having too many people in the household, it was also translated into what we might call "conditional density." For example, with the onset of some undesirable personal condition like a family member's mental illness or delinquency, it was frequently stated that a particular household had become too crowded. This was more than a figure of speech, for the condition was a problem not only for the person who suffered from it, but also for others in the home whose personal space was now infringed upon. Such conditional density, moreover, also signaled trouble for the family writ large.

It is a common theme of Alzheimer's disease's public culture that the disease has two victims: the individual actually afflicted and the caregiver. As the title of a popular handbook for families infers, the home care burden for the caregiver can be like a "36-hour day," expanding into every free moment and the personal space of all concerned. The caregiver virtually becomes a second patient (see Mace and Rabins, 1981). What might have been a perfectly acceptable home before the onset of illness, especially before the disease's progress into its later stages, becomes too crowded to be a home to anyone, raising the prospect of institutionalization.

In this regard, take a typical exchange in one of the Alzheimer's caregiver support groups studied. As part of the discussion of when "it's time" for nursing home placement, the group frequently took the domestic meaning of institutionalization into account. As mentioned in Chapter 4, this involved comparing two locations as possible homes for the patient—the family home and the nursing home. It presented two related questions: As the disease and burden of care progressed, could the family household continue to be a home to anyone, and could a nursing facility provide a home for a loved one? Catherine, a caregiver, had been describing how her increasingly demented mother's presence in the home was affecting the household. At one point, she remarked:

> Well, everyone here knows what I'm talking about; you all have heard it a hundred times. I don't have to tell you how Mother's presence has changed the feel of the place [the home]; it's like no one has any space. I can't tell you how much it makes us all on edge. We're like a pack of caged animals. I hate to think that some day we'll be at each other's throats. We all need space. I realize that more now than I ever did.

Catherine's mother, an 83-year-old widow, had lived in her own apartment near Catherine's home for a number of years. Until the mother's dementia grew severe, she had managed on her own. When Catherine discovered that her mother turned on the heat in the summer and left the windows open on the coldest winter days, Catherine persuaded her mother to move into Catherine's own home. Catherine reported that, at the time, it seemed to be an effective solution, since the two of them had always been close friends anyway and the family members were very fond of their grandmother. Catherine's two-story bungalow was also home to Catherine's husband and their three children. As Catherine pointed out, she had never felt crowded before, even when her mother sometimes spent as long as a month with them: "Even with Mother spending weeks with us, we were like six bugs in a rug—cozy-like and always friendly—and she's always been my closest friend."

Yet as one after another of the participants remarked, some using well-worn clichés, when something like Alzheimer's disease strikes, what had been "company" becomes a "crowd." Various participants implied that crowding soon leads to the breakdown of family life. Indeed, when it was noted that the crowding experienced by those living with a dementia patient was no different from the felt crowding caused by other conditions, it was evident that crowding in general had a distinct place in the descriptive organization of household and family.

In the family discourse concerning personal space, the link between crowdedness and familial disintegration was featured in terms of a familiar metaphor, suggested earlier in one of Catherine's comments: being crowded felt like being caged or confined animals. In contrast, in a related conversation in another support group, the adult son of an Alzheimer's disease victim brought crowdedness, family disintegration, and metaphor together in a somewhat humorous scenario of the "only kind of house that could work under the circumstance." Recalling the large mansions with "hidden" wings that all were said to have either read about or seen in old films, the son joked about such a mansion's being the only place big enough to house a family as well as an Alzheimer's victim, without everyone "becoming animals" and "going crazy" in the process. It was one of those old mansions where one could give Mother or Dad all the room needed to wander "in their own wing." The son added that since none of them was ever going to have that kind of house, they could only joke about the possibility and either live with each other like confined animals and all that meant, or start to think seriously about a nursing home.

There were, of course, some who saw things differently and for that reason continued to care for the demented family member at home. Yet while there were differences of opinion, it was as much what they learned about crowdedness's impact on domestic life as it was understandings of their separate domestic experiences that warranted their interpretations. For example, some cast caregiving as a condition of moral obligation, personal responsibility, companionship, and familial wherewithal. In this regard, what others called "crowdedness" was an intergenerational learning experience centered on what proper families should accomplish for their members. At the same time, it was not uncommon for such opinion to be compared with what, as one caregiver had put it, "everyone seems to think," meaning that conditional density leads to domestic disintegration.

Lack of Supervision

At the opposite end of the spectrum was the condition of too much personal space—in particular, the lack of supervision. This was used in different ways at Cedarview in relation to the families of emotionally disturbed children. Staff regularly argued that lack of supervision revealed something about the family from which such children hailed; namely, that the family lacked responsibility and concern. The argument was also applied to other children in the same households who were not emotionally disturbed. As far as they were concerned, it warned of where a lack of supervision could eventually lead. The single-parent household was a particularly telltale sign of a possible lack of supervision, especially if the existing parent was employed full time. So was the household of the single parent who spent all of his or her spare time with friends or lovers outside the home. "Latchkey" kids represented what could well be a disintegrating family life, which, in turn, could explain why the children lacked self-control.

Lack of supervision also figured in the interpretation of adults' domestic affairs. An important consideration in discharge planning at Wilshire rehabilitation hospital was whether a particular destination offered adequate supervision for the patient. Would a household where few members were ever at home be a supportive environment for a recently paralyzed young adult? On the other hand, would the possibly overwhelming supervision resulting from having too many people in the household shortchange the need to optimize a paraplegic patient's independence? The latter question, of course, ties lack of supervision to its opposite—crowding—in a system of signs of family life.

Supervision also was a critical concern in deliberations over the home care of the demented, especially care of the so-called "wandering" patient. Because wanderers lack a sense of their whereabouts, they must be supervised. In this regard, it was not uncommon in caregiver support groups to hear talk of a sole caregiver as being a possible sign of family troubles—namely, irresponsible kindred. The received wisdom was that, in Alzheimer's, the burden of care was so great that no one person could function as a caregiver for very long without respite and community or family support. Those exceptional enough to succeed in functioning were often celebrated, if they weren't considered to be "denying" the truth of the matter, which was that their relatives "couldn't care less." The related caregiver literature presents the same theme, linking the sole caregiver with inadequate supervision and support from families; caregivers who "go it alone" are a possible sign of unhealthy home situations (see Zarit, Orr and Zarit, 1985). The possibility that the sole, functioning caregiver gains satisfaction from his or her efforts and thus signals familial strength and resilience is rare in the research (see Gubrium, 1988c). The support groups considered the solitary caregiver to be an exception to the rule that viable home care requires a supportive family or, in lieu of that, eventual institutionalization. Even the exceptions had a negative tinge; for while those caregivers who chose to "go it alone" were celebrated by some, others called them "martyrs," if not "deniers."

The degree of supervision was a continual theme, too, in mental hospitalization considerations. As in the other settings, having few persons in the household could be a sign of an ineffective domestic life. For example, when an ex-mental patient's youngest daughter moved out of the family home, leaving just a husband to look after his schizophrenic wife, concern was raised by mental health personnel that there was no longer "any family at all" left in the home. The problem was compounded by the fact that the couple lived in an isolated rural area and the husband was employed far from his place of residence. The family, it seemed, virtually evaporated as its ability to supervise its troubled member diminished.

While these illustrations have been taken from human service settings, all of which presented troubled families of some sort, the descriptive usage of the household was applied equally to the untroubled. Diverse families and households, with and without troubles, were both referred to by and entered into the experience of those studied. The amount of supervision, like crowding, location, and other descriptive usages, were part of a descriptive culture of domestic life, which offered a shared stock of resources for interpreting and explaining the more or less hidden privacies of all households.

Chapter 6

Privileged Knowledge in Practice

The third assumption of the private image holds that, in principle, members of the household have the most authentic knowledge of its domestic affairs. In other words, members have privileged access to family life. This assumption, of course, is tied to the household location assumption. If domestic affairs naturally go on in the home, it stands to reason that its occupants are native witnesses. While outsiders may be acquainted with a family, the knowledge is not grounded in direct experience.

Household occupants vary in their involvement in family affairs. A working mother differs from a full-time homemaker in the perspective she brings to home life, as well as in the sheer amount of time she is involved in household activity. A so-called house dad is around the home for longer periods of time than is his working counterpart. Moreover, some members of households may not be kin. Unrelated occupants may have resided in the home much longer than kindred. Complete strangers may even live in the home; housing boarders was a common practice in the past century. More recently, even researchers have taken up household occupancy to systematically observe the activities and intimacies of families in their native habitats (Henry, 1985).

Variations in household membership suggest that privileged access is only a point of departure for understanding the descriptive organization of related family discourse. While the principle directs the search for domestic truths, especially the pursuit of hidden and secret knowledge, to members of the household, there is no guarantee in practice that members will or can straightforwardly tell the facts. In this chapter, we argue that as far as descriptive practice is concerned, privileged knowledge of domestic affairs is as much a claim as a condition. We examine how such claims about family members' special perspective and knowledge are used by persons in everyday conversation to substantiate their understandings of domestic reality.

Principle Versus Practice

Before considering the organization of claims to privileged knowledge, let us briefly elaborate the distinction between the principle and the practice of privileged access. Philosophers regularly distinguish the question of "what is" from the question of "how we know it," matters of ontology and epistemology respectively. While our purpose in this chapter is hardly that grand, the philosophical distinction does bear on the relationship between the principle and the practice of privileged access.

The principle of privileged access is not just an underlying assumption of formal studies of family life; it is commonly taken into account in everyday descriptive practice. In the field sites, no one cast doubt on the idea that direct access implied seeing something with one's own eyes. The only more authentic witness to experience was the subject of experience himself or herself. For example, it was taken for granted that, in principle, a husband who lived with his wife in the same household knew her in a way that no outsider could. What is more, it was obvious to all that the wife might tell us secrets about herself, say, in the role of mother, spouse, or daughter, that only she held, separate from what her husband of many years knew about her.

The principle of privileged access is informed by a rather mechanical interpretation of authenticity, one that separates the question of "what is" from the question of "how we know it." Those following the household location assumption believe that family life naturally takes place in the home, even while it spills over, of course, into other domains like the workplace and the school. For the most part, the "what is" of family life is that configuration of relationships, sentiments, and activities that takes place in and about the family habitat. "What is" pertains to the domestic life of those concerned, not outsiders, strangers, or bystanders. If we could somehow be "there" where the familial takes place, our presence unnoticed, we would actually see and hear the family for what it really is. The idea of being in a family member's shoes or of being the proverbial fly on the wall of the family home provides two senses of this. In the first instance, one would virtually enter into the experience of family members; in the second, one would be an unobtrusive witness to it all.

Yet while the principle of privileged access is taken for granted, it continually runs afoul of practice. In practice, the principle seems to be a guide to the true family domain, but it seldom produces objective specification. What is assumed to be available in households and known to members must nonetheless *be sought* by someone in some way or other. That is the rub. The ineluctable question remains "How do we know what is?"

Time and again in the various field sites, descriptions of domestic life were combined with questions of authenticity, centered on the issue of whether what was known in practice reflected what actually was. This even applied to family members. While it was assumed in principle that a mother, let's say, knew the details of motherhood in her family like no one else did, at the same time questions could be raised about their insight into her own experience. Whether Mother A really knew what she herself was like or what she was actually doing to her family were questions suggesting that, while she should know better than anyone, her awareness might be clouded or otherwise faulty. Although the mother's sentiments, activity, and social relations contained the facts of her familial role, one might question whether she adequately conveyed them.

Practical exceptions to the rule of privileged access continually proved the principle. In the field, we heard that "a mother would know if she were more aware" or that "family members know more than outsiders but they just don't bother to look at things objectively." Such statements were ethnographic clues to the relation between the principle and practice of discerning domestic affairs.

As we turn to the field data and consider the privileged access assumption in practice, we encounter family discourse as a negotiation of claims. Approaching the data in terms of the question of who speaks for the family, we see that the family does not always recognize its own authentic voice. Diverse claims are made on its behalf, from the claims of experience to the claims of expertise, by both family members and outsiders alike.

Claiming Privileged Knowledge

The assumption of privileged access and knowledge is explicitly used to warrant claims by members and to discount outside opinion. Principle is put into practice, it seems, to authorize members to speak definitively about the intimate details of domestic life.

Consider the claims to insider knowledge and the way the claims were supported and justified by the mother of a 22-year-old, alleged "chronic schizophrenic" during a support group meeting for families of the mentally ill. Shelly Thompson and her husband had been involved in their son Michael's mental health treatment for more than six years. She claimed to have spent over a quarter million dollars on hospitalization and treatment in the finest private mental health facilities in the region, but was now discussing how she had recently resigned herself to "leaving Michael alone." She described how she had agreed to let him discontinue all formal treatments and medications and live on his own on the streets of the city, a plan that Michael had long advocated. This was not an easy decision to make, she informed the group, especially when it directly contradicted the recommendations of all the mental health professionals she had recently consulted. When questioned about the advisability of such a radical departure from her previous approach, Shelly responded at length:

> It's not that we haven't tried everything under the sun. My god, Michael's been to every clinic, seen every shrink, from here to New York, but nothing seems to help. Now this isn't just my guilt speaking, but he hasn't been any better, and this family has suffered just about as much as it can by trying to make Michael one of us. I mean, the psychiatrists tell you to get involved, then they say back off. They say there's no use hospitalizing him and he'd be better off living at home with a lot of attention. But no interference [spoken sarcastically]. Well, they just don't know what he does to this family. We have no life when he's around. Our marriage isn't worth a nickel. Maybe I should feel bad because I won't drop everything when Michael calls or when he comes around, but he just can't be the only thing in our lives anymore. You just can't imagine what it's like to be trying everything, doing everything you can, and have him just hate you for it. You just can't imagine what that's done to this family. . . . So when I hear all the advice, I just have to say, "Well, I'm sorry, but I can see things happening to this family that you can't, and I'm not willing to sacrifice everybody else just to ease my conscience about Michael." I mean, who should know about this sort of thing? I know what we were like and what we were becoming, and I don't think anybody else is in a position to tell me I'm wrong.

In this case, the "what is" of family was portrayed as truly available only to those deeply involved in the family itself. And while the question of who knew what was the best thing to do in the situation was epistemologically complex, the mother justified her stance by reference to the unquestioned assumption of her privileged knowledge. Family members' perspectives were tacitly authorized with no explanation or justification beyond the suggestion that family knowledge is the province of family members. While similar claims were pointedly challenged at other times and in other settings, in this case the assumption stood as a viable, if not unquestionable, basis for launching and assessing domestic claims.

Disclaiming Native Authenticity

For a variety of reasons, family members, even those who had resided there for long periods of time, occasionally disclaimed privileged access to the social order of the household. Still, it was not the principle of privileged access that was discounted, but the lack of a personal means of adequately assessing what was "right there under our very own noses," as it was sometimes put. Such was the recognition by a family member of a theme that was called "hidden knowledge" in Chapter 3, which in practice was something used to warrant what was and wasn't known.

Individuals frequently point out that it is precisely from the vantage point of being outside the home that one comes to realize what he or she has not seen inside. Phrases and comments such as "a different perspective here" and "a new outlook when you're not in the thick of things" suggest that, while the household contains the ultimate truths of domestic life, one can be too close to the actual scene of events to fully grasp their meaning. In the field sites we often heard that, in the household, the minutiae of everyday life tended to occupy one's attention, so that one's sense of the overall family picture might be obscured. As one spouse put it, "You just don't take time out to really think about what your family is really like when you're seeing to this thing or that one."

Disclaimed authenticity and the discoveries of the household were sometimes rather vividly played out. Let us consider two examples, one drawn from Cedarview's parent effectiveness training program and the other from the proceedings of an Alzheimer's caregivers' support group.

During evening hours, Cedarview's parent effectiveness classes brought together the mothers and fathers of the emotionally disturbed boys and girls the agency treated, usually five to ten parents at a time. While the classes aimed to improve parenting skills by means of techniques such as role-playing, home-based behavioral assessment, and the systematic application of household rules and regulations, at the same time there was much discussion of domestic affairs. The social workers who organized and facilitated the classes encouraged the parents to describe the daily routines of the home, the behavior of their children, the parents' responses, and thoughts and feelings regarding their children's successes and failures, among other things. The parents reported in detail what they regularly referred to as what "goes on at home." Some prefaced remarks with incredulous lead-ins like "you wouldn't believe what goes on at home." Yet as they reflected on the everyday meaning of what they seemed to know so well, disclaimers of authenticity often arose. One evening, parents had been asked by a social worker to describe what it was like in the home when their children returned from school. A few conveyed the daily routines of ornery children walking into the house. Some confessed their worry over not knowing when their children would return from school or, indeed, whether the children had gone to school in the first place. Others described the usual mundane activities of snacking and watching television before things settled down for the evening.

In the process, the parents compared their after-school domestic routines. For example, where one commented that things were "pretty hectic" at that time of day, another responded that in her home "things [are] not as bad." It was evident that each household portrayed took its form and substance as much from what each parent learned about his or her home in relation to others' homes, as from what each knew about his or her home in its own right. After-school hours that were, on first mention, "really awful," on subsequent comparison with others could become not as bad as or much worse than previously thought. The proffered facts of each private household stood to be revised, transformed, or confirmed as conversations extended varied bases for interpreting the facts. This social comparison process was commonplace in all field sites.

At one point in the proceedings, a young mother of five children, one of whom was in the day program at Cedarview, made the following remark about the many experiences she had heard about that evening and in previous classes:

> I find that this kind of thing is very sobering. I always thought
> it was just my family that went through the wringer every day.
> Now I see that I'm not the only one. [Several parents acknowl-
> edge her insight.] It's really good to talk these things out. Things
> can be right there in front of your face and you just don't make
> heads or tails out of it. You come here and bang [snaps her
> fingers], just like that, you begin to see what's happening. I've
> been doing a lot of thinking over the last couple of times about
> what you all said and, I'll have to tell you, it sure gives you a
> picture of what kinds of family and kids there are, doesn't it?

Another mother cut in:

> I know what you mean. I come here and I think, "Now why didn't
> I see that?" My husband sometimes makes fun of me when I get
> home and give him an opinion. He asks me like, "Now what're
> you going to say about us? Are we 'effective' parents?" He's so
> sarcastic. I know he's joking, but I tell him that you do learn
> things about your family that you hadn't thought about, really. So
> I know what you mean.

While their exchanges did not lead these parents to develop a formal system of classification for the kinds of families they discovered themselves to be, they did nonetheless categorize themselves into select types of parents, children, and families. In so doing, they discovered new things about themselves as representative of particular types. In reflecting on what they learned about their households in the process, some dis-claimed the authenticity of their prior knowledge or announced their lack of insight into their home life. Where one parent remarked that she hadn't known about, or seen, something until she was out of the home discussing her family, another flatly stated that "You find out when someone puts something across that you wish you'd thought about sooner."

Of course, not all the generalizations and categories put forth were readily accepted, nor did everyone disclaim privileged access. The point of the illustration is not that the parent effectiveness classes in particular nor the communication of experience in general leads to the discovery or reconstruction of domestic order. The point is rather that varied contexts supply alternate visions of experience in general and the household in particular, which in turn provide a basis for reflecting on differences regarding privileged access. Some participants in the parent effectiveness classes insisted that they knew the social order of their own homes better than anyone else. Indeed, it was not unusual for a claim of privileged access to be made by family members. But that claim entered into family discourse with no firmer guarantee of authenticity, on the whole, than did any other claim. Still, as we shall discuss at greater length in Chapter 7, the "organizational embeddedness" of family discourse could place premiums on particular claims. From support groups to treatment facilities and court hearing rooms, there were select informal and formal preferences for accepting certain kinds of authenticity claims, which brings us to the next illustration.

One goal of the support groups for the caregivers of Alzheimer's disease victims was to persuade participants to take into account that their homes were not just caregiving settings but were also households where other family members resided. While many caregivers focused their concern almost exclusively on the patient and the progress of the disease, others said it was the caregiver's own well-being, as well as that of the entire family, that was at stake. As previously noted, the received wisdom was that the home care of the Alzheimer's disease patient can pose a virtual "36-hour day" for the caregiver (see Mace and Rabins, 1981). As such, the caregiver not only is constantly attuned to the daily needs and whereabouts of someone who has experienced "brain failure" (Reisberg, 1981), but also can become so preoccupied with the minutiae of care that he or she ignores the family as a whole. Thus, the support groups placed a premium on being open to considerations of the entire household, "for the sake of all concerned," as they often said.

Caregivers typically entered support groups with many unanswered questions. They could be confused by many things, not the least of which was what was happening to their relationship with a loved one, usually a spouse or a parent. Many said that the support group provided some respite from the daily burden of care; it also became clear in the fieldwork that the support group was a place to take time out to consider the broader background of the home care situation. There was a more or less urgent desire to make sense of what was happening at home. And it was the household that, by and large, located the Alzheimer's disease experience for the caregivers.

While support group members assumed that caregivers were, of course, at the scene of home care like no one else and thus, in principle, were the most direct witnesses to the caregiving situation, it did not mean that they fully or even minimally understood the experience. In this regard, others frequently attempted to get the caregivers to understand what was happening to them and others in the household. To that end, the caregiver's direct or indirect disclaimer of native authenticity was an important step in becoming a successful support group participant.

Disclaimers of native authenticity could be emotionally intense. In one session of a support group, proceedings had settled on the many details that had to be handled and monitored in the home care of the Alzheimer's disease patient. Muriel, the 77-year-old caregiver of Casper, her demented husband, began by remarking:

> Sometimes, it's just too much, more than anyone can do. I try to fix my hair in the morning and no sooner than I'm in the bathroom, he [Casper] walks in and wants to go out. Or like Paul [another support group participant] said, he [Casper] starts to walk out of the house and I know that if I don't stop whatever I'm doing right then and there, he'll wander off and there'll be hell to pay for it the rest of the day. It's worse than having a kid. At least with a kid you can plunk them down in front of the tube. You know Casper. He'll sit there for a minute or two and, well, you know he's not comprehending what's going on and will just get up out of the blue and walk somewhere. God knows where. You've just got to be sharp to what's going on all the time.

As usual, other participants shared their own experiences of the need to be vigilant in attention to details and the need to avoid taking the victim's behavior or expressions for granted. As the commentaries unfolded, each participant increasingly centered his or her attention on the dread intensity of the daily experience. What one would say was like not being able to come up for a breath of air, another reported as like not seeing the forest for the trees. In the process, several commented on what a welcome relief from the burdens of care it was to be in the group. The comments lent credence to the joint workings of two purported missions of the support group—namely, to combine a respite from the caregiving experience with the opportunity to gain a broader perspective on it.

Reflecting comments made in other support groups, several participants admitted that they just did not know what was happening to "us." "Us" pertained to their relationship with the victim, on the one hand, and their feelings about themselves, family members, and significant others, on the other. It was the kind of reference to the family and domestic affairs that, like other phrases such as "not knowing who we are any more" and "trying to make sense of it all," signaled a disclaimer of native authority.

Occasionally, disclaimers were combined into touching pleas for support and help in sorting things out. Responses showed that the more emotional the expression, the more genuine the disclaimer was taken to be. This was especially the sentiment of facilitators who were responsible for nurturing the sharing and support. At one point, the distressed husband and caregiver of a 72-year-old wife with Alzheimer's spoke of his own quandary:

> I'm seeing her every day get worse and worse. She's slipping away and away, farther and farther. I try all the time to do everything. No time for myself, all for Katya [the wife]. No time for the children, for my grandchildren. No time for no one. All for Katya. That's life. But what kind of life? [As he shakes his head, he begins to quietly weep.] This one is angry. That one tells me, "Papa do this and do that." [Describes how they help, too.] I get angry with Katya, with my children, with everyone. What's happening to us? I never was angry with Katya, with my children.

His comments revealed uncertainty and confusion regarding his own experience and were received with much sympathy.

In the course of the proceedings, participants noted that the feelings conveyed were "sure signs" that those expressing them were in need of advice and understanding, referring not only to the need for sympathy but also to the need for a broader understanding of the caregiving experience. As one facilitator put it, "They can get a handle on things" and start to consider the domestic picture, not just care or cure.

While not denigrating weeping and other emotional expressions as genuine in their own right, it is important to note that in relation to the question of how privileged knowledge of the private household is communicated, emotional expressions served as signs of validity. The cultural connotation of feelings is that their expression reveals a deeper layer of experience than mere testimony does. As far as descriptive practice is concerned, the depth of the feelings expressed served as a kind of standard by which participants in the support groups evaluated the genuineness of claims and disclaimers. Indeed, emotion was a sign of the appreciation of privileged knowledge in general, whether or not it served a disclaimer, as it did in these proceedings, or a claim, as it does when a member of the household vehemently claims to know better than anyone else what goes on at home because he or she resides there.

Claiming Objectivity

At times, family members' claims to privileged knowledge were countered with other claims. One important counterclaim cited objectivity as a basis for seeing domestic matters more accurately than family members. Counter-claims did not dispute the native experience of households, thus safe-guarding the principle of privileged knowledge. Rather, they contested the manner by which privileged knowledge was appreciated.

One justification for the counterclaim of outsider objectivity was that because family members were "so close" or "too close" to what was going on at home, they were not likely to see things clearly. It was common to note further that a family member had too much emotional involvement in his or her own domestic affairs to provide a balanced view. Sometimes perspective was the culprit. Some said that because the particular family member or household occupant claiming privileged knowledge held a particular role in the home, he or she was seeing things exclusively from that point of view. For example, a husband who claimed to have impeccable knowledge of his own family life might be told, "That's the way *you* are seeing things; what about what your wife thinks?" At times, the greater objectivity of outsider experience in dealing with domestic matters served as a general counterclaim. One who had "seen so many cases like this" could claim to know "these things" even better than a particular family member who knew only his or her own household intimately. The ostensibly privileged knowledge of the insider was too specific to detect a pattern, much less to appreciate the general significance of what happened in the home. All told, from emotional involvement to the lack of perspective and experience, the household member's domestic vantage point could be quite biased; there were practical grounds for replacing the privileged knowledge of the insider with the clearer vision of the outsider.

Consider the issue of aging and nursing home placement in connection with the claim of objectivity. The issue arose in many family-related discussions among staff and family members in the nursing homes, the rehabilitation hospital, and the Alzheimer's disease support groups studied. An important question was whether a demented elderly person's care could be managed at home—in particular, whether the burden of care was too great to maintain the elder outside an institution. For elderly patients already in a nursing home, the issue was connected to changes in the availability of outside support or in the patient's developing nursing needs. For those in physical rehabilitation, the staff's discharge planning took into account, for example, whether a stroke victim's continued care could be managed at home or in the household of kindred, or whether it required the services of a nursing home. In support groups for the caregivers of Alzheimer's disease patients, an enduring question was how much longer caregivers could continue to cope with the growing burdens of a demented elder at home and when it was time to seek nursing home placement.

In each setting, participants discussed the topic in terms of the changes in domestic life that came with home care. They raised a range of related questions in the process. What is the family like? Is the family strong enough to handle the growing burden of care? Are family members realistic about their strengths and weaknesses? Who best knows the situation? The questions centered on the social order of the household.

In a typical session of one of the support groups, participants turned their attention to Barbara, who requested help in deciding whether to continue caring for her increasingly confused and agitated husband at home. Barbara was assisted by her three daughters but refrained from burdening them too much with what she believed to be her own problem. She explained that even though the daughters lived nearby, they had families of their own to care for. The decision under consideration was familiar enough, part of the general question of the adequacy of family support.

As the discussion unfolded, Barbara offered details of her husband's daily activities. As participants asked for elaboration, they occasionally questioned whether Barbara had perhaps overlooked something or not taken it sufficiently into account. They were gentle challenges, put forth to get Barbara to see and report her home care experiences accurately. As Barbara respectfully and kindly pointed out in response to one such challenge, "I've been there and know from experience what we've [her family] been through, what we can and can't do for him [husband]."

Some time later in the proceedings, following a facilitating social worker's unrelated comment that some families "just can't see the forest for the trees," another caregiver, Beth, recalled Barbara's concern. Prompted by what Beth now spoke of as "hints" about Barbara's family that were dropped in Barbara's earlier remarks, Beth turned to Barbara and asked whether an outsider might help her to sort things out, to assess more realistically the home situation, and to consider whether a nursing home placement was perhaps more urgent than Barbara considered it to be. Beth framed her suggestions in terms of the objectivity of an outsider, implying that insiders most intimately acquainted with family life were likely to be biased. While Barbara initially presented personal experience as the basis for a claim to privileged knowledge, she later entertained the rhetoric of objectivity, casting doubt on some of her earlier assertions. Indeed, at one point, as Barbara listened closely to Beth's comments and description of what "could actually be going on" and what Barbara might not have bothered to think about, it was evident in Barbara's testimony that the facts of the home situation she had originally conveyed now took a new twist. Barbara began to consider how her familiar household might feature a different social order than that she had initially presented.

This is not to say that the matter simply ended there. Objectivity was not automatically accepted over personal experience as the final arbiter of authenticity. As the proceedings of this and other support groups showed, claims and counterclaims produced considerable oscillation in what was accepted, in practice, as the distinct domestic order of the households under consideration. The household's ostensibly distinct social order was produced out of quite varied and unrelated circumstances. Indeed, the descriptive culture of every circumstance was, in a sense, a virtual index of each social order (see Garfinkel, 1967).

Yet the construction of domestic order was not arbitrary, for what one circumstance produced, another regularly did not. For example, while outsider objectivity was a commonly used claim in the Alzheimer's disease support groups to challenge native authenticity, the privilege of expertise was not. Expertise was a more common claim of participants in Cedarview's psychiatric staffings and in the community mental health settings studied, although it was presented in the support groups when "expert" opinion was at hand. As we shall discuss in greater detail in Chapter 7, family discourse's organized circumstances systematically influence the articulation of social order.

Claiming Expertise

Expertise differs from objectivity in that those concerned offer the claim against a background of formal training, academic degrees, and/or professional credentials. It is the category of claims that seems to be uppermost in the minds of those who, like Lasch (1979), criticize the professional "siege" of the household. In the broader context of descriptive practice, it is nonetheless one claim out of many.

Consider the manner in which expertise enters into the proceedings of involuntary commitment hearings as a claim against the authenticity of family members' experience. Tricia Marsh, 24 years old, sought release from hospitalization, claiming that she would live with her parents. In her testimony in Metropolitan Court, Tricia remarked that her parents were willing and able to take her into their home. The representative of the District Attorney's (DA's) office, who was arguing for commitment, considered Tricia's claim as he proceeded with his cross-examination:

> You say you're going to live at home with your parents? Am I right? Now that doesn't seem too realistic, does it? [Tricia responds, "Yet it is."] Your doctor doesn't seem to think that you're well enough to leave the hospital and, frankly, I'm not sure things are all that open to you at home. It says here [referring to Tricia's psychiatric report] that the [hospital] social worker has talked with your folks and she seems to think that they are in no shape to handle you right now. Don't you think she knows a bit about what might happen in a family like yours?

Tricia objected to the suggestion and underscored her earlier claim by insisting that she knew her parents "pretty darn well" and there was not going to be any problem if she rejoined the family. The DA moved to other topics, but returned to the family placement question and indirectly to the issue of privileged knowledge in his closing summary:

> Your honor, this story about living with her parents flies right in the face of what the hospital staff are saying. She [Tricia] says she'll be all right with them, but we've got one professional opinion that says she's not well enough to leave [the hospital] and another saying that she will be very disruptive to that family if she stays with them. It seems to me that under the circumstances, we better take a hard look at who is telling us what. Tricia seems very well-intentioned, but I think she's doing a bit of wishful thinking. In light of all this, I've got to ask you to find her gravely disabled and continue her stay [in the hospital].

The appeal to professional expertise was compelling, especially since the court routinely sought guidance from the human service professionals who dealt with candidate patients. But, at the same time, the court was not a rubber stamp for expert opinion. As the judge discussed his options, he took issue with aspects of the DA's argument:

> We have to keep in mind what we are trying to accomplish here and I, for one, don't like to see the State foot the bill for treatment any more than is necessary. Now, granted the hospital says the family might not be the best option, might not be up to handling the stress, but they [the parents] seem to disagree. The question is, "Who do we believe?" I'm sure the social worker has her reasons, but a parent has a pretty good idea what he's in for, too.

The judge considered a variety of factors as he contemplated his decision, but the proceedings made clear the ways in which claims and counterclaims appealed to the various interpretations of authentic family knowledge. Insider knowledge was played off against expert opinion; membership was pitted against professional status as the basis for privileging one version over the other.

As another illustration, consider one of the regularly held patient care conferences at Murray Manor, a nursing home with several levels of care. The patient care conference is a meeting of treatment and care staff for the purposes of establishing long- and short-term goals for the patient and reviewing continuing patient problems. The conference under consideration was scheduled in part because Helen Curry, an 81-year-old right-foot amputee with complications of diabetes, had been demanding to be discharged. She wanted to go home. However, the proceedings showed that it wasn't clear which home that meant. Was Helen well enough to go home and which home would it be? In attendance were the home's social worker, staff nurses and aides, the pastoral counselor, the dietitian, and the activity director.

The conference began in the customary fashion, with a reading of the diagnosis, a brief medical history, and a description of the immediate problem. The charge nurse from Helen's unit asked for advice about what to do about Helen's "constant demanding to go home." According to the nurse, it wasn't the usual kind of whining "you get from some of them [patients]" because the family had come into the picture. As the nurse explained:

> It's not an easy one. You know how Mary [another patient] is always whining to go home. Well, this isn't the same thing you get from some of them [patients] because you just can't ignore it that easily. Her [Helen's] sister's been up to the desk a lot lately and asking us if we think she can manage Helen in her apartment. The sister seems to feel that she might be able to do it alone, but she's not real sure about it. [The nurse remarks at length about the sister's request and conduct.] I think, really, that Helen's been doing a number on her [the sister], and the sister's just on a real guilt trip about it. I don't know. What do all of you think?

In the subsequent deliberation, staff members discussed both Helen's ambulatory and self-care status against a background of opinions about the sister's apartment as a possible discharge destination. As the charge nurse had noted, it was not altogether clear whether the sister actually wanted to take Helen home. It seemed to those gathered in the conference that the sister was looking to the staff for advice in the matter. Helen's daughter also had expressed interest in taking her mother home "if nothing else can be worked out," as the daughter was reported to have stated. The financial constraints of the case were judged insignificant. The physician was ready to order whatever the staff and the family considered to be in the patient's best interest. Except for Helen's demand to be discharged, it seemed that the onus of the decision was on the staff.

As staffers discussed the possibility of discharge, bits and pieces of information were put together to form pictures of the contending discharge destinations. No one had actually been in either household, but everyone knew something about one or the other—their social composition, the size and accessibility of each, the amount of time anyone was at home, the ability of occupants to care for a handicapped elder, the neighborhood situations, among a host of conditions taken to be pertinent to the questions under consideration.

At one point, a unit nurse seemed to favor the sister's option, stating that she, the nurse, understood the sister's dilemma, but that, from what the nurse knew, she believed that living with the sister would do both Helen and the sister "a world of good." The nurse added that she believed the sister wanted to be told it was the right decision. The sister presumably was a rather indecisive person. However, the social worker interjected:

> I know what you're saying, Grace [the unit nurse], but you have to remember who you're hearing this from. I've been in that kind of [apartment] complex, with all those kids around and all the noise. From what I've read and learned, you just can't easily mix

people like that. As a social worker, I think I know a bit about this kind of thing. Believe me, I'll bet the sister's having a hard enough time herself coping in that environment. She really shouldn't be living there; it's just not for older people. If Helen moved in with her, everything would come apart. I really feel that when you take everything into account, Helen is better off right here.

There was much speculation and deliberation about what it would be like for Helen to live with her sister in that apartment and environment. This was compared with what was felt would happen if Helen were taken in by her daughter. Staff construed the envisioned domestic orders of both discharge destinations as much from what they knew of the compositions of the households, their physical appearance and environs, as from the staff's acquaintance with the character and social relations of the respective family members.

While admittedly speculative, knowledge of the impending domestic orders of the households under consideration was evaluated in relation to the claims made on their behalf: Helen's reported beliefs about where she rightfully should be housed; the unit nurse's ostensibly firm understanding of the two sisters' relationship; the social worker's expert interpretation based on her professional training and experience; and the many comments from those who, in the role of impartial outsiders, conveyed their readings of the two potential discharge destinations. In contrast to the deliberations of participants in the Alzheimer's disease support groups and the involuntary commitment hearings, the embeddedness of family discourse in the care conference, in practice, granted privilege to professional expertise as much as it did to objectivity and native authenticity. The relation between Helen's repeated requests, on the one side, and the domestic order of two possible homes, on the other, was anything but a straightforward matter of figuring a best fit. Rather, both what we referred to in Chapter 5 as the descriptive usage of the household and what we in this chapter describe as the claims of privileged access served to articulate the domestic order of the households considered.

Antiprofessionalism

While some say expertise and professionalism have become the claims of last resort in contemporary life, it is important not to overstate their predominance. Although doctors, for example, must formally sign medical orders, in practice it is not always their expertise that produces diagnoses or recommendations. Claims to expertise were not always affirmed in the field sites. Ostensible experts occasionally disclaimed their own credentials, deferring instead to the "native expertise" of those who were said to know best from actually having lived in the households under consideration. At times, in mental commitment hearings and in Alzheimer's support groups, patients' rights were pitted against expert opinion. And, on occasion, the distinct antiprofessionalism built into the public culture of the Alzheimer's disease movement flavored support group proceedings.

The antiprofessionalism in some of the caregiver support groups created considerable tension with participants' medical orientation to the disease experience. The received wisdom was that the natural history of a support group should move from participants being cure-oriented, which was considered to be a normal initial state, to a self-help orientation, where equal emphasis was placed on the well-being of the caregiver. Since Alzheimer's is a disease with no known cause or cure, and thus the patient is expected to experience continued mental decline, the caregiver herself or himself is a major subject of support and care. While antiprofessionalism could be seen as a natural, final outcropping of the history of a support group, strains of it nonetheless could appear across deliberations at any stage. Like expertise and objectivity, the anti-professionalism of the Alzheimer's support groups was a kind of claim regarding privileged knowledge of domestic affairs. Rather than disclaiming native authenticity, antiprofessionalism forcefully asserted it against its counterclaims.

Antiprofessionalism was one product of a particular mode of attention to the disease experience. When support group proceedings became didactic or focused on so-called medical breakthroughs, caregivers' attentions centered on what could be done for the disease, the patient, and the caregiver. In this "ameliorative mode," expertise and professional experience weighed heavily in persuading those concerned how to interpret domestic affairs in general and the home care situation in particular. In this mode, the disease experience was treated as relatively well-structured. Caregivers and others spoke of the varied courses of the illness, the natural history of caregiving, and other configurations. When support group proceedings became mired in the seemingly hopeless news that there was no known cure, that all medical breakthroughs were either tentative or suspect, and that the course of illness was highly variable, the "tribulation mode" led to considerable resignation and self-pity, understandable as they were. In this mode, the disease experience was conveyed as being completely unstructured. Caregivers referred to the illness as having no "rhyme or reason" or stated that "there's just no sense to it" and that "you can't get a handle on it." They might say that no two patients were alike, nor for that matter were any two caregivers' experiences. It was in the tribulation mode that antiprofessionalism arose as an embellishment to the discourse of privileged access. In the tribulation mode, often heard was that none of the experts or the professionals really knew what was going on.

However, it is important to note that, while antiprofessionalism was not a part of the amelioration mode, antiprofessionalism did not always accompany the tribulation mode. In some of the support groups studied, the tribulation mode was simply characterized by despair and considerable emotional expression. Communication and personal testimony tended to be cathartic as facilitation succeeded in turning caregivers' attentions to themselves. In other support groups, the tribulation mode readily lead to antiprofessionalism. Communication and personal testimony were decidedly assertive, with facilitation aimed at self-reliance. Like tribes and nations, the support groups had local cultures of their own.

Antiprofessionalism, then, could be a context for depreciating professional advice concerning the effect of the disease on the family. It might prompt reconsiderations of what was often seen as a perfunctory recommendation to seek nursing home placement, or it might counter some other target. In general, the argument was that because no two cases were alike and no two caregiving experiences identical, only those actually involved could possibly know what was happening in the household. In their own way, caregivers knew that service providers, as experts of sorts, retained knowledge of *general* principles of illness and care as a basis for expert and rational interventions. When it became too evident to caregivers that there was nothing general about any of it—nothing having any "rhyme or reason"—the disease experience in effect was destructured and reclaimed for the individuals concerned. The primacy of personal knowledge was thus restored.

Antiprofessional comments were not merely assertions of knowing better because home caregivers actually resided in households; they also often accompanied invidious comparisons with what outsiders, especially "the doctors," actually did not know. Some said that no outsider could possibly know how it felt to have a family member lose his or her mind before one's very own eyes. In this context, caregivers asserted that only family members knew how, and to what extent, the illness affected them. As caregivers frequently put it, "You just have to be there" to know what really is going on. What typically followed was a version of the comment "and the professionals haven't been there." Caregivers said that each of them had to organize home care according to his or her own wits, feelings, and domestic situation.

On occasion, not even native testimony could capture what only caregivers themselves knew (Gubrium, 1988d). There were no words available to convey what it was like. At such times, caregivers seemed to admit that the knowledge they held was unavailable even to themselves. Of course, this did not mean that it was more available to outsiders, only that even those who carried what was known could not retrieve it and convey it completely. This communicative stance was quite different from the common professional assertion that those in-the-know sometimes cannot admit to what they know full well or that they admit to something other than what they know is true, a situation to which we now turn.

Denial

Bearing on the topic of privileged knowledge, denial is a claim that has become increasingly persuasive in contemporary society. It is a psychological state said to characterize those who refuse to recognize what they know about an aspect of their experience. The claim does not take issue with privileged knowledge in principle, for it assumes that, in the case of domestic affairs, those who are direct witnesses to the goings-on of the home know better than anyone what is really happening there. What is questioned is the truth of what is *communicated* about what is known. Falsehood in the form of denial is distinguished from lying; deniers are not liars because deniers don't know they are hiding the truth from themselves and others. Denial is more than a matter of pitting one version of domestic reality against another, for denial places the command of what is known by direct witnesses of domestic affairs into the hands of those who claim that denial is taking place.

Denial was a common claim in each of the field sites studied, commonly used by service providers against family members. Sometimes it was used by family members against other family members. Occasionally, outsiders used it against occupants of households under consideration. Its usage could take the form of formal psychological or psychiatric language, or it could be used casually to "get [someone] to admit" what was really happening in the home.

The family discourse associated with denial aimed to achieve a kind of one-sided communication. Putting it in Foucault's (1978) terms, those accused of denying the realities of the household were "incited to speak" of their domestic lives in terms presented to them as more authentic than their own. Frequently, a so-called denier might be said to have overcome his or her problem when he or she successfully admitted that the perspective of those claiming denial was indeed correct. A denier who resisted the incitement to speak preferred domestic truths might become part of the family problem under consideration; in the final analysis, denial itself became pathological. It was not uncommon to hear denial constructed into the problem par excellence in the arena of family troubles.

Consider the use of denial in relation to a claim to privileged knowledge at Wilshire, the rehabilitation hospital, regarding to the discharge and placement of spinal-cord-injured patients. These patients were mostly adolescents or young adult males who had sustained cord injuries form motorcycle, automobile, swimming, and work-related accidents. Whether low-level paraplegics or high-level quadriplegics, they would be handicapped for the rest of their lives, many confined to wheelchairs.

Discharge planning began soon after admission for all rehabilitation patients. A major consideration for the spinal cord-injured was the subsequent life-style of the young adult. It was evident that whatever household was to serve as the patient's home and whoever were to be its co-occupants, "things couldn't be the same as they were before the accident." Various parties to related decisions could have different ideas of impending life-styles. The patient had a point of view, as did family members, so-called significant others (which often included a girlfriend, boyfriend, or close acquaintance), and the hospital rehabilitation team. It was common for family members or team members to differ among themselves.

As usual in discharge planning, questions related to the domestic order of prospective households or discharge destinations formed major topics of consideration. Could a young adult, formerly employed male return to his apartment to live with his girlfriend? Could the life-style they had established before the injury accommodate the new situation? Was an adolescent's family strong enough to handle the psychological distresses of a lifelong handicap? Was a mother or father ready to believe that things would be different in the future for a son or daughter? Was the family prepared to adjust itself to the needs of a member confined to a wheelchair? Were family members at odds or at one in their views of what had occurred, how they now fit into the picture, and what the injured's future would be like? The interrelated questions were complicated by their many points of view.

The question of the discharge destination, then, was no simple matter of whether and when to return the patient home. After the injury, home could mean rather different things than before. For example, while home before the injury might have been a family household, a new option might be a wheelchair-accessible apartment complex for young adults or the supportive environment of a girlfriend's two-bedroom lower flat. Neither housing, familial options, nor their related points of view presented themselves as pristine bits of information and opinion; they were combined with the diverse rhetorics of descriptive practice. While the patient might, say, claim to know best what "his chances were" or how his family would react because he had, after all, lived with them for twenty-five years, a close friend might claim less bias in the matter as a not-too-distant outsider and outline an entirely different scenario for the future.

At Wilshire, staff took it for granted that the patient would engage in considerable denial about his own future and impending life-style. The family and significant others also could be characterized as denying. If family members and outsiders did not know the language of denial before the hospitalization experience, they soon took it up, too, and applied it to the patient and sometimes to each other. Patients likewise learned the language and routinely spoke of each other and select family members as denying what they claimed otherwise to be clearly the truth of matters under consideration.

While clinically compelling, denial did not consistently rise above related claims. Where a social worker might suggest that a mother was denying the family's lack of psychological preparedness to take in a formerly independently living, adult son, the mother might respond that she knew her family's strengths better than anyone and that what might seem to be denial to the social workers was actually, say, her well-known habit of not wanting to confine her children but rather letting them make their own life decisions. In the hospital's support groups for spinal-cord-injured patients, it was not unusual for one patient who was charged with denial by another to react, in turn, with a counteraccusation of denial.

Regardless of its claimants, denial was just as likely to pertain to perceptions of the domestic affairs of the household as it did to the psychological adjustment of the patient. The conventional wisdom in these matters at the hospital was that family, home, and household were each important ingredients in the total rehabilitation picture and that, to the extent each was seen clearly and its true picture not denied, realistic plans could be developed for the patient's optimal functioning.

Because the claims for privilege are categorically diverse, it is important to point out that each category further complicates family discourse's potential for multiple spokespersons. Not just one, but several family members may claim or disclaim native authenticity, for different reasons. While one outsider may claim the objectivity of the stranger, another may counterclaim the equal objectivity of intimate acquaintance without sentimental attachment. One professional's expertise may engage another one's claimed credentials. In practice, privileged knowledge is virtually a principle at work, its manifold, everyday laborers putting their authenticating skills and resources to work to produce the distinct domestic order of the families and households concerning them. In the next chapter, we turn to the organizational embeddedness of descriptive practice as a further, public complication of family and home.

Chapter 7

Organizational Embeddedness and Family Diversity

Contemporary discussions of the family often contest its mono-lithic depiction. Commentators from all perspectives note that groups of various shapes, sizes, and arrangements pass for family at one time or another. Dispute arises when the discussion turns to whether the diverse forms are all entitled to be called "family." From the left comes the plea to acknowledge the variety of families into which persons organize themselves. In turn, this position legitimizes the differentiation of family experience (Thorne and Yalom, 1982) and allows that no single family structure is best for all people in all situations (Zinn and Eitzen, 1987). From the right comes the insistence that nontraditional family forms, not being real families at all, threaten the social fabric (see Melville, 1983). The central issue is family diversity.

The controversy over whether alternate forms are valid, how-ever, presupposes a definition of family tied in some way to concrete group structure, typically articulated, at least partly, in terms of house-holds. The dispute can ultimately be reduced to a definitional contest over which kinds of household can, and should, be assigned family status. Given our stance that domestic reality is constantly in the making, the issue of family diversity is analytically fascinating, but not because we are concerned with specifying family's legitimate or authentic forms. Rather, the dispute itself publicly reveals the construction of family, quite separate from domestic settings. This, of course, is part of descriptive practice—the application of family image, the use of family discourse, and the articulation of its rhetoric.

We make our own claims regarding family diversity, however. If family is a way of thinking about social relations and domestic order, family diversity extends to the various ways and places that the family image is applied. Family's diverse forms are as much connected with usage as with diverse familial life-styles. Describing a gathering of grandparents, parents, brothers, sisters, aunts, uncles, children, and grandchildren as a family get-together tells us of the kinship that unites the collectivity. But assigning family status in other ways, for example, in the manner that members of racial or ethnic groups, or even fraternity and sorority members, refer to each other as "brothers" and "sisters," is no less authentically descriptive of the social relations inferred.

Family assignment is a practical, interpretive matter and, like all interpretive work, is responsive to context (Garfinkel, 1967). Yet, as we noted earlier, context is not a set of arbitrarily ordered background conditions of interpretation, but is itself socially organized, its discourse socially distributed. This chapter considers how circumstance and its interpretive conditions shape the construction of the familial.

Organizational Embeddedness

Interpretations of family are not uniquely formulated each time domestic matters are engaged. Domestic order is construed with reference to preexisting, locally available images of family life. For example, saying that a group of friends and caregivers is "like a family" to a client of a community mental health program calls upon shared understandings of family ties to convey the palliative and supportive nature of the social network. At the same time, it is the therapeutic milieu of community mental health care that promotes the definition of "family" as one of caregiving, as opposed to, say, one of kinship or intimacy.

Representations of the familial, then, are situationally sensitive. Family usage is *organizationally embedded* (Gubrium, 1987a). Family assignment in caregiver support groups, for example, embeds the articulation of family in local discursive conventions so that family is not likely to be presented in the same terms and forms as it would be in household, medical, or legal settings. Other contexts realize different domestic orders according to their varied descriptive offerings and agendas. While a child's parents may feel that the child's long-time babysitter is "like the child's grandmother," personnel at the child's school may deny the babysitter's status when it comes to participation in the school's family activities. The alternate understandings reflect more than the simple desire of one party to be "technical" about the matter. The circumstances, constraints, and priorities that circumscribe the diverse activities involving the child, the babysitter, the parents, and the school staff shape the ways that the babysitter's relationship can be understood.

It is important to note that we intend "organizational" to be construed in its most general terms. The social organization of all settings and circumstances shapes, and is shaped by, descriptive practice within them. The embeddedness of family discourse thus reflects any and all organized circumstances of its use. While most of our examples are taken from formal social service organizations, our analysis would also apply to circumstances that were organized along different lines, say by reference to age or ethnic groupings.

While circumstances provide interpretive resources for assigning meaning to the familial, embeddedness does not dictate official or formal assignment. A community mental health center, for example, may have an explicit treatment policy, but it also may employ a variety of therapists and other human service workers who bring different perspectives on mental health, illness, and family life to the program. Other differences, rooted in a specific profession's approaches and missions, provide further resources for shaping the ways troubles and remedies are formulated. And other organizational circumstances, like gender, race, or social class crosscut and underpin descriptive practice. Thus, from one perspective, a mental health clinic client may suffer from long-standing psychosexual disorders grounded in childhood family relations, while another approach may suggest that trouble stems from dysfunctional communication patterns in the existing family system. And the client's mother may be convinced that the client's troubles would abate if he just came home for Sunday dinners with the family. Such interpretations may simply coexist or they may be thrust into competition in, say, the formulation of a coherent team treatment plan that involves family members. Images of the family and its role in the situation are continuously open to modification as perspectives collide and working solutions are negotiated. What embeddedness does circumscribe is a local culture of family meanings—both official and unofficial, formal and informal, old and new—that characterizes domestic affairs in its own distinctive way.

We must remember, then, that while their descriptive practices are organizationally conditioned, practitioners of family usage are not "judgmental dopes" (Garfinkel, 1967) who merely react to circumstances and obvious structural imperatives. Rather, they are constantly interpreting the recognizable features of everyday life, sifting through cultural instructions, articulating available models with everyday experiences to assemble the coherent social realities they inhabit.

As we attend to how family is interpreted against the diverse contexts of its consideration, our analysis in this chapter highlights the organizational embeddedness of family usage. Family assignments might differ as a chronic schizophrenic's circle of intimates is considered, first by a therapist in a community mental health center, then by a judge of an involuntary commitment hearing. The former may describe a potentially rich, emotionally supportive family environment where the latter sees no one who is capable of taking full familial responsibility for a potential troublemaker. In the following sections, we examine the diversity by considering two fundamental questions often raised about family: who is family and what does it mean to be family? In the process, we show how the institutional contexts that embed domestic affairs can virtually "think" (and "talk") the familial into diverse shapes and forms (Douglas, 1986).

Who Is Family?

Consider the following scenario and events in, and about, one of the community mental health settings studied. The South City police department's community service officer had just responded to a civilian complaint that a young black man, Rodney Keats, was disrupting a residential neighborhood, ranting incoherently, and brandishing a broom-stick at concerned onlookers and passers-by. Officer Jones approached the youth cautiously, talked him into sitting down under a shade tree to discuss the problem, and convinced him to surrender the broomstick. As Jones tried to decipher the circumstances that led to the bizarre, but unsettling, incident, she searched for a practical solution to the question at hand: what was she going to do with Rodney?

Keats appeared to be psychiatrically impaired—disoriented, agitated, and delusional. Local statutes made it possible to transport a dangerous mentally ill person to the county hospital—involuntarily if necessary—for the purpose of observation and treatment. Hospitalization, however, was contingent upon the availability of a bed on the emergency psychiatric ward. Jones knew that only six such beds existed and that, in all likelihood, Rodney would be turned away. The city jail was not equipped to handle persons with psychiatric problems and would almost certainly refuse him as well. Under the circumstances, the best Jones might have done was to negotiate some sort of community custody for Rodney, securing the help of a responsible resident to look after him and make sure that he sought immediate treatment at a community mental health center.

To that end, Officer Jones asked Rodney where he lived. He said he lived down the street and directed Jones to a small duplex in a row of modest, slightly deteriorating houses. Jones asked Rodney who he lived with and Rodney responded, "My momma." A middle-aged woman answered the door and, after inquiring into the circumstance of Rodney's "arrest," asked what she could to to "keep Rodney out of trouble." The following exchange took place:

JONES: Are you the boy's mother?

WOMAN: As much as he's got.

JONES: Well, where is his mother? Where does she live? Does the boy have a family?

WOMAN: She lives across town, but she don't have nothing to do with him.

JONES: Well, who are you?

WOMAN: Esther Franks. I'm his momma.

JONES: Just a minute. Who's the mother? What are you saying?

WOMAN: I'm Rodney's momma. I raised him since he was a baby. He's mine to look after, so I got to claim him.

As Officer Jones considered Rodney's family ties, she sought more clarification of family status. Most importantly, she looked for signs of who was "really" responsible for Rodney's care and supervision. For the moment, it was of little concern to her that the woman had only tenuous kinship ties to Rodney. (She was the former common-law wife of Rodney's deceased uncle.) Jones's immediate purpose was to find Rodney's "family," which, in this situation, meant someone who would care for him in a familial manner. As far as she could tell, Esther Franks better met that status than did Rodney's "mother," who had long since abandoned him.

After a lengthy discussion regarding Rodney's problems and detailed instructions on how to enroll him in a community mental health program, Jones left Rodney with Esther Franks and returned to the police station. She called the mental health center and made arrangements for Rodney to be seen the next day, telling a therapist that Rodney's "mother" would accompany him on the intake visit. Jones then filed a police report on the incident, indicating that after restoring order to the situation, she left Rodney at home with his "family" and arranged for his "mother" to call her, Jones, if any further trouble arose.

Esther Franks's family status was debatable on both legal and biological grounds, yet within the circumstances confronting Rodney Keats and Officer Jones, "motherhood" was unequivocally assigned. Esther and Rodney talked of each other as mother and son, and while the legal details of their relationship were of passing interest to Officer Jones, her sense of who Rodney's mother was—his family, as it were—oriented to matters other than kinship. The organized circumstances of her encounter with "mother" and "son" made caretaking the salient and consequential familial dimension. It was clear to Jones who Rodney's family was at the moment. The agenda and outlook Jones brought to the situation contained a model of family that could be fit, for all practical purposes, to the relationship that she encountered.

The issue of who belongs to a (particular) family is clearly more than a technical or theoretical matter. Any set of social relations is continuously subject to conflicting or changing interpretation as the context of assessment varies. Consider the definitional complications that arise in discharge planning for elderly stroke patients at Wilshire, the rehabilitation hospital studied. While Wilshire successfully guides recovery, postpatients are rarely fully recovered when they depart. Discharge planning raises issues of the advisability of home or extended care, typically including the need to define who the family is for related practical purposes. The question is not at all academic, for under consideration is who is to be assigned family status for the purpose of assisting with continuing care. Biological or legal ties are only candidate qualifications for membership. Above all, what is being sought is a "family-for-discharge purposes." In this circumstance, the family form that guides the assignment of membership is embedded in the rehabilitation enterprise.

It was evident that those concerned—human service providers, kin, significant others—entered into deliberation with fairly concrete understandings of what they believed to be familial. They took seriously the task of deciphering who could be taken to "really" be a family member and who might only appear to be. Following one Wilshire family conference, two members of an elderly stroke patient's rehabilitation team—a physical therapist and a social worker—met to discuss the patient's discharge destination. They agreed that the patient would not return to her own home because she could no longer get around the large old house by herself, nor deal with the neighborhood's changing social character. The patient's son had already put the house up for sale. The patient would either go to live in her younger, widowed sister's home or to her son's large house. Both had offered to provide a home.

As the case was discussed, it became clear that the team members were engaged in more than simply choosing between two seemingly adequate placement options. They were seeking *familial* care, their deliberations taking into account what each claimed to know about the sister's and son's family status. As they repeatedly reminded one another, their main concern was over who the patient's "real family" was. The physical therapist had done an environmental assessment of both households, and while she found the son's house more wheelchair-accessible, she was skeptical about placing the mother with the son because, she contended, the son "certainly didn't act like one." The therapist explained that everything she had seen and heard led her to believe that the so-called son considered his mother to be just so much human baggage, soon to be tucked away in a bleak back bedroom where she would not interfere with *his* family's daily life. The therapist made special note of how the son kept referring to what his family needed as opposed to what his mother required, interpreting this to mean that the son did not really include his mother in the family. Furthermore, the therapist continued, the son's eagerness to sell his mother's house confirmed the therapist's feeling that he wasn't properly sensitive to his mother's needs; he was no son at all. The therapist believed that it would be in everyone's best interest to plan for discharge to the patient's ostensibly capable sister.

The social worker, however, focused on two other considerations. She believed that she knew more about both the son and the sister, having frequently dealt with them by telephone and in office visits during the patient's hospitalization. Both the son and the sister appeared very concerned for the patient, she noted, keeping track of the patient's progress and offering to do what they could to facilitate recovery. The social worker also pointed out that both sister and son took active part in the hospital's support group for families of stroke victims. She concluded that either could provide an adequate home for continued care. The social worker did acknowledge a "subtle prejudice" against the son, stemming from the son's alleged cold manner, but she argued that team members should take care not to let their prejudice affect their judgment, lest it lead the son to justifiably "make a federal case of it," thereby dividing the family against itself.

Other team members assessed the discharge plans as well, assigning family status to the son and sister in their own ways, reflecting their own biographical, professional, and organizational entrenchments. The physical therapist had seen signs of family membership in the different household plans that had been proposed, while the social worker had read signs of membership in the ways the son and sister had kept in touch with her about the patient's progress and welfare. To the social worker, the son's eagerness to sell his mother's house represented efficient goodwill, not selfishness. The physician on the team uncovered signs of membership in the family's medical history and comparable "typical" families she had known in related experiences. Other team members assembled and assigned their own family bonds out of diverse interpretive orientations. The patient's eventual discharge destination hinged on staff assessments of family status articulated from the various organized concerns in which considerations of membership were embedded. Ultimately, family status derived as much from the contexts of its assessment as it did from kinship ties.

Kindred are not always on the sideline as membership is assigned. Indeed, their interests and orientations can be as consequential as their biological ties for the assignment of family status. Such was the case for Maida Wood, a patient at Lakeview, a nursing home. Gossip had it that Maida was placed in the home when she was abruptly ushered into a medical courier van under the pretext of being taken to the doctor for an examination. Her daughter and son explained to the staff, and later to Maida, that it was the only way they could get Maida admitted, because, as the daughter put it, "Mother just wouldn't hear of it."

At first, Maida was totally confused; she reported that she did not know where she was even though she had been repeatedly reminded that Lakeview was her new residence. She said she had no idea why she had been left in the facility after the "medical people" had finished with her. She tried to compose herself, get her bearings, and find a reasonable explanation for what had happened. Lakeview staff considered her conduct somewhat disoriented, a common postadmission status.

As time passed, Maida grew resentful of the abrupt, unforeseen placement. When she learned that her children had planned it, she felt betrayed and resigned herself to the filial disloyalty. The children's visits were decidedly uncomfortable, even though both son and daughter apologized for their actions and explained that they felt they had no other alternative. They were considerate and never relented in being concerned for Maida's welfare, visiting her often and frequently taking her out.

At the same time, Maida was drawn to a small circle of other patients in the home, two women and a man. They became fast friends, so close and visible that they were known throughout Lakeview by staff and many other residents as "Maida's group." When a member of the group became ill, the others would be highly solicitous and wary of staff intervention. When any of them was temporarily absent from the home, the others became anxious about how things were going for the missing member. There was even a recognizable division of co-concern among them that both staff and the group itself referenced in kinship terms. Freda, for example, was the oldest and said to be the "mother" or simply "grandma Freda." Group members routinely spoke among themselves of Sara, who was sixty-eight years old and at least ten years the others' junior, as "the baby," a reference that Sara relished and used herself to describe her role in the group. Maida was the group organizer and advocate, and Harold the purveyor of needed resources—"a very, very handy man," they claimed.

Still, the group was not simply "one big happy family," certainly not from all points of view. Maida's children bristled at the quasi-kinship, irritated by the group's constant presence and reports of members' genuine familial concern for each other. Maida did not hesitate to remind the children that she had a "genuine" family: Sara, Freda, and Harold were her family now. Maida claimed that no real children would have done what the son and daughter had done in placing her in a "final resting place" against her wishes.

Needless to say, the children were not pleased to hear this and began to interpret Maida's "family-like" conduct as a sign of further disorientation—growing confusion in filial sensibility. They complained to the Lakeview social worker and frequently sought the support of sympathetic nurses, at one point even trying to have members of Maida's group transferred to different floors. When Maida's group infringed on what staff took to be the customary order of the floor, staff members, too, grew resentful. When the children's and staff's irritations coincided, they openly discussed disbanding the group because, they argued, all its members were just patients and had caring families of their own to think about. When irritations did not coincide, the family-like alliance was less likely to be considered a source of trouble.

It was clear that who Maida's family was in practice was not simply a matter of kinship. As far as Maida and sympathetic others were concerned, Maida's son and daughter were filially derelict. Sara, Freda, and Harold, on the other hand, proved to be just what was expected of family. The son and daughter pitted their actual family status against their mother's ostensibly confused counterclaims. Maida and friends, on occasion, responded that the son and daughter were no family at all. The practical familial structure of the group rose and fell with the challenges to its self-assigned integrity, taken by some to be signs of Maida's further disorientation or held as a model of real familism by others, according to perspective, purpose, and sympathies. Family membership—who is family—could not be disentangled from the differential claims and claimants embedded in the diverse institutional circumstances of the concerned parties. Their understandings and arguments derived from the contingencies of those circumstances. Kinship could be cited to authorize claims to family status, but warrant for family assignment was also embedded in the existing culture and discourse of the nursing home.

What It Means to Be Family

Answers to the question of what it means to be family distinguish preferred and undesirable responses. Participants in support groups for the Alzheimer's caregivers often entertained the question. While the Alzheimer's disease experience for caregivers typically entailed myriad daily burdens, personal sacrifices, and the looming problems of caring for increasingly demented patients at home, institutionalization was a pervasive contingency of care and custody that was faced with trepidation. Diverse care-related matters were likely to be considered in relation to the question of the extent and limits of familial responsibility. Caregivers had to deal with the issue of how an ostensible family can decide to institutionalize a loved one when to be family commonly connotes "taking care of one's own."

Despite the well-intentioned interest in Alzheimer's disease voiced in many quarters—medical, psychological, legal, custodial—it was widely believed to be the patient's family who would offer the kind of love and attention needed to cope with a disease that "steals bright minds" and is "like a funeral that never ends." Support group members felt that professional service providers could offer "only so much"; at the same time, they were reminded repeatedly that there was a limit to what they could offer as family members.

What being family meant in light of the mental demise of a loved one underpinned many questions: What should a family do for the victim? How much was enough? What is too much? What should be expected from any member? Each question raised the possibility that one's concern would be judged unfamilial, not adequate for a worthy family member. The concern and questions, of course, are not unique to the Alzheimer's disease experience. They are challenges to anyone dealing with responsibilities regularly linked with the family—coping with juvenile delinquency or mental illness, for example. Responses to the challenges are equally diverse. Yet the organizational embeddedness of the concern can provide virtually formulaic options and solutions to the interpretive puzzles. In the Alzheimer's disease experience, the Alzheimer's Disease and Related Disorders Association (ADRDA) furnishes a formal interpretive context for assigning meaning to the disease and caregiving in general and, in particular, to what it means to be family in conjunction with them. ADRDA support groups offer institutionalized guidelines for assigning familism to the activities of those concerned. What makes familial understandings within these support groups different from individual assignments in other forums is the distinct public culture of definitions and interpretations of the disease experience made available by virtue of the organizational ties with the ADRDA. Is it a realistic group that considers both the patient and the ongoing lives of other family members? Or does the decision to institutionalize mean one has abandoned the patient, with kindred becoming no "real" family at all to the one so in need?

The public culture of the Alzheimer's disease movement combines with a family-as-a-final-haven sentiment to offer a tense stock of options in grappling with the meaning of being family. On the one hand, all concerned are repeatedly reminded that, in the final analysis, for a disease such as Alzheimer's, it is the family that matters most as a source of care. Caregivers are told that only the family can make sense of the progress of the disease, the burdens of care, and the interests of the patient. Indeed, as noted earlier, there is a distinctly antiprofessional tone undergirding the ADRDA's self-help emphasis. Thus, caregivers identify the family as a source and network of unlimited devotion and care: what a family should be.

On the other hand, presented by way of the ADRDA, through its newsletters, self-help books, and other community awareness efforts, caregivers also encounter widespread portraits of ostensibly realistic families, said to have become aware that, also in the final analysis, institutionalization is the most humane course of action and, in any case, inevitable. While a true family puts it off as long as possible, offering whatever care it can, loving and concerned kindred, as true family, know what ultimately is in the best interest of all concerned and act responsibly. To prevent caregivers themselves from becoming totally incapacitated, the public culture suggests that being family eventually means optimizing self-help by displacing the burden of care and offering up an "empty mind" to those suited to harboring its vestige. Ironically, some suggested that, if the demented patient were aware of it, he or she would recognize that the disease eventually prevails on a family to act in the most familial way possible—that is, to decide in favor of what all members would desire and deserve in the end.

These options for interpreting what being family is entered into Alzheimer's support group proceedings and confronted members with alternate senses of what really being family could mean. For example, at a gathering of victims' spouses in one of these support groups, a discussion of marital satisfaction came to center on a particularly distraught and overburdened wife, Kitty. It was Kitty's and John's second marriage, and while she and John had no children of their own, he had brought two daughters from his first marriage to the second one. She loved John's daughters as her own, having been mother to them for more than thirty years. Presenting this background, Kitty added that she and John had become totally devoted to each other over the years. It was "like a marriage made in heaven," she remarked. Tearfully, Kitty described in devoted detail the ways in which she and John expressed their love. She reported that John was at the point where she had to tend to all his needs— eating, toileting, dressing, grooming, and moving about—reminding her listeners of what all had heard and expressed many times before, that daily care entailed putting in a "36-hour day." It was a familiar story of a spouse's and family's total devotion to one of its members.

Others sympathized with Kitty as she compared her own experience to those less devoted and vented her apprehension about an institution's ability to "handle him right and feel for him as I can." Kitty's devotion was taken to exemplify true loving concern and care. Other participants presented similar instances of devotion, offering evidence of the wide range of particulars that signaled what a family should be. The caring family thus took concrete shape from members' descriptions.

One of the group facilitators, Rhoda, an experienced caregiver who had already placed her patient in a nursing home, asked Kitty if she had given any thought to the possibility that she was overburdening herself. Rhoda explained that, while she recognized and understood Kitty's devotion, perhaps Kitty was ignoring herself and the rest of the family. Was it not conceivable, Rhoda asked, that Kitty's family was actually breaking down while John, as Rhoda put it, was "really in never-never land," completely oblivious to himself, to what was being done for him, and even who was involved? Kitty listened intently, agreed that she had occasionally asked herself the same question, but concluded that she could not admit that John was totally unaware. Perhaps, deep down inside, he was still actually there, "maybe cold and lonely and really trying to reach out." She rhetorically asked those attending whether any of them could really admit that their spouses, even though evidently demented, were totally gone.

Rhoda's response was pointed, asserting that it sounded like Kitty was "denying," not being willing to admit that she was destroying herself and the rest of her family by refusing to acknowledge that John was gone. In the process, Rhoda referenced the kind of family that never fully realizes what it means to be family in these matters and that doesn't face the fact that it is time for the patient to be institutionalized. She argued that caring enough meant giving up what now was really "just the shell of a former self."

It was evident that Kitty, Rhoda, and others were articulating, each in her own fashion, the caring family by means of themes not wholly consistent, yet still representative of what a caring family should be. On the one hand was a family image drawn from the common understanding that family is one's final refuge. On the other hand was an image, informed by the Alzheimer's disease movement's related public culture, that institutionalization was a sensible family's only final option. Whatever Kitty's eventual decision would be, in the context of the support group, the meaning of family in relation to Kitty's actions and sentiments was framed in terms of socially organized alternatives and experiences.

Family Usage and Institutional Thinking

Mary Douglas (1986) has elaborated the Durkheimian view that reason is organized and expressed through social structures, suggesting that institutions virtually "think" for their participants, providing models of social order through which experience is assimilated and meaning is constituted. In particular, formally organized settings "think" and "talk" for participants through their conventional modes of discourse, practical agendas, and available images. In this regard, consider the interpretations of family in the following exchange between a community mental health center psychiatrist, Dr. Conrad, and the judge of an involuntary commitment hearing in Metropolitan Court (Holstein, 1988b). Note how vividly professional roles and organizational affiliations assist the various participants in articulating the meaning of the familial.

Dr. Conrad was arguing for the release of his patient, Tyrone Biggs, contending that Biggs's therapeutic program would be completely undermined by hospitalization. He claimed that Biggs did not meet the grave disability criteria for involuntary hospitalization because Biggs was able to function adequately in a community setting. The judge was interested in Biggs's living arrangements and asked for further details, which led to the following exchange:

DR. CONRAD: Tyrone lives with his family. They have an apartment in Lawndale.

JUDGE: I thought Mr. Biggs was divorced last year.

DR. CONRAD: He was, your honor. But he's moved in with his girl-friend and their two children. They share a place with her aunt. He really seems to be getting along fine.

JUDGE: Now who is it that takes care of him? You say these two ladies are going to be able to keep him out of trouble. How long has he lived with them? What happens when he gets delusional again?

DR. CONRAD: We're hoping that's under control. His medications seem to be working. I think it's important to understand that being close to his family is extremely important to Tyrone's [treatment] program. His family wants him there and they make him feel like he belongs. He needs that kind of security—the family environment—if he's ever going to learn to cope, and he's not going to get it from anyone but his family.

JUDGE: That may be so, but you still haven't told me who will keep him under control. Who's going to make him take his medication? He's fallen off before. We have these incidents, and I just don't see any family there to look out for him. You say this is his girlfriend and *her* aunt? How old is this woman [the aunt]? How are they going to handle him? I'm sorry, doctor, but this just isn't the kind of situation I can feel good about. I really don't see much of a family here at all. If I thought there were people there who could really be responsible for this man, it might be different.

The judge and the psychiatrist came to this case from separate and distinct interpretive domains. Their situationally relevant notions of family were clearly tied to, and shaped by, professional and organizational backgrounds, orientations, and mandates. Dr. Conrad engaged in a discourse of therapy as he oriented to improving Biggs's mental health. Conrad voiced a therapeutic concern as he articulated family in terms of support for the psychiatric treatment program; people who provided a supportive environment were "family." In contrast, the judge was concerned with controlling the trouble that he anticipated Biggs would cause. His orientation was to managing trouble so that further incidents stemming from Biggs's schizophrenia might be avoided. He saw no family in Biggs's life because there was no one available who could take responsibility for controlling him.

As articulated by the participants in this setting, family embodies the practical and professional outlooks and interests of the parties and organizations involved. Family usage was thus institutional—psychiatric and legal institutions "thinking" and "talking" in contrasting ways through their respective spokespersons. In effect, judge and doctor voiced separate organizational understandings of the place of family in the situation at hand. Across the settings in which involuntary mental hospitalization was studied, judges consistently voiced concern in custodial terms, seeking assurance that mentally ill persons released to live in the community could be kept under surveillance so they would not cause further trouble. When family matters became topical, they were typically interpreted with an eye to how "family" might help contain and control the behavior of a released patient. In many instances, "family member" became synonymous with "custodian" so that the assignment of family membership was likely to be withheld if the candidate was not seen as capably filling this role. Similarly, mental health care organizations and professions speak both for, and through, their personnel. Dr. Conrad, for example, displayed professional, remedial concerns as he described Tyrone Biggs's "family" in therapeutic terms. The same arrangement in which the judge could find no family to speak of became a "family environment" through the inter-pretive voice of the psychotherapeutic community.

Time after time, in discussions where legal and psychiatric opinions collided, one could see and hear contrasting institutional realities produced out of the same candidate circumstances. Embedded as it was in the respective institutions' interpretive procedures, family was repeat-edly reproduced in terms of the alternate conventions, reiterating the inability of legal and therapeutic personnel to "see things the same way."

Institutional "thinking" does not just distinguish the family depic-tions of alternate professional disciplines but also extends to job orienta-tion. Consider, for example, the contrasting family constructions that emerged by way of the competing investments of casework, as a Commu-nity Support Program (CSP) social worker in Northwoods County sought collegial advice regarding Harriet Baker, the 47-year-old mother of three adult children who had all moved away from Northwoods (Holstein, 1988b). The CSP was mandated to provide practical assistance to chroni-cally mentally ill persons who were attempting deinstitutionalized living. While CSP personnel were concerned with the emotional and psychiatric well-being of their clients, their day-to-day task was to help clients accomplish the routine tasks of community living—managing a household, shopping for groceries, keeping various appointments, and so on.

Harriet Baker's husband had reported several times that Harriet had been extremely agitated and claimed to hear voices in her head. She had become forgetful, negligent, and had lost the patience required to complete even the simplest household tasks. Twice she had wandered away from the house into the surrounding woods. Her absence was not noticed until her husband returned from work to find her missing with no indication of her whereabouts. Both occasions required the sheriff's department to search the woods until Harriet was found. Although Harriet was unharmed, and did not harm anyone else, she could not say where she was going, what she had been doing, and when she had intended to return from her excursions. She would only say that she needed to get out of the house because it was "closing in on her."

The social worker was concerned because Harriet had been her CSP client for several months and had not improved in her ability to run the household. Indeed, Harriet's competence in managing her daily affairs seemed to be declining. The CSP social worker began to doubt the feasibility of allowing Harriet to remain at home and sought the advice of a colleague—a county Department of Social Services (DSS) social worker—who was familiar with Harriet's problems. In their discussion, the CSP social worker tentatively proposed Harriet's involuntary hospitalization:

> We just don't have any other way of looking out for her. Harriet's really isolated out there and we just can't keep track of her. I visit as often as I can and her support worker goes at least once a week, but we can't replace her family. All she has is Jack [Harriet's husband] and he's not there during the day and sometimes not even at night. Her family should look out for her, but since Janie [Harriet's youngest daughter] moved, nobody's there. Harriet really needs more help if she's ever going to learn to live with her problem and now she seems to need someone watching her day and night. It's either her family or the hospital, and right now the hospital may be more family than she's got at home.

The CSP social worker's suggestion to commit Harriet oriented to the practical problem of "looking out" for Harriet, which was cast at least in part as a familial responsibility. As the social worker described Harriet's domestic relations, however, Harriet's family was portrayed as virtually nonexistent for purposes at hand and the mental hospital offered as "more family than she's got at home."

The DSS social worker was not convinced that hospitalization was a good idea. Although Harriet was not technically his client, he had as the DSS mental specialist and as a practicing therapist provided Harriet's family with informal "family counseling" for several years. He had an investment in keeping the family together as a unit. His concern was for how Harriet might respond emotionally to being hospitalized fifty miles away:

> She really does need to have someone look after her, but I'm not so sure that she wouldn't get worse if she was sent to Milford [the psychiatric hospital]. If she was put away, she'd have nothing left. No house; no family. She'd think nobody cared and she wouldn't have anybody to care about. I'm afraid that having no family at all would make her mighty unhappy. She doesn't have much of a family now, but it's more than Milford would be. She could really get messed up.

The DSS social worker's concern for the affective component of Harriet's mental health moved custodial and remedial concerns to the background as he focused on how hospitalization would disrupt Harriet's already unstable life and decimate the family. Hospitalization was framed as an unappealing response to Harriet's troubles because it could not be "family" to her, at least not in an affective sense.

The social workers offered understandings of Harriet's problems and how they should be handled that were informed by, if not patterned after, their notions of what constituted a healthy living environment. Their respective investments in, and professional associations with, the case led them to construe family in different ways. Family assignment was responsive to priorities established in the related casework—custodial concerns in one instance, therapeutic in the other. The household held no family in one social worker's report, but was represented as more familial than the hospital in the other. The disagreement was not merely about whether or not Harriet had a family (although this was implicit in the conflicting assessments of the situation), but also represented a clash of descriptive domains.

If we attribute family diversity to the organizational embeddedness of family usage, the household is no longer the express geographical location of domestic order. As we reveal family in its assignment practices, family's geography is transformed. The meaning of familial experience is attached not to the private household as a site for "family," but rather to the diverse domains of family usage. This does not discount the household's importance, but it does invalidate the assumption that it is the ultimate experiential location of domestic order.

As diverse descriptive domains and interpretive orientations clash, a "politics of description" emerges to complicate the meaning of the familial. To understand the social organization of claims, counterclaims, and practical resolutions, we need to consider family usage as a facet of social control (see Foucault 1972, 1977), to which we turn in the following chapter.

Chapter 8

Family Usage and Social Control

A colloquium at an annual conference of the Society for the Study of Social Problems was about to convene. It was the last day of the conference, Sunday morning, 8:30 A.M. There were more people seated at the presenters' table than in the audience. As the chair of the session stood to start the proceedings, there was an almost palpable disappointment, even embarrassment, shared by those present at the seemingly resounding lack of interest the colloquium had generated. The fact that it was the last day of the conference also figured in the dismay. Undaunted, the chair mounted the rostrum and greeted the meager assembly:

> I'm pleased and gratified to see all of you this morning, early as it might be. We've got quite a nice family gathering here that makes coming all the way to Chicago even more worthwhile to share our work with one another.

The comment presented a subtle yet conscientious attempt at framing a gathering otherwise beyond managerial control. For most of those present, the moment represented the culmination of considerable work done in obscurity that would finally be brought to light after traveling thousands of miles and spending hundreds of dollars. For the colloquium papers to be presented to a sea of empty folding chairs would have been an unfortunate denigration. But there was recompense of sorts in the chair's introduction, for while the forthcoming presentations would be heard by few, that handful of listeners—that "family gathering"—was cast as special, a group with extraordinary interest in a common concern, whose opinion was highly valued, and whose evaluations would be tempered by a rule of gratuitous support. Casting that morning's gathering as a family was an act of sentimental control over the meaning attached to the courtesies of a social occasion. It publicly confirmed an audience of academic kindred, as it were, not distant critics, who would be "at home" with each other.

If family reality is the product of descriptive practice, family discourse can be understood as a form of social action through which aspects of social life not only are assigned meaning but also are organized and manipulated—that is, controlled. Family usage is a means of accomplishing social order; as such, family discourse is both expository and rhetorical (Gubrium and Lynott, 1985). Family usage creates and simultaneously controls the social order it purports to describe (see Foucault, 1980). And this control is indeed profound. While the features of family reality are interactionally produced and sustained, the processes that produce that reality—descriptive practices—pass largely unnoticed. Because they are practically invisible, we are often oblivious to the interpretive control they insinuate in our everyday lives. A family image may recommend particular social relations and arrangements as "normal" or "expectable," while proscribing others. As the public sentiment of the chair's comment at the annual conference implied, those gathered could be counted on to express the attitude of family members, discernibly conducting themselves like family in response to the presentations. The comment, of course, did not guarantee familism, but it did set a background against which infractions would occur.

This chapter takes us beyond the data of the field settings to explore family discourse and social control in diverse applications, from academic conferences to contemporary political rhetoric and industrial relations. While the applications are varied, the focus is on descriptive practice in relation to the intended realities of family.

Contemporary Family Ideology
As Normative Control

What is most remarkable about the contemporary public culture of the family is that, despite the "surprisingly protean nature of the central concept of 'the family'" (Bernardes, 1985a, 192), the family image remains so unflinchingly monolithic and moral in character. Indeed, it is especially noteworthy that the concept which Bernardes and others (see Thorne and Yalom, 1982) accordingly write as "The Family" retains its stature as an ethical or normative prescription despite its relatively short history and our increasingly apparent inability to empirically verify its contemporary existence as a distinct social form.

The family studies literature indicates that what passes for family life (at least for twentieth-century North America and the United Kingdom) is extraordinarily varied. The traditional nuclear form is currently a minority experience, with most persons' family lives departing in some significant way from the model. Given the absence of the traditional family type from most of our experiences, Bernardes (1985a, 196) notes how curious it is that we, as scholars and lay observes, "have ever believed that there existed a single central dominant 'type' of family." Clearly, "The Family" cannot be treated as a literal signifier.

Evidently, ubiquitous reference to "The Family" is motivated by something other than its alleged empirical referent. A variety of commentators and critics of family life and family studies (such as Gittins, 1986; Skolnick, 1983; Thorne and Yalom, 1982) contend that "The Family" is both the artifact and fundamental underpinning of a highly valued symbol system that advocates as much as conveys particular states of domestic life. But because the discourse of "The Family" is taken to be merely descriptive, its basically partisan character and motivations are obscured.

Bernardes (1985a, 1985b, 1987) recapitulates these arguments and suggests that we take them seriously and begin to examine and understand the discourse of "The Family" as *ideology*. We can discover what is literally accomplished by the designation "family" by examining how our use of "The Family" influences and informs the ways that people interact with one another and understand the circumstances of their social lives. Bernardes (1985b) suggests that ideology encompasses the many processes by which individuals construct a sense of familial reality, for both themselves and others. The essence of "The Family" as ideology lies in the way the concept permeates our understanding of everyday circumstances and simultaneously persuades us of its presence, absence, or limited existence in our lives. Because it forms a "cornerstone of our mutual sense of [domestic] reality" (Bernardes, 1985a, 209), perceptions of ourselves and others as individuals and groups are constructed in terms of the typical family roles and idealized relations conjured up by the image. And because we tend to see "The Family" as "a 'natural' and universally present feature of all human societies, an 'institution' which is positively functional and the basis of morality" (Bernardes, 1985b, 279), we tend to treat it as a prescriptive or normative referent. In various ways, subscribing to the discourse of "The Family" underscores a set of constraints on, as well as enablements of, social interaction. Its use promotes a sense of what ought to be as much as it suggests what actually exists.

Drawing from one of the field sites, consider the normative implications of the way the chaplain of a state psychiatric hospital presented the treatment and rehabilitation philosophy used on an all-female ward at the facility:

> We're trying to help some very sick people. It's hard to talk about curing them, but we'd like to see them get just a little normalcy, make their lives a little less troubled, cut back on the trouble for the people they live with. You might say we're trying to preserve the family. We hope it's possible for these women to go back to being wives and mothers, to be able to manage a household, do the shopping and the cleaning. We know that there really aren't good cures for the kinds of problems they have, but we hope that we can help them live relatively normal lives back home.

While Reverend Miller's reference to the family might appear almost incidental to his comments, its use in relation to a standard of ostensible "normalcy" is noteworthy. He enumerated a set of activities and roles typical of (women's) family life, then explicitly suggested that their competent performance constituted "normal lives." He thus established psychiatric normality in behavioral correspondence to the assumed features of women's participation in "The Family"—being wives and mothers, managing a household, shopping, and cleaning. In application, "The Family" became a practical influence over the lives of the patients on this psychiatric ward as it specified the parameters of mental health and the criteria for the eventual resumption of life outside the hospital.

Some have argued that "The Family" is a coercive image for women, a culturally shared interpretive structure that posits and supports the traditional, single male wage-earner at the center of a nuclear family. It is an ideal against which actual experience is compared and evaluated. In application to ourselves and others, the image articulates attitudes and sentiments. As Bernardes (1985b) argues, the presumed naturalness of "The Family" asserts a biological basis for family life, assumed to manifest itself in traditional family forms and functions. Thus, the image and ideology undergird determinate assessments of domestic and gender roles, structuring our perceptions of one another in terms of gender-appropriate behaviors. Patterns of superordination and subordination, as well as gender roles, appear natural and functional as "The Family" is elevated as the only desirable and legitimate domestic living arrangement (Thorne, 1982).

Geraldine Ferraro's experience as the Democratic Party's 1984 vice-presidential nominee is instructive in the usage of "The Family" image. Ferraro's nomination represented a first in American public life; the vice-presidency was the highest office to which a major political party had nominated a woman. In one sense, Ferraro stepped beyond conventional gender and domestic roles as well as political tradition, apparently defying the vestiges of a patriarchal political and family system. In another sense, her behavior was held thoroughly accountable to "The Family" image. Ferraro's competence, as well as her commitment to being a wife and mother, were questioned perhaps as often as were her professional activities in the U.S. House of Representatives or the New York District Attorney's office. Questioning by the mass media and the electorate, for example, often placed Ferraro in the position of pronouncing that her commitments to public office would not undermine her family commitments—that is, her continuing devotion to being, first and foremost, a wife and mother. Repeatedly, over the course of her campaign, she was asked in one way or another what she would do if family responsibilities conflicted with the demands of the vice-presidency. Invariably, she indicated that her duties as wife and mother would always remain her top priority. As a routine part of her campaign, she made a point of referencing her motherly plans and activities, showing explicitly how she fit family into her political schedule (*Time*, 7/30/84, 28).

An implicit challenge to Ferraro's commitment to the family permeated her public scrutiny. Explicitly, of course, she was asked about family policy matters. But just as consequentially, her personal integrity as a woman was placed on trial in terms of her ability and willingness to display how her private life fit into a political career. This seems to be a commonplace campaign challenge, particularly to female candidates. For example, in the 1988 Wisconsin senatorial campaign, candidate Susan Engeleiter was questioned about her parenting and family responsibilities. She responded that she was not shirking her duties as a mother of two preschoolers by running for Senate: "My family comes first in my life. . . My family is young and flexible. . . ." Her opponent, Steve King, a father of three, seized the opportunity to impugn Engeleiter's family commitment, while underscoring his own: "If my family were young, if my family were preschoolers, I wouldn't be making this race" (*Milwaukee Journal*, 9/1/88).

In a sense, Ferraro experienced the paradox of having to convince the electorate that she was more committed to her domestic affairs than to public office if she was to be considered fit to be vice-president. In a culture so tightly bound to the ideology of "The Family" in both private and public policy spheres, a woman who would abandon her traditional family responsibilities would be seen as violating normative, if not natural, prescriptions. She would be acting in a socially deviant fashion. And of course this would be unacceptable for a leader committed to supporting "The Family." The ideology of "The Family" clearly informed the political discourse surrounding candidate Ferraro, exerting a profound moral control over who and what she could be and do, both publicly and privately. This control extends into the more typical lives of women outside the political spotlight as well, for they too are held accountable to the ideal form.

Political commitment to openly proclaimed family values is apparently an unstated requirement for political success. More often than not, this commitment takes the form of support for "The Family," as 1988 presidential candidates Bush and Dukakis made evident in their explicit and repeated proclamations of support for "family values" and "The Family" itself. And consider the furor that arose over a White House conference to discuss and recommend policy measures to implement "family values" during the Carter administration (Skolnick, 1983). The conference was thwarted from the very start by a controversy concerning the appointment of a divorced mother to chair it. The appointment, it was argued, would symbolically undermine family values by tacitly condoning divorce, which is clearly not a feature of "The Family's" image. The appointment was rescinded. Equally to the point, note the implications of the following "pro-family" claims made by a candidate for the U.S. Senate:

> I oppose any federal program that encourages something other than full-time motherhood. . . . I don't think the government should be in a position of providing incentives for people, in this case women, to work outside the home. (*Milwaukee Journal*, 6/28/88)

Supporting "The Family" in this case meant explicit preference for a particular domestic arrangement.

"The Family" is so thoroughly implicated in "family values" that one calls critical attention to his or her moral character with the slightest deviation in attitude or activity. Because this constrains personal beliefs and behavior, it plays a large role in maintaining contemporary social and economic structures and hierarchical relations. As Bernardes (1985a, 209) notes:

> Family units . . . are literally an ideal arrangement both for producing wage-labourers and for the purchase and consumption of material and nonmaterial goods. . . . The individual struggle to achieve a family life which comes even remotely close to the image portrayed in family ideology is surely one of the most powerful stimuli to ensure 'conformity' to standards of social and economic behavior in contemporary society.

We can find the family image utilized as an ideological form of control beyond the Western cultural context. Take, for example, the control implicit in family usage in contemporary Japan. Thomas Rohlen's (1974) ethnography of a Japanese bank describes the use of family imagery and ideology to convey an ideal pattern of interpersonal relations within the firm. Profound social control, he suggests, is embodied in the practice of referring to the bank as "one great family." The implications of the image are extensive. The bank, like the Japanese family, is an entity within which the interests of members or employees are considered secondary to the interests of the family as a whole. Individuals are subservient to the collectivity; everyone must work for the well-being and reputation of this "home." In turn, the family exists for the benefit of all its members. The family imagery conveys an ideal pattern of interpersonal (private) relations between bank employees: warm, giving, understanding, and cooperative. As in a family, leaders and followers, old and young, men and women occupy different roles and have varying degrees of authority. Yet the differences are interpreted in terms of mutual respect and loyalty to one's place in the grander scheme of things. As Rohlen (1974, 46) concludes, "The family ideal is clearly a rich source of inspiration and the high esteem and respect for the institution of the family, combined with its emotionally appealing image, invest the metaphor with considerable persuasive power." The power of the imagery has not escaped American corporate interests, as witnessed, for example, by the self-characterization of the "Beatrice Family," a foodstuffs conglomerate.

Interpretive Control and Social Influence

Deviance and normality, sickness and health, jobs, as well as gender roles may be shaped or constrained by family imagery. Efforts to conform to the blueprints of "The Family" influence our performance of myriad activities, even some that might initially seem completely unrelated to domestic matters. Recall, from throughout this book, the numerous examples of family description that have carried with them express or implicit approval or condemnation of social relationships. Family terminology can provide the very essence of what meaningful social relations are about. To describe a blood relation as "no family at all," to claim that "the mental hospital is more of a family to her than she has at home," or for a parent to say to a son or daughter that "I have no family," is a powerful way of passing judgment or exerting influence.

Two now-classic studies of the social organization of close ties— Stack's (1974) *All Our Kin* and Giallombardo's (1966) *Society of Women*— capture the profound influence that the family image can have as an articulation of social relations. The studies describe how references to "fictive families" or kin-like relations with non-kin are common features of daily life in an impoverished black community and in a women's prison. Indeed, these studies might be considered prototypic examinations of the articulation of social order and control through family discourse because they demonstrate how social structures like community and social integration are constructed through the voicing and assignment of family status.

Stack (pp. 58–61) notes how everyday social relations are reflexively described, categorized, and evaluated in terms of kinship. Persons portray as kindred those "with whom they have had good social dealings" and whom they feel are reliable and responsible, using terms such as "going for sisters," "play daddies," "uncles," "aunts," and "cousins." The familial meaning of the terms accords more with interpretations of social relations than it does with formal kinship. Giallombardo presents similar practices among female inmates, findings echoed in Jones's (1986) more recent study of female inmates. The studies illustrate how the parameters of relational rights and obligations are informed by the family metaphor and established through family usage. By conferring or claiming family status, one defines one's place in relation to the lives of others as well as within the larger entity of which all are a part.

The ways in which these practices exert control is clear. For an inmate to enter into a "marriage" with another inmate or to take on an identity as another's mother or daughter signals a certain kind of involvement in, and commitment to, the relationship:

> Sometimes you get close enough to a resident that she feels like a sister, or you look up to a resident as you would a mother. You just feel close enough to them that you feel like they are part of your family. (Jones, 1986, 77)

To be considered "going for kin" (Stack, 1974) underscores the mutual trust and obligation that characterize a relationship. As Becker (1964) might put it, varieties of "side bets" are made based on the characterization and understanding, tying culture to concrete commitment. Control extends to all who connect to the investment. Inmates hearing that another is a member of a particular family group, or is "married," act in ways that are accountable to the understanding conveyed or risk contending with sanctions attached to infractions of the understanding. The ostensibly private, domestic lives of those concerned are approached and shaped in collective terms, what it means to be "at home" virtually being on public display.

The power of the family image can be irresistible. Stack (1974, 21), who is a white female, commented on the compelling character of the "family" status she achieved with Ruby, one of her black informants:

> When Ruby's youngest child was sick in the local hospital, we went to visit her. The first day, the white nurse on duty stopped me—the rules stated that only close relatives could visit. Ruby told the nurse angrily, "Caroline here is my sister, and nothing's stopping her from visiting this baby." Ruby's claim went unchallenged and we were able to visit the baby every day.

The question of whether or not the black woman and the white woman could, in fact, be sisters, was, for all practical purposes, moot in this instance. More consequentially, by characterizing Stack as her "sister," Ruby conveyed the strength and centrality of their relationship, letting the attending nurse know in no uncertain terms that the person accompanying her to see her sick child was indeed an important and highly appropriate visitor.

Family is also used to convince others of both the "deviant" and "normal" aspects of behavior. In one of the community mental health systems studied, for example, a psychotherapist argued with his supervisor that a young, male client of his was not "chronically mentally ill" and hence not appropriate for inclusion in a community support program for chronic patients. Part of the argument hinged on the question of the "persistence" and "severity" of the client's "distorted thought patterns." In speaking to the issue, the therapist finally concluded that the client was

> not really all that paranoid. It's almost a family trait with him. They're all a bit suspicious. Distrustful, you might say. Maybe it comes from being so isolated . . . call it 'self-sufficient' . . . but it's really not that much of a problem. I wouldn't call him a chronic on that basis.

Family background was invoked as a framework for understanding the cognitions and behaviors of the person in question in such a way that the person could be excluded from consequential deviance.

Similar practices may be seen cross-culturally, as in the following discussion of deviance in the workplace in the People's Republic of China:

> If the family background of the worker who was responsible was "worker" or "poor peasant," then we would criticize him and this would be considered a small problem. But if his class background was not good, then they would turn this into a struggle-criticism session [a more severe sanction]. (Walder, 1986, 142)

While this set of assessment procedures seems highly political and prejudiced to most Westerners, suggesting distortions of reality, it is in many ways identical with the immediately preceding account. Family provides a reference point that is commonly shared and tacitly agreed upon, against which other relations and behaviors are interpreted. In either case, features of the person in question are invested with a particular meaning in light of the family context mobilized for purposes of interpretation.

The Unassailable Family Account

We have seen that the family image is frequently invoked to constrain social behaviors and relations, but we can also find it mobilized to warrant a wide range of behavior and circumstances that may be called into question. When U.S. Representative F. James Sensenbrenner, Jr., front-running candidate in early voter preference polls, announced that he would not be the Republican candidate for the U.S. Senate from Wisconsin, he explained his decision, at least in part, by claiming that family commitments were his principle priority: "I will be able to spend more time with Cheryl [his wife] and my two sons" (*Milwaukee Journal*, 10/30/87). A newspaper headline read: "Sensenbrenner won't seek seat: Declines to make bid for Senate because of family. . ." (*Milwaukee Journal*, 10/30/87). The account presents a commonplace and acceptable reason for retirement from public office (Clint Eastwood, Mayor of Carmel, California, is another recent, prominent example who retired from public office because of "family" commitments). It also serves as a suitable account for refusing more mundane responsibilities ("I really can't serve as chair of the department because of my family responsibilities right now.") or moves to greener pastures ("It's just time for a change. I owe it to my family to take this opportunity.").

In the case of Congressman Sensenbrenner, his decision not to pursue higher office might have been questioned, as indeed it was, on a number of grounds. He was apparently popular with the voters. Many saw him as the best candidate for the office, had begun to actively support him, and contributed to his unannounced campaign. He disappointed many Republican party officials, who viewed him as the most electable candidate. Faced with the necessity of publicly accounting for the decision, Sensenbrenner opted for an explanation that was, in many ways, unchallengeable in the contemporary American context. By using family concerns as the warrant for his decision, he rendered the decision reasonable, compassionate, and—for all practical purposes—unassailable. The account aligned Sensenbrenner with "family values" and their persuasive public image. It ostensibly made his priorities clear, understandable, and honorable. We would be hard pressed to find outer reasons that might be so succinctly communicated, yet so universally compelling.

The versatility as well as the power of the family account is documented throughout this book. We seem to hear it everywhere troubles arise or explanations are demanded. The world of sports, where public commentary and explanation have become as much a part of the experience as the game itself, offers repeated instances of family usage. It is difficult to attend to media-oriented sports without hearing family used to signify the togetherness or mutual caring and concern that are offered as the hallmark and foundation of a team's success. Consider, for example, the now familiar refrain of a college basketball player who was asked to account for his outmanned team's surprising success against a highly favored opponent:

> We didn't think things were so bad. We have a good family atmosphere going. . . . The fellows banded together to show that things are fine here at [university]. (*Milwaukee Journal*, 11/15/87)

Typically, such accounts are used to explain how the ultimate product—the team performance—has somehow managed to exceed the sum of its individual contributions. The 1979 Pittsburgh Pirates baseball team became a national phenomenon as it won the National League pennant and the World Series to the theme "We are family," adapting the lyrics of a currently popular song to the explication of the team's somewhat surprising success.

Family usage also can illuminate breakdowns and defeats, typically by depicting the ways in which the team lacks coherence or clear definition of purpose. This can be seen in the accounts of defeats offered by two coaches, one for a professional football team and the other for college basketball:

> Individually, we're making progress, but we've got to start working together as a unit, as a family. That's what we're lacking right now. Your successful teams develop that sense of family that we have to get before we really arrive. (WLUP Radio, Chicago, 10/17/87)

> We've tried to create a family atmosphere that will pull us through some of these hard times. We're just not there yet. We break down and start to go in five different directions at once. (WISN Radio, Milwaukee, 12/4/87)

Troubles may be explained in terms of family's absence, but they also may be normalized in family terms. Typically, athletic success and failure command vastly more attention than do the ups and downs of daily family living. The family image can be used to establish some "perspective" on teamwork, providing reassurance that matters are not as bad as they might seem. Consider what is attempted in the coach's explanation of a college basketball team's recent poor performance on the court that was reportedly the result of dissatisfaction among team members concerning playing time and their team roles:

> We're having some problems right now, but nothing we can't handle. You know, it's like any family. Things don't always go exactly like you planned them. But just like any family, we're going to work things out. (WTMJ Radio, Milwaukee, 1/10/88)

The family imagery is applied to simultaneously acknowledge the already apparent troubles and minimize them by placing them in the context of the routine difficulties that family members regularly encounter and overcome. The team's imperfections are likened to those of "any family," which normalizes them and at the same time suggests that they are not insurmountable. Indeed, their correction is depicted as all but inevitable because team members, like a family, care for one another and will work together on behalf of the collective good rather than personal gain.

Family imagery may be utilized to account for and normalize even the most serious personal or relational troubles. A heated argument and shoving match between Kansas City Royals baseball players Willie Wilson and George Brett, for example, was called "just a little family fight" by team manager John Wathan (ESPN-TV, 7/18/88). Later, Wilson himself dismissed the incident, saying, "It's like two brothers fighting. How many brothers do you know who never fought?" (*Milwaukee Journal*, 7/19/88). The potential seriousness of the conflict was interpretively circumscribed by casting it in familial terms; even discord and violence are "normal" family relations. By articulating the family character of the dispute, the various parties could reassure their audience that the team (family) would not be torn apart by the altercation. Families, it was implied, survive even bitter quarrels between members.

Framing the fight in terms of family conflict not only normalized the antagonism and dissension, thus minimizing their seriousness, but also offered the possibility that the argument was actually a sign of a healthy, caring relationship. The family imagery implied that deep emotional involvement and commitment lay behind—even caused—the fracas. As Wilson noted in conjunction with his use of the "arguing brothers" metaphor, people who are together for a long time have their differences. The absence of such flare-ups, he suggested, is a sign of "two guys who don't care." The fight, he said, "might be the best thing that ever happened to this team" because it demonstrated the intensity of the relationship and the passion the two combatants maintained for achieving their common goal (*Milwaukee Journal*, 7/19/88).

The assumptions of the private image are also mobilized to manage the meaning of interpersonal troubles. Privacy and privileged access, for example, are asserted to insulate and distance alleged family matters from public scrutiny and judgment. Consider the implications of the following comments made by a college basketball coach regarding allegations of off-court troubles and disciplinary problems involving one of his players:

> Michael [the player] has been going through some tough times, but this is a family matter, and we're gonna handle it like family. Things have been pretty rough and I think he may be frustrated, but we just have to deal with it as a family. (WISN Radio, Milwaukee, 2/8/88)

> That's family. That's family stuff. I don't want to get into that. (*Milwaukee Journal*, 2/9/88)

In one sense, the family characterizations can be seen as attempts to convey the caring concern that was being exercised in this situation. As unsavory or disruptive as things may have been, they would be handled solicitously and compassionately. In terms of the family imagery, one does not abandon or condemn a family member, even when he takes a wrong turn or makes a mistake. But just as importantly, the family image is used to establish the private nature of the problem. As a family matter, the player's transgressions and the coach's responses to them were framed not only as matters for care and concern, but also as matters between intimates that were rightfully hidden from public scrutiny. In a virtual methodological coup, the privileged access of members was invoked to retain and deal with what we, as outsiders, can only infer was happening at home.

Our use of examples from the sports world is not meant to trivialize family usage. Nor should one surmise that the family image is merely being used as part of self-serving, bad faith public accounting. Rather, the illustrations demonstrate how family discourse deeply penetrates the diverse realms of public life. Players and coaches, bosses and workers, officials and private citizens routinely draw upon the discourse and imagery to give a particular tone to their circumstances and behaviors. Perhaps most importantly, as family increasingly confers value on social relations, family becomes an almost universally effective account (see Scott and Lyman, 1968).

Formal Control and Commonsense Theorizing

In the remaining section of this chapter, we turn to studies of formal aspects of control in human service settings other than our field sites. While the central concern of the research we draw upon has not been family usage as such, it is evident nonetheless that family provides an important and ubiquitous social control rhetoric. In discussing the research, we consider how family is literally theorized by those concerned.

The concept of social control is typically thought of in relation to "troubles" or "deviance" (see Emerson and Messinger, 1977). As casual observers, victims, or more detached social analysts, our interest generally focuses on assigning causes and proposing remedies for the interpersonal troubles that all too frequently seem to beset us. Given the centrality of the family concept to the organization of our daily lives, it is not surprising that theories about the family as well as theories about features of family life and its role in human development are paramount in explanations or accounts of troublesome behaviors and circumstances. While much of this theorizing has been incorporated into professional and academic literatures, our interest here is in *native* uses of theories about the family—"commonsense theorizing." Native theorizing may or may not be informed by hypotheses that professionals and researchers have been accustomed to apply.

The history of remedial responses to juvenile delinquency is instructive regarding the ways that family theorizing has shaped our approaches to dealing with trouble. According to Schlossman (1977), in the early nineteenth century the notion that the family was the most consequential influence on human development had just taken hold. The response to juveniles with behavior problems was to remove them from the "bad" families that were acting as inadequate socialization agents, placing the juveniles in alternate institutional settings where they could be taught appropriate values and behavior patterns. The institutional embodiment of this correctional philosophy—the "House of Refuge"—was felt to be a literal sanctuary from bad family influence. By mid-century, family life had become even more romanticized, with affective, sentimental dimensions paramount. Accordingly, juvenile corrections adopted a sentimental family orientation as well, not only removing delinquents from unhealthy home environments, but ostensibly treating them with the love and compassion of surrogate parents in "Family Reform Schools." Finally, by the twentieth century, the centrality of family as a developmental influence had become so widely accepted that our correctional philosophy shifted from merely attempting to rehabilitate children to widespread institutional attempts to "fix the family" as well as the child through the juvenile court and probation system. The notion that juvenile troubles have family causes (and hence were family troubles) became concretely institutionalized as rehabilitation and social control philosophies and policies adopted a decidedly domestic orientation.

Indeed, based on the historical record, we might conclude that "The Family" has emerged as an institutionalized resource to meaningfully account for a range of problematic conditions and circumstances. While today we often hear that the family has all but disappeared from our lives, we can argue that precisely the opposite is the case. Family has entered into such diverse applications—as an account and explanation—that it seems to figure in nearly all aspects of social life in one way or another. Its diffuse ascendence as a cultural hallmark has eliminated any distinct and recognized organizational basis family might have claimed.

Studies of social control decision making continually point to family matters as focal concerns of the police, psychiatrists, judges, parole officers, and correctional personnel who attempt to formulate practical understandings of the cases they encounter. Cicourel's (1968) work on juvenile justice, for example, suggests that family imagery is central to police appraisals of juvenile delinquency. When putative delinquents attract the attention of the police, considerable discretion is exercised in deciding how to interpret the juveniles' activities as well as in determining what to do about them. In the course of dealing with the various accounts and explanations that typically arise, the police are routinely presented with multifaceted evidence of the juvenile's conformity, which stands to be contrasted with, and undermine, imputations of deviance. When putative delinquents or their parents can mobilize favorable family appearances, Cicourel argues, law enforcement officials find it difficult to make a case for criminality because the ostensible appearance of the case and its "family" circumstance—for example, an intact home with reasonable, respectable parents—does not fit officers' conceptions of typical delinquency. As instances of "informal" decision making in the context of formal control, agents employ commonsense theories of good and bad family life as interpretive frameworks within which cases come to be understood and processed.

Similarly, Emerson's (1969) *Judging Delinquents*, an ethnographic study of juvenile court, suggests that family imagery has a profound influence on judicial decision making. His analysis of the court management and processing of delinquency cases considers the "pitches" and "denunciations" that are employed to establish versions of "what kind of youth [we are] dealing with here" (pp. 89–90). Case dispositions, Emerson argues, orient to the presumed delinquent's "moral character." As cases are presented, delinquent characters and careers are assembled not only out of general patterns of behavior, but also from depictions of fam- ily circumstances associated with the conduct under consideration. Thus, the "good family" or "bad home situation" may be invoked as part of the pitches and denunciations that establish moral character for purposes of adjudication. As Emerson points out, "the court's assessment of the delinquent's moral character is fundamentally shaped by the *reports* made of his family situation" (p. 131; emphasis added). Family rhetoric, then, in the form of what Dorothy Smith (1984) would call a "mediated-text," is central to the activities of the court. As the family theories of court personnel whose opinions are sought, as well as those of report-writers who document court cases, provide the interpretive context for character assessments and the practical outcomes that emanate from them, we find family discourse and imagery orienting the decision-making process.

Recent studies of decision making in adult courts also show family to be a central interpretive resource. In ways similar to those just noted, family imagery may be invoked to provide a context for understanding what has transpired and what has to be done as courts offer verdicts and sentences. Eaton (1983, 1985), for example, describes the influence of "family ideology and rhetoric" on magistrates in a London court. One recurring theme is the ways in which depictions of defendants as deeply integrated into conventional family life are used by defense attorneys to illustrate the defendants' commitment to acceptable social relations. According to Eaton (1983), if family commitments are apparent, criminal activity may be seen as a temporary aberration, something for which the defendant should not be held fully responsible even though he or she may in fact be guilty of a criminal act. By way of illustration, Eaton cites testimony from a case involving two brothers who plead guilty to assault charges. In asking for a lenient sentence, their counsel argued that:

> these men were members of a "close-knit family." They contrib-
> uted to the financial support of an invalid father and a mother who
> had only recently recovered from TB. Their mother took the stand
> to testify to their goodness and kindness at home. (p. 389)

The magistrate apparently shared the implied idea that the defendants were not serious criminals because he handed down a very lenient sentence.

Similar findings emerge from Daly's (1987) study of U.S. criminal courts. Here, too, court officials consistently draw on theories of family to explain the outcomes of their decisions. For example, when discussing factors that influenced sentencing, one judge revealed the following orientations:

> Is he or she employed and what is the employment history? If you have a defendant who has worked at the same job for five years, has a wife and two children, I would be less inclined to put him in jail than one who is not working and doesn't have a wife. (p. 273)

Leniency towards defendants who have the appearance of commitment to family is justified on the grounds that these defendants seem to be more stable and have more to lose by getting into further trouble. One prosecutor quoted by Daly (pp. 273–74) revealed the interpretive influence of the family image when he suggested, "There's a maxim: There's more stability in these defendants because they have a family." And a judge, echoing the reasoning described in Eaton's studies, concurred with the prosecutor, "I am loath to incarcerate the family man and woman. . . . They are already conforming to society and the norms that we have at this time in society" (p. 277). The family image may thus serve as the foundation for interpretations that focus on the fundamental conformity of defendants who are believed to have uncharacteristically deviated. In light of such interpretations, control and sanctioning are often felt to be unnecessary.

Some have argued that the exercise of formal social control varies inversely with the amount of informal social control that can be exerted over violators (Black, 1976). Informal, noninstitutional responses to trouble may help achieve social order in ways that are considered more efficient, less socially disruptive or costly, or more humane than formal means. To the extent that family relations and domestic settings can be portrayed as capable of regulating, restraining, and rehabilitating troublesome individuals, family can be offered as a practical resource for social control—an alternative to formal sanctions, treatments, or detention.

For example, in a recent study of the judicial disposition of 129 criminal cases, Allen (1987, 102) reports that "the family was frequently presented as the ideal agency for providing whatever control and surveillance was needed." As illustration, Allen quotes a psychiatric report summarizing the case of a woman who admitted to committing arson and repeatedly threatened to murder her husband. The report characterized the family setting as the best social control response available and recommended placing the woman with her family in the community:

> I would not feel her admission to Rampton is justified. For many years she seems to have coped reasonably well when living with

her family having outpatient treatment. . . . I think she could be satisfactorily looked after in the community. (p. 102)

Eaton and Daly found similar reasoning and practices in criminal courts. According to Daly (1987), court personnel believe that control and rehabilitation of law violators can be more effectively and humanely secured in the family than in prison. She quotes a representative of the District Attorney's office to make her point: "There is no way a state can do what a family can do better" (p. 275). In a sense, the family is viewed as the ultimate resource, which is suggested in another prosecutor's guidelines concerning what he looks for in deciding how to pursue sentencing of a case:

> Family contact—do they have concern from parents or siblings? If concern is shown, then the defendant will be on double proba-tion. . . . Other family ties are very important, the family support is important: Will someone be at home to keep an eye on the defendant? (pp. 275–76)

The promise of care and control also shapes the sentencing decisions of London magistrates. Eaton (1983, 391–92) illustrates this with an example of a thirty-year-old woman convicted of theft. A number of mitigating circumstances were cited during arguments pertaining to her sentence, but the magistrates' ruling ultimately indicated that the woman's impending marriage to a responsible man who would provide for her and keep her out of further trouble was the deciding factor. They waived the option of imprisonment "as she is getting married to someone who will look after her."

Eaton (1985, 127) notes the common belief that "It is the con-ventional nuclear family which is seen to provide the social and economic support necessary for 'normal' life." This family imagery provides a com-monsense basis for considering the family unit as a resource for social con-trol. But if the family is to provide the normalcy—the stability and order—of social life, it must itself be sustained and nurtured. So while family is clearly implicated in controlling and caring for individual community members, social control practitioners are themselves solicitous of family stability as well. In native reckoning, family imposes order upon the lives of its members as the "touchstone of normality" (Eaton, 1983, 389), the foundation upon which interpretations of conformity as well as restoration projects are built. Consequently, concerns for family stability orient de-cisions toward how control and sanctions are to be allocated.

Consider, for example, the dilemma posed by a public de-fender who was seeking a resolution to a drunk driving charge through a plea bargain:

> See, here's the problem . . . he supports his family, wife, and kids.
> . . . And if he does seventy-five days straight time [the sentence

> the district attorney was seeking], he's going to lose his job, his
> wife's going to be on—kids, you know—family's going to be on
> welfare. (Maynard, 1984, 157)

Implicit in the argument is the belief that more harm than good
would come from incarcerating the offender—a family man—because his
domestic life itself would be destroyed in the process. It is tacitly being
argued that the family must be preserved if greater trouble is to
be averted.

Daly (1987) also finds the theme of protecting the family—both
the individual family and the institution—to be an implicit agenda in
sentencing decisions. She cites numerous accounts for decisions in which
concerns for keeping families together and maintaining familied defendants' support for their families (that is, men's wage labor and women's
homemaking and caretaking labor) were highlighted. The negative consequences of jailing familied defendants were repeatedly referenced. One
defense attorney routinely argued for leniency for his clients by trying to
demonstrate that if the defendant is

> supporting the household and a couple of kids, you are trying to
> show the judge that he will be hurting other people. He should
> pay for it, but not other people. . . . Who is going to pay the price
> if we send them away? Does he pay the price or does the family?
> Do the kids pay the price? (p. 274)

Of course, the negative consequences of lodging a troublemaker
in the midst of a vulnerable family are also a concern. The family may "pay
the price" by having to cope with the disruptions of a member whose
presence can no longer be tolerated. Involuntary-commitment decision
making, for example, closely scrutinizes the conditions of family life and
speculates on families' abilities to accommodate the troubles that candidate
patients bring to the home (Holstein, 1987b). If the belief is that the family
cannot survive with the troublemaker in its midst, that person is likely to
be excluded, probably institutionalized, despite the prevailing sense that
family care is preferable to institutional treatment. Thus the family itself
becomes the momentary object of judicial concern.

Family concerns are typically and explicitly guided by the model
nuclear family. Daly argues that the court's aim is to maintain the
conventional family roles and relations from which, it is assumed, responsible social behaviors emanate. This orientation is illustrated in the words
of a judge commenting on what he looks for in a family environment as
he tries to decide if a family unit should be left intact:

> Male and female, mother and father. Are you following through
> on that responsibility? . . . For men, I want to know: Is he holding
> the home together as best he can? Does he contribute to the

support of the family? A woman has a different function. Is she
fulfilling her obligation as a mother? (Daly, 1987, 278)

Social control agents preserve a commonplace family image at
the same time they use it. Those whose lives and actions are congruent
with the conventional image are themselves understood, basically, as
conventional. Their deviant behaviors are not as likely to be treated as
fundamental violations of their conformity, but rather are seen as temporary or transient aberrations. By respecting and supporting those who
occupy conventional family arrangements, the arrangements are themselves promoted, tacitly advocated as proper ways of living. Jurists grant
privilege to traditional homemaker roles for females, for example, when
they make special allowance for violators who nonetheless conform to the
role requirements of wife and mother, as Allen (1987, 104) contends in the
following summary of judicial attitudes towards female offenders:

> Home and family are her proper place. Caring for her husband
> and children are her rightful activities. Tenderness towards her
> child is her natural emotion. The technical possibility of disrupt-
> ing this domestic idyll by the preventive detention of the woman
> is dismissed in half a sentence.

Traditional family structure, then, is institutionalized through judicial practice; social control serves the conventional family's interest. Indeed, support of this family image is virtually codified as we can see in the
following excerpt from a 1977 publication of the British Home Office:

> To send a woman to prison, or indeed to any residential institu-
> tion—even a hospital—is to take her away from her family. . .
> which can lead to the breakup of the home even where there is
> a stable marriage. (Morris, 1987, 93)

Still, it is important to note that these are the applications of a
prevalent *contemporary* image of domestic order and tranquility. It is
entirely possible, with the diffusion of feminist and alternative ideas of
family order, that "enlightened" judges, prosecutors, and others concerned with law, social life, and domestic affairs will, for better or worse,
apply "The Family" to other social arrangements. Regardless of what social
arrangements come to be hailed as familial or derided for their absence,
it is still the discourse of domestic life that articulates and assigns meaning
to the differences—a discourse that is a hallmark of our times.

We have argued throughout this book that there is no literal
correspondence between family discourse and imagery, on the one side,

and the realities they purport to convey and represent, on the other. The forms and associations that pass for family in everyday life are myriad and, as we have noted, situationally and organizationally embedded. Yet despite our inability to empirically establish family's singular form, our everyday lives proceed as if a distinct family were obvious to us. Moreover, family's elusive character does not seem to detract from the power or durability of family ideology. Against this background, we turn in the concluding chapter to the broad question of the nature of family's place in contemporary life.

Chapter 9

The Descriptive Culture of Domestic Life: Considerations and Prospects

In presenting a new perspective for family studies we listed five terms—family, house, household, home, privacy—that are central to the discourse of domestic life. The terms specified a configuration of concern focused on the familial. Taken together, they signaled diverse constellations of meaning as well as wide-ranging political preferences, from the emphasis on privacy and traditional family values to gender domination and exclusion. In this concluding chapter, we take stock of the configuration as an important domain of understanding for relationships.

Following the ideas and illustrations presented earlier, we ask in general what the current status of "family" is and in particular how that status links with domestic privacy. This offers a basis for addressing the issue of whether the family as a social form is disappearing or diminishing in importance. We argue that as long as family is a public concern, it will be a distinct and important part of everyday experience. Current obituaries of the family notwithstanding, family is an increasingly viable and vital aspect of our lives.

A Configuration of Concern

The set of terms that constitutes a configuration of concern provides an important framework for drawing together and conveying what our social relations mean to us. They pattern a range of ideas and sentiments so that, as we borrow one term to describe experience, we are urged on to borrow from the rest. There are myriad configurations of concern in public life: for example, work/career/ambition/opportunity/success and sex/pornography/smut/Satan/sin. Adapting what Durkheim (1938) might have said, they are *patterns* of collective representation, ways of putting together both ideas and experience to mirror who we are and what we do.

A configuration of concern links sentiments as well as ideas. We not only perceive links between family, house, household, home, and privacy, but have feelings about them as well. As matters of American public life, domestic affairs convey important preferences about who we are, were, and will be as families. They generate deep feelings about the place of the familial in everyday life, the privacy of the household, and the meaning of house and home. In other words, the private image and the larger configuration of concern of which it is a part penetrate the heart of the familial.

Whatever is celebrated or lamented, desired or avoided, is more or less done against *shared* patterns of understanding. This is precisely what the private image of the family accomplishes, drawing together common assumptions about the bounds of the familial, its natural place in everyday life, and who has access to it. Consequently, it is not just the private goings-on of one broken home or another that is used to explain, say, Jimmy's delinquency as opposed to Timmy's acceptable behavior or Harriet's mental disturbance as opposed to Cora's life satisfaction. It is equally the shared understanding that the life of the family in-the-large is a cradle for the life of the mind. Shared patterns of understanding explain why there is little confusion when a football coach says his team wins because they have faced adversity like a family, or when a student says she really enjoyed her American Lit class because the family atmosphere was conducive to exploring her feelings about the books she read.

Our sense of the privacies of the household derives from a distinctly public concern for the familial, a concern evident in family discourse. We say that our own home lives are such-and-such as opposed to the particulars of other households. We hint at what we are really like when we are "at home" and contrast that with what we might seem to be to outsiders. The private household is made visible through the public discourse of the familial. At the same time, public discourse assigns privacy to domestic life, putting home and family off limits to public scrutiny. Regardless of the concrete particulars that we associate with family living, we share a common orientation to what we present to each other. Such is the descriptive culture of domestic life.

The Configuration of Concern in Application

While the configuration of concern is public and shared, it does not exist in an abstract world separate from everyday life. Rather, it is a feature of family discourse—a working language—one we use to sort the particulars of the familial, categorize them, and assemble a sense of social order. In that regard, the configuration is abstract only to the extent that it provides the general outlines of a domain of interest. The configuration tacitly links "household" to "family," "family" to "privacy," "house" to "home," and so on. The configuration does not inform us of how its connections are to be concretely made. Application is *guided* by the configuration, not *determined* by it. It is one thing to hear references to any one term in connection with the others; it is quite another thing to derive the actual substance of the connections.

For example, how the household signals family life in one organization such as a nursing home is at considerable odds with how household signals family in a residential treatment center for emotionally disturbed children. While there are repeated references in both organizations to the household as a sign of domestic affairs, field data show that the household for nursing home staff is typically perceived as a home longed for and reluctantly left, while the household for the treatment staff in residential care for disturbed children typically is looked upon as a source of personal troubles. The links between family, house, household, home, and privacy guide how those concerned figure the meaning of domestic life in relation to both settings, but the links take on their concrete meaning from the particulars at hand.

We must take care not to over determine the place of configurations of concern in everyday life. Field data from all the settings studied suggest that the experiences of family, house, household, home, and privacy are subject to the interpretive conditions of their application, which are matters of descriptive practice. As we showed in Chapter 7, the organizational embeddedness of domestic affairs suggested connections between household, home, and family depending on specific local interests and conditions. The descriptive culture of domestic life is not so encompassing as to define what its empirical connections are across the board. Each application and reapplication defines and redefines what actually is shared, stopping short of the totalized, determinant status that culture commonly is given. In application, the descriptive culture of domestic life is a multiplicity of concrete interpretations informed by shared understandings. The multiplicity is as detailed and disjoint as the varied contexts in which familial affairs arise.

Indeed, family meanings are so tied to practice that producing a catalog or typology of meanings associated with family is impossible without simultaneously cataloging all the possible contexts and motivations for family usage.   Moreover, our practical interpretive procedures present us with tremendous interpretive freedom, allowing us to link image with experience in the most oblique, paradoxical, or ironic fashions. It is through practice, for example, that exceptions to common family understandings can nonetheless "prove the rule" underlying the common understandings.   By way of illustration, a sportswriter once mobilized unusual family imagery in response to some of the more clichéd familial references that were being used to salvage the image of the New York Yankees, a team that was, at the time, rife with jealousy, bickering, and name calling.   Ron Fimrite of *Sports Illustrated* wrote, in response: "The Yankees . . . are a family.   A family like the Macbeths, the Borgias, and the Bordens of Fall River, Massachusetts" (Nelson, 1984). We understand full well the negative connotations that were intended, yet our sense of "family" is left intact, because rhetorical technique played out shared understandings against well-known deviant cases. The facetious comment relied upon a shared sense of family to provide the background for violation.

Local Cultures

It has been a common habit of cultural studies to separate culture and social organization, a practice that regularly "totalizes" culture.   Culture becomes a complete field of meanings, separate and distinct from the organization of social relations.   From Marxian conceptualizations (see Jay, 1984) to functionalist accounts (see Parsons, 1951), culture seems either to betray or beset social relations, as if each category had a life of its own. Regarding domestic life, this is one of the main contentions of an important collection of feminist papers on rethinking the family edited by Thorne and Yalom (1982).   Throughout the anthology, the authors refer to "The Family" in a capitalized format, clearly implying that "The Family" is an unwarranted totalization or reification of the diverse experiences of the familial, taken to be a global entity separate from its practices.

We, too, wrote earlier about the family as an abstract entity in the large.   Yet we were careful to call the entity a "family project," thereby avoiding its reification.   We took care to show that what "The Family" was, is, or could be, is a descriptively practical undertaking.   Rather than construing family as a thing in its own right, separate from practice, our analysis has treated "it" as a thing *used*.   Rather than dismissing family altogether as no longer being a useful way to understand close relationships (see Scanzoni et al., 1988), we reclaimed it as a means of social organization.

While we refrain from overdetermining the familial, we must not underdetermine it either.   Family terminology and meanings cannot be applied to just anything helter-skelter. We have tried to show throughout, notably by way of the concept of "organizational embeddedness," that the ways in which the familial is construed and conveyed are socially organized. Because the everyday discourse of the familial is understood in relation to varied concrete applications of its configuration of concerns, its practice does not resemble what Derrida (1977) described as a continuous play of difference. The familial is not so much an undisciplined, unfettered interpretive brainstorm as it is a reasonably ordered and recognizable set of articulations. As an ensemble of entities, the familial is the by-product of the family-for-this-purpose, the family-for-that-purpose, and so on in further hyphenated form, as Borg entertained at the start. Ideological tone aside, we might suggest that the familial is regularly constructed by way of its everyday modes and relations of production. The social construction is far from being a mere artifice of imagination.

As Geertz (1983) noted in his attempt to detotalize culture by attending to its "local" understandings, "local knowledge" brings culturally conceived "wholes" into the concrete and particular purviews of those concerned. In the same way, organized circumstances of modern American life provide local knowledge for interpreting family matters and household privacies. This is all very public. Indeed, with a simple substitution of terms, we might alter Geertz's phrase "local knowledge" to produce "local cultures," the implication for family being that each local culture conveys "The Family" in its own terms. Accordingly, if we think of the descriptive culture of domestic life as the concrete applications of a common configuration of concern, we preserve both the total and the particulars of the familial.

From Entity to Practice

As we have shown throughout, to refer to *the* family, or even "The Family", tells us that family is a thing with distinct shape and form. While there are alternate and diverse versions of this distinct entity, varying according to time and place, the entity that varies nonetheless is taken in principle to exist apart from acts of perception, interpretation, and description. As a separate and distinct entity, not a hyphenated construct, those concerned with it proceed to locate its bounds and characteristics. Having done so, they move on to trace its relationships to other things like delinquency, personal ambition, and stress.

This activity constitutes a very large share of the theory and research that currently constitutes family studies. Perusing any family textbook, we find two kinds of treatment of the family entity. One is the obligatory introductory chapter that either attempts to define or characterize *the* family or, having described the very wide range of forms it can take, laments the difficulty of defining it. The other kind of treatment is found in the chapters that follow. The reader is presented with *the* family in its various social, psychological, cultural, and historical connections. It is precisely the assumption of the entity-status of the family, as a separate and distinct thing, that makes such a textual presentation reasonable.

Yet the hyphenated form of family, not "The Family", suggests that family is an entity only in a special sense. That sense has to do with perspective, image, and practice. If we consider any one family and attempt to discern its characteristics, such as whether it is socially integrated, happy, or nurturant, we begin with a thing and hope to end with a representation. But, at the same time, we know that someone or other must *discern* these or other characteristics, which raises the question of where to look or whom to ask about them, questions of whose perspective to take. To detach the entity from the process of discernment would seem impossible, requiring us to forget perspectival sources—a kind of failure of social memory. The more those concerned forget the perspectival sources of one description or another, the better formed and distinct the entity will be—in other words, the more concrete and reified it will become.

The issue under consideration—of family's status as an entity—is far from being merely philosophical or academic. For example, in arriving at select characteristics of a family, are we to take the father's point of view, the mother's, the child's, or that of someone more distantly related? Perhaps we might judge insiders to be too subjective to provide unbiased accounts and seek the opinion of someone more objective—say, a family therapist or a family scholar. We might even conclude that any real life observer, whether or not a member of the household, would hold biases of one sort or another; and therefore we might decide to apply nonsubjective or unobtrusive measures. We might even set the standard of unbiased perception to accord with the perspective of an imaginary extraterrestrial. Reiss and Lee (1988), in one of American's most respected family textbooks, conscientiously set out to define the topic of their studies "empirically." They contend that they are pursuing a "real" definition of family that states the essence of the concept. The test of their definition would then be "whether most people in a society do indeed define a concept by terms that we use in our definition" (p. 15). Such a definition-by-consensus approach ignores both perspective and context, two of the most significant influences on the diverse ways people think and talk about the familial. Regardless of the alternative chosen, it seems, perspective persists, whether the perspective of a family member, a combination of members, an independent observer, or the researcher who undertakes objective inquiries. Alas, even Borg has a perspective and is as human as the rest of us! (Recall that Borg was, after all, Caswell's Borg.)

The attempt to discern the family as an entity is not only taunted by perspective, but also by image. This brings us full-circle to the private image and family/house/household/ home/privacy as a configuration of concern. While the production of the family as entity would seem to depend on a kind of perspectival forgetfulness, not everything is forgotten. What is not forgotten is that the family is a thing, not a figment of our collective imagination, not an image of social relations, not a shared myth, but a thing. In that regard, it is like other things: the person, the mind, the state, the community, the neighborhood. What is more, family is a thing that seems to be readily and intelligibly connected with other things, like the household, the home, and privacy. The familial configuration of concern seems to be a natural part of public life, whose culture secures it for everyday usage.

Can it be that culture works against the various hyphenations we listed earlier? Recall that the hyphenations implied that whatever the family is, it is always simultaneously a by-product of the way someone, some agent, some organization or other saw or imagined it to be. What culture seems to do for family (and other things) is to draw our attention away from descriptive practice, perspective, and image and toward the things themselves that are represented in particular collective understandings. As such, the private image and the configuration of concern—as cultural entities—seem to be at the very heart of *the* family as we know it, not in its particular versions, but as a thing.

Anything (any thing) that can be constructed can be deconstructed. This book has been an attempt to deconstruct the family entity. We have tried to show both conceptually and empirically how the family materializes through usage. Having deconstructed family into its hyphenations, we can hardly say that it is just an entity. But what then is it? Can we be satisfied to speak of it as an image or a configuration of concern? This would suggest that family is purely an abstraction, a set of recognizable ideas. Or is the family a grammar; that is, a recipe for assigning meaning to social relation? In that regard, it would be a set of rules for organizing our conduct as we interact with each other according to what is and is not held to be familial. Are we prepared to leap from entity to idea, from the concrete to the abstract?

What the descriptive practices we have illustrated in the various chapters show is that the familial seems to be as much idea as concrete entity. It is *practice* that unifies ideas and things. Accordingly, we would do well to consider descriptive practice as a basis for answering our questions. As an object of descriptive practice, family is neither just a thing or objective set of bonds, nor merely an idea about the quality of social relations. It is, rather, an object that is interpretively assembled out of experience. In describing the familial, we find those concerned virtually working at the everyday sense of their social relationships, which they derive more or less definitively, until the matter is taken up again for further consideration. Their labor is not a continuous process of definition but rather seems to be patterned by circumstance. Occasions that challenge otherwise taken-for-granted understandings of their familial bonds prompt what we called the "family project." Those concerned are social constructionists, yes, but ones whose labors are definitely circumscribed by the conditions of description, such as those arising around dinner tables, on street corners, in hospitals, treatment centers, counseling agencies, and family courts.

The Private Image in Use

While the everyday experience of the familial is at odds with the assumptions of the private image, this does not mean that the private image has no place in domestic affairs. In practice, it is central. Rather than being a set of assumptions about the nature of the family, in practice the private image is something people *use* to discern and define the familial. It is used by all concerned, from students of domestic affairs to members of households. Its assumptions guide the articulation of the configuration of terms discussed earlier. To assume that the family is a thing allows us to reasonably decipher its characteristics and its relationship to other things. It can be treated as a substantive part of the world in which we live our lives. To assume that the family is found in the home reasonably brings the household into account in figuring the details of domestic life. To assume that insiders have privileged access to the home provides a compelling claim to knowledge of its privacies. Accordingly, the private image presents us with what Ryle (1949, 7) might have called a kind of "logical geography" of the family—that is, a way of thinking and making claims about the place and connections of family, house, household, home, and privacy in experience. In other words, the private image offers both conceptual anchors and rhetorical grist for seeking the contemporary familial experience (see Gubrium and Lynott, 1985).

 Time and again in our daily lives and across the field sites studied, we heard descriptions of domestic life. They varied in their details, of course, as well as in the force and passion by which they were conveyed. Still, the details and connections of domestic life were never so totally enticing as to eclipse the distinct-entity assumption. It is this entity that a corporate employee spoke about, for example, when he noted that he had "a family to look out for" when he announced he was taking a better-paying job with another firm. And participants of family conferences often tried to persuade each other with a claim like "Well, after all, we're not talking about bricks and siding here, we're talking about *the* family!"—even when they were mired in the minutiae of everyday domestic affairs. Whatever the particular setting, all understood the declaration that the family was a thing it its own right, not to be confused with other matters, even though it was equally evident that other matters could infringe on the clarity of what ultimately was under consideration.

 The assumption of the household as the natural location of family life offered a basis for claims-making (Spector and Kitsuse, 1977). Cases were regularly presented for or against the household as the location of authentic familial facts or information. It was not unusual for the authenticity of descriptions of family life to be questioned because, among other claims, it was said that those who offered ostensibly factual descriptions "hadn't even been in the home." We heard innumerable arguments over who had the most intimate knowledge of the household. A teenage daughter, for example, once railed against her father's policy regarding household chores, concluding loudly that "you're not home enough to know what's going on in this family anyway." Even those who offered the counterclaim of expertise in family matters as a way of overriding the household location claim revealed the locational assumption of the private image when they asserted that experts were exceptions to the rule, thus underscoring the rule itself. Again we recognize the status of the private image as a *resource* rather than as a determinant of descriptive practice.

As illustrated in Chapter 6, the assumption of family members' privileged access was variously used by those concerned. Membership did not so much determine whose domestic experience would be taken as most authentic as it was a kind of working epistemological principle used to judge knowledge of matters familial. Once more the exception could prove the rule. Although a husband or wife might very well have been the head of a household for thirty years and, in principle, have the most authentic knowledge of its domestic order, a claim suggesting that the knowledge was "totally confused," or a matter of "not seeing the forest for the trees," could beset its validity. While privileged access is denied in this case, the idea that the husband or wife would have "naturally" or normally possessed the most authentic knowledge if he or she had not been confused is not.

We have spoken indirectly of discursive power throughout this book. Following Foucault (1980), we find the power of the family as a social form everywhere it is used to designate the nature of social relationships. To make a claim is not simply to describe, but also to assert—a combination of depiction and desire. An outsider's claim to know a family better than members is both a statement of "fact" (though not necessarily factual) and an attempt to control. To the extent a claim becomes shared, the common description tends to overwhelm alternate claims and interpretations. Control over interpretation, then, involves a kind of discursive power (see Foucault, 1981) that revolves around the rhetorical organization and promotion of descriptions. Much of the contemporary controversy over the place of the family in modern society can be understood as clashes between countervailing claims about what voice should be allowed to speak for, and about, the family. Certainly, with the proper adjustments, Lasch's (1979) *Haven in a Heartless World* could be read as an attempt to reveal the growing descriptive infringement by expert outsiders on what he believes would best be treated as the incommunicable privacies of the household. It is but one example of the many current efforts to secure control over family and the lives it describes and organizes.

Is the Family Disappearing?

Concern about the condition of the family seems to be gaining momentum. Social and religious commentators lament family's decline or demise, citing the rising divorce rates and the number of children born out of wedlock as evidence that the family is in danger of disappearing. Many family scholars echo the sentiment. While not everyone agrees that the family is under siege or in retreat, and some—notably some radical feminists—urge the institution's demise, the debate about the state of the family increasingly commands the public spotlight.

If family is not some distinct entity, but rather is a way of assigning meaning to social relationships, then the question of its disappearance takes an interesting, if not ironic, twist. The more we hear the voices of the familial or speak of the family ourselves, even if it is to decry family's existence or to lament its passing, the more attentive we are to its objects and events. The more pervasive family discourse is in both public and private affairs, the more domestic meanings organize our lives. Almost paradoxically, contemporary misgivings about the family have underscored family's importance as an interpretive cornerstone of American life. It seems to capture our attention at every turn. To the extent the voices of the familial are professionalized or certified, domestic life literally becomes a business, an occupation as well as a preoccupation. Indeed, as Zaretsky (1982, 192) argues, the welfare state has not destroyed "'the family' in the conventional sense of a private, self-supporting nuclear unit, [but] to a large extent, 'the family' was created, or at least reconstituted, by the modern state. . . ." On a smaller scale, Miller (1987) argues that family therapists are virtual authors of the family and its problems, an observation confirmed by our own research in other human service settings. In this sense, the besieged domestic life that Lasch decries is not so much a shriveling refuge as an expanding domain of application. It is not that the privacies of the household are being invaded, but that the familial is spreading well beyond what Lasch and others of similar opinion believe to be its proper domain—namely, a particular version of the home. Today, it seems that family is being "produced" everywhere. In this context, what alarms Lasch is not a changing social arrangement but a cultural explosion—the expanding utility of family and its connections as a configuration of concern.

Many of those who argue that family is becoming a less important aspect of Western society and culture tie their assessments to the assumption that the family is a discrete entity. They define the parameters of the "thing" they are concerned with and then suggest ways in which the thing has been shunted aside or changed for the worse. The assessment focuses more on physical properties of the entity that is defined as "the family" than on the meanings that are conveyed. Popenoe's provocative monograph, *Disturbing the Nest: Family Change and Decline in Modern Societies* (1988), is exemplary in this regard. Setting aside, for the present, the author's compelling observations regarding trends in child rearing, childbirth out of wedlock, and marital dissolution, let us examine the way Popenoe "constructs" the family whose decline he intends to demonstrate.

The nest imagery can be thought of as a rhetorical device, but our tendency to reify the family as an entity and accept such characterizations without challenge conceals its rhetorical nature. In this particular instance, the nest imagery ties the notion of family's decline or disappearance to evidence of alterations in the family-as-nest. Changes in living and child-rearing arrangements signal deterioration of the nest and hence a decline in family. The author thus argues that family decline is a social reality because there are fewer marriages, more marriages break up, more children are raised outside of two-parent households, and so on than in times past.

Without disputing these trends as characteristics of contemporary Western societies, we must nonetheless point out that it is a particular set of living arrangements that are "declining" but not necessarily the concept of family or the familial relationship. Popenoe writes that groups that he claims are family's real world referents are losing influence over our daily lives, but the argument cannot extend to a claim that the idea of family, with its associated and diverse social attachments as it were, is unimportant.

Popenoe does argue that a value he calls "familism" is encountering an adverse cultural climate, but he characterizes the value itself as a concern for the perpetuation of the family *unit*. Once again this ties his argument to the rise and fall of a particular thing. Interestingly, Popenoe does briefly attempt to analyze family decline in terms of its discourse and offers an insightful observation concerning Swedish/American differences. Comparing the political platforms of Swedish and U.S. political parties, he notes the liberal use of family rhetoric on the American side while pointing out that the discourse of Swedish political debates is one primarily of individualism. From our perspective, this is more revealing of the relative importance of family in U.S. and Swedish cultures than are the relative divorce rates or the prevalence of unwed mothers.

It is with considerable conviction, then, that we argue that the family is not at all disappearing from American culture. It is emerging and being embellished at the very time political, social, religious, and academic commentators debate and lament its demise. The greater the public discourse of the familial, the more numerous and complex are the categories we hear and have to interpret the meaning of our relationships, both in and out of households. Each category of, claim to, or question about, the familial provides a new challenge for defining who we are in relationship to each other. When, for example, feminists call for the diversification of the living arrangements that legitimately pass for family and the fundamentalist religious community or members of the political right respond by decrying those very changes, we find family commanding vast public attention. Such debates reveal the familial potential of countless aspects of our experience, invite reflection upon the familial in our own lives, and underscore the extent to which matters familial are important in the larger scheme of American society. With each claim that the family is finished, with each call to reassert traditional family values, family is secured as a cultural hallmark.

The constant public debate over the decline in "family values" highlighted during the Reagan administration as well as the almost childish insistence on the part of 1988 presidential candidates Bush and Dukakis that each was more committed to family values than the other signal just the opposite. Family, its seems, has never been more central to our culture, as a guide to understanding and arranging our lives together. Family, of course, is an old discourse, but it has not always been a prominent one, as we noted in Chapter 2. It is clear that, as a construct which organizes our lives and commands our attention, family is considerably more important in contemporary society than it was in the past. As the discourse increasingly claims our attention, it simultaneously directs our interest to its objects of reference. Such is the experiential connection between the contemporary public family and the private image. In Chapter 1, our extraterrestrial visitor, Borg, had considerable difficulty finding the "thing" that was *the* family. But once she began to listen in order to see, she found family everywhere.

The perspective on family offered in this book suggests a new direction, a new program for "family studies." The program centers on questions of culture, discourse, interpretation, and descriptive practice. Yet, while we have scrutinized the assumptions of conventional family studies—indeed, we have made these assumptions topics of our own inquiries—we are not recommending that traditional topics be abandoned. We should continue to explore, describe, and explain relations between husbands and wives, parents and children, brothers and sisters. We should retain an interest in the effects of social context on the lives of individuals and living groups. But, in addition, we urge students of the familial to seriously consider the interactional basis of domestic meanings. As we have tried to show, the diverse aspects of domestic life that we often take for granted as concrete features of social relations are better understood as artifacts of family usage.

We would do well to trace the social organization of public categories of the familial in relation to the ostensibly private domains of experience. The studies reported in this book are one beginning. But there are innumerable contexts in which the familial is embedded. In examining the social distribution of family discourse, we stand to make visible the manifold ways that descriptive practice reveals the family, domesticity, and the home. To some degree, the public categories of the familial have a life of their own. This, too, is fertile ground for study. As the title of Tufte and Myerhoff's (1979) anthology suggests, we might trace the "changing images of the family" as a means of further revealing the possibilities of domestic life. Just as novels and poetry provide us with prospects of what family could be, historical and cultural records can continue to inform us of what family has always been—as much idea as thing.

References

Adams, Bert N. 1986. *The Family: A Sociological Interpretation.* New York: Harcourt Brace Jovanovich.

Aldous, Joan. 1978. *Family Careers: Developmental Change in Families.* New York: Wiley.

Allen, Hilary. 1987. *Justice Unbalanced: Gender, Psychiatry, and Judicial Decisions.* Philadelphia: Open University Press.

Anderson, Elijah. 1976. *A Place on the Corner.* Chicago: University of Chicago Press.

Anderson, Michael. 1980. *Approaches to the History of the Western Family.* London: Macmillan.

Anderson, Stephen A. & Dennis A. Bagarozzi. 1983. "The use of family myths as an aid to strategic therapy," *Journal of Family Therapy 5*: 145–154.

Aries, Phillippe. 1962. *Centuries of Childhood: A Social History of Family Life.* New York: Random House.

Bagarozzi, Dennis A. & Stephen Anderson. 1982. "The evolution of family mythological systems: Considerations for meaning, clinical assessment, and treatment," *Journal of Psychoanalytic Anthropology 5*: 71–90.

Bagozzi, R. P. & M. F. Van Loo. 1981. "Decision-making and fertility: A theory of exchange in the family." Pp. 91–124 in T. K. Burch (ed.), *Demographic Behavior: Interdisciplinary Perspectives on Decision-making.* Boulder, CO: Westview Press.

Ball, D. W. 1972. "The 'family' as a sociological problem: Conceptualization of the taken-for-granted as prologue to social problems analysis," *Social Problems 19*: 295–307.

Barrett, Michele & Mary McIntosh. 1982. *The Antisocial Family.* London: Verso.

Becker, Howard. 1960. "Notes on the concept of commitment," *American Journal of Sociology 66*: 32–40.

Becker, Howard. 1964. "Personal change in adult life," *Sociometry 27*: 40–53.

Bellah, Robert N. 1973. "Introduction." Pp. ix–lv in Robert N. Bellah (ed.), *Emile Durkheim on Morality and Society.* Chicago: University of Chicago Press.

Bennett, Linda A. & Katherine McAvity. 1985. "Family research: A case for interviewing couples." Pp. 75–94 in Gerald Handel (ed.), *The Psychosocial Interior of the Family.* New York: Aldine.

Berardo, Felix (ed.). 1980. *Decade Review: Family Research, 1970–1979.* Minneapolis: National Council on Family Relations.

Berger, Peter L. & Hansfried Kellner. 1970. "Marriage and the construction of reality." Pp. 50–72 in Hans Peter Dreitzel (ed.), *Recent Sociology No. 2*. New York: Macmillan.

Berger, Peter L. & Thomas Luckmann. 1966. *The Social Construction of Reality*. Garden City, NY: Doubleday.

Bernardes, Jon. 1985a. "Do we really know what 'the family' is?" Pp. 192–211 in P. Close & R. Collins (eds.), *Family and Economy in Modern Society*. London: Macmillan.

Bernardes, Jon. 1985b. "'Family ideology': Identification and exploration," *Sociological Review 33*: 275–297.

Bernardes, Jon. 1987. "'Doing things with words': Sociology and 'family policy' debates," *Sociological Review 35*: 679–702.

Bernardes, Jon. 1988. "Founding the *new* 'family studies,'" *Sociological Review 36*: 57–86.

Black, Donald. 1976. *The Behavior of Law*. New York: Academic Press.

Bott, Elizabeth. 1957. *Family and Social Network*. New York: Free Press.

Broderick, Carlfred (ed.). 1971. *A Decade of Family Research and Action*. Minneapolis: National Council on Family Relations.

Buckholdt, David R. & Jaber F. Gubrium. 1985. *Caretakers: Treating Emotionally Disturbed Children*. Lanham, MD: University Press of America. (Originally published in 1979 by Sage Publications)

Burgess, Ernest W. 1926. "The family as a unity of interacting personalities," *The Family 7*: 3–9.

Burr, Wesley R., Reuben Hill, F. Ivan Nye, & Ira L. Reiss (eds.). 1979. *Contemporary Theories about the Family I and II*. New York: Free Press.

Carroll, Lewis. 1873. *Alice Through the Looking-Glass*. London: Macmillan.

Cicourel, Aaron V. 1968. *The Social Organization of Juvenile Justice*. New York: Wiley.

Clifford, James & George E. Marcus (eds.). 1986. *Writing Culture: The Poetics and Politics of Ethnography*. Berkeley: University of California Press.

Daly, Kathleen. 1987. "Structure and practice of familial-based justice in a criminal court," *Law and Society Review 21*: 267–290.

Demos, John. 1970. *A Little Commonwealth*. New York: Oxford University Press.

Derrida, Jacques. 1977. *Of Grammatology*. Baltimore, MD: Johns Hopkins University Press.

Dingwall, Robert, John Eekelaar & Topsy Murray. 1983. *The Protection of Children: State Intervention and Family Life*. Oxford: Blackwell.

Donzelot, Jacques. 1979. *The Policing of Families*. New York: Pantheon.

Douglas, Mary, 1966. *Purity and Danger: An Analysis of the Concepts of Pollution and Taboo*. New York: Pantheon.

Douglas, Mary. 1978. *Implicit Meanings: Essays in Anthropology*. London: Routledge & Kegan Paul.

Douglas, Mary. 1986. *How Institutions Think*. Syracuse, NY: Syracuse University Press.

Durkheim, Emile. 1938. *The Rules of Sociological Method*. New York: Free Press.

Durkheim, Emile. 1947. *The Division of Labor in Society*. New York: Free Press.

Durkheim, Emile. 1961. *The Elementary Forms of the Religious Life*. New York: Collier-Macmillan.

Eaton, Mary. 1983. "Mitigating circumstances: Familiar rhetoric," *International Journal of the Sociology of Law 11*: 385–400.

Eaton, Mary. 1985. "Documenting the defendent: Placing women in social inquiry reports." In Brophy, Julia and Carol Smart (eds.), *Woman-in-Law*. London: Routledge & Kegan Paul.

Elias, Norbert. 1978. *The History of Manners*. New York: Urizen Books.

Emerson, Robert M. 1969. *Judging Delinquents*. Chicago: Aldine.

Emerson, Robert M. and Sheldon Messinger. 1977. "The micro-politics of trouble," *Social Problems 25*: 121–134.

Ferreira, Antonio J. 1963. "Decision-making in normal and pathologic families," *Archives of General Psychiatry 8*: 68–73.

Ferreira, Antonio J. 1966. "Family myths," *Psychiatric Research Reports of the American Psychiatric Association 20*: 85–90.

Foucault, Michel. 1972. *The Archaeology of Knowledge*. New York: Pantheon.

Foucault, Michel. 1977. *Discipline and Punish*. New York: Pantheon.

Foucault, Michel. 1978. *The History of Sexuality*, Volume I. New York: Random House.

Foucault, Michel. 1980. *Power/Knowledge*. Edited by C. Gordon. New York: Pantheon.

Foucault, Michel. 1981. "Truth and power." Translated by Garth Gillian. Pp. 293–307 in Charles Lemert (ed.), *French Sociology*. New York: Columbia University Press. (Original work published 1969)

Garfinkel, Harold. 1967. *Studies in Ethnomethodology*. Englewood Cliffs, NJ: Prentice-Hall.

Geertz, Clifford. 1973. *The Interpretation of Cultures: Selected Essays*. New York: Basic.

Geertz, Clifford. 1983. *Local Knowledge: Further Essays in Interpretive Anthropology*. New York: Basic.

Gerth, Hans & C. Wright Mills. 1953. *Character and Social Structure*. New York: Harcourt, Brace & World.

Giallombardo, Rose. 1966. *Society of Women*. New York: Wiley.

Gittins, Diana. 1986. *The Family in Question*. Atlantic Highlands, NJ: Humanities Press.

Glaze, Bobbie. 1982. "A never-ending funeral," *Generations 7*: 42 & 52.

Goffman, Erving. 1959. *The Presentation of Self in Everyday Life*. New York: Doubleday.

Goffman, Erving. 1974. *Frame Analysis*. New York: Harper & Row.

Grusky, Oscar, Kathleen Tierney, James Holstein, Renee Anspach, David Davis, David Unruh, Stephen Webster, Steven Vandewater, & Harris Allen. 1986. "Models of local mental health delivery systems." Pp. 159–95 in W. Richard Scott & Bruce L. Black (eds.), *The Organization of Mental Health Services*. Beverly Hills, CA: Sage.

Grusky, Oscar, Kathleen Tierney, Renee Anspach, David Davis, James Holstein, David Unruh, & Steven Vandewater. 1987. "Descriptive evaluations of community support programs," *International Journal of Mental Health 15*: 26–43.

Gubrium, Jaber F. 1975. *Living and Dying at Murray Manor*. New York: St. Martin's.

Gubrium, Jaber F. 1980a. "Doing care plans in patient conferences," *Social Science and Medicine 14A*: 659–667.

Gubrium, Jaber F. 1980b. "Patient exclusion in geriatric staffings," *Sociological Quarterly 21*: 335–348.

Gubrium, Jaber F. 1986. *Oldtimers and Alzheimer's: The Descriptive Organization of Senility*. Greenwich, CT: JAI Press.

Gubrium, Jaber F. 1987a. "Organizational embeddedness and family life." Pp. 23–41 in Timothy Brubaker (ed.), *Aging, Health and Family: Long-Term Care*. Newbury Park, CA: Sage.

Gubrium, Jaber F. 1987b. "Structuring and destructuring the course of illness: The Alzheimer's disease experience," *Sociology of Health and Illness 3*: 1–21.

Gubrium, Jaber F. 1988a. *Analyzing Field Reality*. Newbury Park, CA: Sage.

Gubrium, Jaber F. 1988b. "The family as project," *Sociological Review 36*: 273–295.

Gubrium, Jaber F. 1988c. "Family responsibility and caregiving in the qualitative analysis of the Alzheimer's disease experience," *Journal of Marriage and the Family 50*: 197–207.

Gubrium, Jaber F. 1988d. "Incommunicables and poetic documentation in the Alzheimer's disease experience," *Semiotica 72*: 235-253.

Gubrium, Jaber F. 1989a. "The domestic meaning of institutionalization." In Eugene Thomas (ed.), *Adulthood and Aging: The Human Sciences Approach*. Albany, NY: SUNY Press.

Gubrium, Jaber F. 1989b. "Local cultures and service policy." In Jaber F. Gubrium and David Silverman (eds.), *The Politics of Field Research: Sociology Beyond Enlightenment*. London: Sage.

Gubrium, Jaber F. & David R. Buckholdt. 1977. *Toward Maturity: The Social Processing of Human Development*. San Francisco: Jossey-Bass.

Gubrium, Jaber F. & David R. Buckholdt. 1982a. *Describing Care: Image and Practice in Rehabilitation*. Boston, MA: Oelgeschlager, Gunn & Hain.

Gubrium, Jaber F. & David R. Buckholdt. 1982b. "Fictive family: Everyday usage, analytic and human service considerations," *American Anthropologist 84*: 878–885.

Gubrium, Jaber F. & James A. Holstein. 1987. "The private image: Experiential location and method in family studies," *Journal of Marriage and the Family 49*: 773–786.

Gubrium, Jaber F. & Robert J. Lynott. 1985. "Family rhetoric as social order," *Journal of Family Issues 6*: 129–152.

Gubrium, Jaber F. & Robert J. Lynott. 1987. "Measurement and the interpretation of burden in the Alzheimer's disease experience," *Journal of Aging Studies 1*: 265–285.

Haley, Jay. 1967. "Experiment with abnormal families," *Archives of General Psychiatry 17*: 53–63.

Hammersley, Martyn & Paul Atkinson. 1983. *Ethnography: Principles in Practice*. London: Tavistock.

Handel, Gerald (ed.). 1985. *The Psychosocial Interior of the Family*. New York: Aldine.

Henry, Jules. 1971. *Pathways to Madness*. New York: Random House.

Henry, Jules. 1985. "My life with the families of psychotic children." Pp. 51–66 in Gerald Handel (ed.), *The Psychosocial Interior of the Family*. New York: Aldine. (First published 1965)

Hess, Robert D. & Gerald Handel. 1959. *Family Worlds*. Chicago: University of Chicago Press.

Hodgson, J. W. & R. A. Lewis. 1979. "Pilgrim's progress III: A trend analysis of family theory and methodology," *Family Process 18*: 163–173.

Holstein, James A. 1984. "The placement of insanity: Assessments of grave disability and involuntary commitment decisions," *Urban Life 13*: 35–62.

Holstein, James A. 1987a. "Mental illness assumptions in civil commitment proceedings," *Journal of Contemporary Ethnography 16*: 147–175.

Holstein, James A. 1987b. "Producing gender effects on involuntary mental hospitalization," *Social Problems 34*: 301–315.

Holstein, James A. 1988a. "Court-ordered incompetence: Conversational organization in involuntary commitment hearings," *Social Problems 35*: 801–816.

Holstein, James A. 1988b. "Studying 'family usage': Family image and discourse in mental hospitalization decisions," *Journal of Contemporary Ethnography 17*: 247–273.

Holstein, James A. & Gale Miller. Forthcoming. "Rethinking victimization: An interactional approach to victimology," *Symbolic Interaction*.

Howell, Joseph T. 1973. *Hard Living on Clay Street: Portraits of Blue-Collar Families*. Garden City, NY: Doubleday.

Jackson, Don D. 1957. "The question of family homeostasis," *Psychiatric Quarterly 31*: 79–90.

Jackson, Don D. 1965. "Family rules," *Archives of General Psychiatry 12*: 589–594.

Jay, Martin. 1984. *Marxism and Totality*. Berkeley: University of California Press.

Jones, Richard S. 1986. *Mitchelleville: A Study of the Adaptation Responses of Women in Prison*. Unpublished doctoral dissertation. Iowa State University: Ames, Iowa.

Kantor, D. & W. Lehr. 1975. *Inside the Family*. San Francisco: Jossey-Bass.

Katz, Daniel and E. Stotland. 1959. "A preliminary statement to a theory of attitude structure and change." In S. Koch (ed.), *Psychology: A Study of a Science*, Volume 3. New York: McGraw-Hill.

Kennedy, David. 1970. *Birth Control in America*. New Haven: Yale University Press.

Krech, David and R. S. Crutchfield, and E. L. Ballachey. 1962. *Individual in Society*. New York: McGraw-Hill.

Kübler-Ross, Elisabeth. 1969. *On Death and Dying*. New York: Macmillan.

Kuhn, Thomas. 1962. *The Structure of Scientific Revolutions*. Chicago: University of Chicago Press.

Laing, R. D. 1969. *The Politics of the Family*. New York: Random House.

Laing, R. D. & A. Esterson. 1964. *Sanity, Madness and the Family*. Baltimore: Penguin.

Lakoff, G. & M. Johnson. 1980. *Metaphors We Live By*. Chicago: University of Chicago Press.

LaRossa, Ralph, Linda A. Bennett & Richard J. Gelles. 1981. "Ethical dilemmas in qualitative family research," *Journal of Marriage and the Family 43*: 303–313.

LaRossa, Ralph and Jane H. Wolf. 1985. "On qualitative family research," *Journal of Marriage and the Family 47*: 531–541.

Lasch, Christopher. 1979. *Haven in a Heartless World*. New York: Basic.

Laslett, Barbara. 1973. "The family as a public and private institution: A historical perspective," *Journal of Marriage and the Family 35*: 480–494.

Lewis, Oscar. 1959. *Five Families*. New York: Basic.

Lewis, Oscar. 1961. *The Children of Sanchez*. New York: Random House.

Liebow, Eliot. 1967. *Tally's Corner*. Boston: Little, Brown.

Lynott, Robert J. 1983. "Alzheimer's disease and institutionalization: The ongoing construction of a decision," *Journal of Family Issues 4*: 559–574.

Mace, Nancy L. & Peter V. Rabins. 1981. *The 36-Hour Day*. Baltimore, MD: Johns Hopkins University Press.

Manning, Peter K. 1979. "Metaphors of the field: Varieties of organizational discourse," *Administrative Science Quarterly 24*: 660–671.

Maynard, Douglas. 1984. *Inside Plea Bargaining*. New York: Plenum.

Melville, Keith. 1983. *Marriage and Family Today*. New York: Random House.

Miller, Brent C., Boyd C. Rollins & Darwin L. Thomas. 1982. "On methods of studying marriages and families," *Journal of Marriage and the Family 44*: 851–873.

Miller, Gale. 1987. "Producing family problems: Organization and uses of the family perspective in family therapy," *Symbolic Interaction 10*: 245–265.

Miller, Gale & James A. Holstein. 1989. "On the sociology of social problems." Pp. 1–16 in James A. Holstein & Gale Miller (eds.), *Perspectives on Social Problems*, Volume 1. Greenwich, CT: JAI Press.

Miller, Gale & James A. Holstein. Forthcoming. "Social problems work as rhetoric." In Gale Miller (ed.), *Studies in Organizational Sociology*. Greenwich, CT: JAI Press.

Miller, Leslie. 1987. *Violent Families and the Rhetoric of Harmony*. Paper presented at the Western Social Science Association Annual Meeting.

Miller, Leslie. Forthcoming. "Safe home, dangerous street." In Gale Miller & James A. Holstein (eds.), *Perspectives on Social Problems*, Volume 2. Greenwich, CT: JAI Press.

Mills, C. Wright. 1940. "Situated actions and vocabularies of motive," *American Sociological Review 5*: 904–913.

Mills, C. Wright. 1959. *The Sociological Imagination*. New York: Oxford University Press.

Mitterauer, Michael & Reinhard Sieder. 1982. *The European Family*. Chicago: University of Chicago Press.

Moerman, Michael. 1965. "Ethnic identification in a complex civilization: Who are the Lue?" *American Anthropologist 6*: 1215–30.

Moerman, Michael. 1974. "Accomplishing ethnicity." Pp. 54–68 in Roy Turner (ed.), *Ethnomethodology*. Baltimore, MD: Penguin.

Morris, Allison. 1987. *Women, Crime, and Criminal Justice*. Oxford: Basil Blackwell.

Neal, A. G. & H. T. Groat. 1976. "Consensus in the marital dyad: Couples' perceptions of contraception, communication, and family life," *Sociological Focus 9*: 317–329.

Nelson, Kevin. 1984. *Baseball's Greatest Insults*. New York: Simon & Schuster.

Nicholson, Linda. 1988. *The Age of the Family*. Paper presented at the Symposium on Literature and Family. Milwaukee: Marquette University, Institute for Family Studies.

Nye, F. I. & A. E. Bayer. 1963. "Some recent trends in family research," *Social Forces 41*: 290–301.

Parsons, Talcott. 1951. *The Social System*. New York: Free Press.

Perlmutter, Morton S. & James M. Sauer. 1986. "Induction, trance and ritual in family mythologizing," *Contemporary Family Therapy 8*: 33–43.

Pollner, Melvin. 1987. *Mundane Reason*. Cambridge: Cambridge University Press.

Popenoe, David. 1988. *Disturbing the Nest: Family Change and Decline in Modern*

Societies. New York: Aldine De Gruyter.

Raffel, Stanley. 1979. *Matters of Fact.* London: Routledge and Kegan Paul.

Reisberg, Barry. 1981. *Brain Failure.* New York: Free Press.

Reiss, David. 1967. "Individual thinking and family interaction: I. An introduction to an experimental study of problem solving in families of normals, character disorders, and schizophrenics," *Archives of General Psychiatry 16*: 80–93.

Reiss, David. 1981. *The Family's Construction of Reality.* Cambridge, MA: Harvard University Press.

Reiss, Ira L. & Gary R. Lee. 1988. *Family Systems in America* (4th ed.). New York: Holt, Rinehart & Winston.

Rodgers, Roy. 1964. "Toward a theory of family development," *Journal of Marriage and the Family 26*: 262–270.

Rohlen, Thomas P. 1974. *For Harmony and Strength.* Berkeley, CA: University of California Press.

Ruano, B. J., J. D. Bruce, & M. M. McDermott. 1969. "Pilgrim's progress II: Recent trends and prospects in family research," *Journal of Marriage and the Family 31*: 688–698.

Ryle, Gilbert. 1949. *The Concept of Mind.* Chicago: University of Chicago Press.

Safilios-Rothschild, Constantina. 1969. "Family sociology or wives' family sociology: A cross-cultural examination of decision-making," *Journal of Marriage and the Family 31*: 290–301.

Scanzoni, John, Karen Polonko, Jay Teachman, & Linda Thompson. 1988. *The Sexual Bond: Rethinking Families and Close Relationships.* Newbury Park, CA: Sage.

Schlossman, Steven. 1977. *Love and the American Delinquent.* Chicago: University of Chicago Press.

Schultz, Richard & Gail Brenner. 1977. "Relocation of the aged: A review and theoretical analysis," *Journal of Gerontology 32*: 323–333.

Schutz, Alfred. 1970. *On Phenomenology and Social Relations.* Chicago: University of Chicago Press.

Schwartz, Howard & Jerry Jacobs. 1979. *Qualitative Sociology.* New York: Free Press.

Scott, Marvin B. and Stanford M. Lyman. 1968. "Accounts," *American Sociological Review 33*: 46–62.

Shorter, Edward. 1975. *The Making of the Modern Family.* New York: Basic.

Silverman, David. 1987. *Communication and Medical Practice.* London: Sage.

Simmel, Georg. 1950. "The metropolis and mental life." In Kurt H. Wolff (ed.), *The Sociology of Georg Simmel.* New York: Free Press.

Skolnick, Arlene S. 1983. *The Intimate Environment.* Boston: Little, Brown.

Smith, Dorothy E. 1984. "Textually mediated social organization," *International Social Science Journal 34*: 59–75.

Smith, Dorothy E. 1985. "Women, class and family." Pp. 1–44 in V. Burstyn & D. Smith (eds.), *Women, Class and Family.* Toronto: Garamond.

Spector, Malcolm and John I. Kitsuse. 1977. *Constructing Social Problems.* Menlo Park, CA: Cummings.

Speedling, Edward J. 1982. *Heart Attack: The Family Response at Home and in the Hospital.* New York: Tavistock.

Stack, Carol. 1974. *All Our Kin.* New York: Harper & Row.

Stone, Lawrence. 1977. *The Family, Sex, and Marriage in England, 1500–1800.* New York: Harper & Row.

Strauss, M. A. 1964. "Measuring families." In Harold T. Christensen (ed.), *Handbook of Marriage and the Family.* Chicago: McNally.

Strodtbeck, Fred L. 1951. "Husband-wife interaction over revealed differences," *American Sociological Review 16:* 468–473.

Thomas, D. L. & J. M. Calonico. 1972. "Comparative family study through multiple member measure: A methodological note," *Journal of Comparative Family Studies 2:* 292–295.

Thomson, Elizabeth & Richard Williams. 1982. "Beyond wives' family sociology: A method for analyzing couple data," *Journal of Marriage and the Family 44:* 999–1008.

Thorne, Barrie. 1982. "Feminist rethinking of the family: An overview." Pp. 1–24 in Barrie Thorne & Marilyn Yalom (eds.), *Rethinking the Family.* New York: Longman.

Thorne, Barrie & Marilyn Yalom (eds.). 1982. *Rethinking the Family.* New York: Longman.

Tobin, Sheldon S. & Morton A. Lieberman. 1976. *Last Home for the Aged.* San Francisco: Jossey-Bass.

Tufte, Virginia & Barbara Myerhoff (eds.) 1979. *Changing Images of the Family.* New Haven: Yale University Press.

Walder, Andrew G. 1986. *Communist Neo-Traditionalism: Work and Authority in Chinese Industry.* Berkeley, CA: University of California Press.

Waxler, N. E. 1977. "Review of Power in Families edited by Ronald E. Cromwell and David H. Olson," *Social Casework 58:* 315–316.

Weber, Max. 1947. *Theory of Social and Economic Organization.* New York: Free Press.

Whyte, William Foote. 1943. *Street Corner Society.* Chicago: University of Chicago Press.

Wiley, Norbert F. 1985. "Marriage and the construction of reality: Then and now." Pp. 21–32 in Gerald Handel (ed.), *The Psychosocial Interior of the Family.* New York: Aldine.

Wirth, Louis. 1938. "Urbanism as a way of life," *American Journal of Sociology 44:* 1–24.

Zaretsky, Eli. 1982. "The place of the family in the origins of the welfare state." Pp. 188–224 in Barrie Thorne & Marilyn Yalom (eds.), *Rethinking the Family.* New York: Longman.

Zarit, Steven H., Nancy K. Orr, & Judy M. Zarit. 1985. *The Hidden Victims of Alzheimer's Disease.* New York: New York University Press.

Zinn, Maxine B. & D. Stanley Eitzen. 1987. *Diversity in American Families.* New York: Harper & Row.

Index